D0484853

(Continued)

Learning to Read

Beyond Phonics and Whole Language

Edited by

G. Brian Thompson
and Tom Nicholson

Foreword by
Celia Genishi and
Dorothy Strickland

International Reading Association
800 Barksdale Road
Newark, DE 19714

Teachers College
Columbia University
New York and London

Published simultaneously by Teachers College Press, 1234 Amsterdam Avenue, New York, NY 10027 and The International Reading Association, 800 Barksdale Road, Newark, DE 19714

Library of Congress Cataloging-in-Publication Data

Learning to read : beyond phonics and whole language / edited by G.
  Brian Thompson and Tom Nicholson; Foreword by Celia Genishi and Dorothy Strickland
    p. cm. — (Language and literacy series)
  Includes bibliographical references and index.
  ISBN 0-8077-3792-5 (cloth). — ISBN 0-8077-3791-7 (pbk.)
  1. Reading. 2. Word recognition. 3. Reading comprehension.
4. Literature—Study and teaching.   I. Thompson, G. Brian (George
Brian), 1938–   . II. Nicholson, Tom. III. Series: Language and
literacy series (New York, N.Y.)
LB1050.B382   1998
372.4—dc21   98-30943

ISBN 0-8077-3791-7 (paper)
ISBN 0-8077-3792-5 (cloth)
IRA Inventory Number 9127

Printed on acid-free paper
Manufactured in the United States of America

06 05 04 03 02 01 00 99   8 7 6 5 4 3 2 1

Contents

Foreword

As the editors of the Language and Literacy series, we are pleased to have the opportunity to introduce G. Brian Thompson and Tom Nicholson's *Learning to Read: Beyond Phonics and Whole Language*, a collection of recent work from New Zealand. We wish to frame it historically and instructionally by referring to the ideas of John Dewey, a philosopher, and Jeanette Throne, a kindergarten teacher. Both have written about the complexities of the classroom and the hazards of holding "either–or" theoretical positions. Throne writes:

> Curriculum reforms that put educators into opposing camps, such as direct teaching versus discovery learning, phonics versus whole language, or a child-centered curriculum versus a content-based or teacher-directed curriculum, move the field of education back and forth to the extreme ends of the pendulum. The educational debates that often ensue promote one ideology or the other and prevent educators from engaging in the back-and forth dialectic that could help them better understand teaching and learning. (Throne, 1994, p. 206)

Sixty years ago Dewey wrote: "At present, the opposition, so far as practical affairs of the school are concerned, tends to take the form of contrast between the traditional and progressive education" (Dewey, 1938/1963, p. 17).

Both writers capture a perennial dilemma in education and the academic world in general: the polarization of theoretical and practical positions that seems to hinder a deeper understanding of teaching and learning. Throne notes that in the classroom particular children are inevitably left struggling when one theoretical approach is chosen to the exclusion of others. Her solution has been to reject the extremes and make judgments based on knowledge of curricular approaches, of her own teaching, and of the individual learner's thinking and learning.

In the field of literacy learning, theoretical polarization can be especially severe. In 1997, several states and the U.S. Congress introduced legislation to mandate phonics instruction in primary-grade classrooms. The legislation is a reflection of where the controversy is most pronounced—

in the disagreement about how beginning reading should be taught. The debate generally positions systematic, intensive instruction against holistically oriented approaches. Briefly stated, those promoting systematic, intensive phonics advocate an emphasis on phonics that is highly sequenced, skills- or code-driven, and initiated early in the child's schooling. Children begin by learning about the parts of words and build toward whole words. Correct identification and automaticity of response are stressed. Much of the research cited to support this view is grounded in experimental studies in which children's demonstration of performance is based on the results of standardized tests (Adams, 1990; Chall, 1983).

Holistically oriented approaches include philosophies and practices frequently associated with terms such as *whole language, integrated language arts*, and *literature-based curricula*. In operation, these terms share certain characteristics; however, they are not synonymous. Trends in literacy education that stress greater emphasis on writing and its relationship to reading, greater use of trade books, increased attention to the integration of the language arts, and greater reliance on informal classroom assessment are visible at least to some extent in virtually all teaching where a holistic orientation is espoused. However, implementation and adherence to various philosophies varies widely from teacher to teacher. Those who endorse a meaning emphasis are likely to cite basic research on how children learn to read and write as well as classroom-based studies on long-term effects (Krashen, 1993; Weaver, 1994).

Our experience suggests these differences are evidenced to a much lesser extent in the classroom than they are in the debate. In practice, teachers who advocate holistic approaches are apt to include strong word-recognition programs with phonics as a key tool for word recognition; and teachers who support intensive, systematic phonics often employ instructional strategies, such as reading aloud to children and the encouragement of invented spelling. Although the matter of emphasis is not to be taken lightly, it is unlikely that you will find classrooms that reflect polar ends of an instructional continuum. Fortunately, throughout the debate there have been moderate voices reminiscent of Throne's and Dewey's—for example, Richard Allington, Kathryn Au, David Pearson—who have reminded us that polarization and politicization of theoretical and instructional stances are neither necessary nor helpful to our presumed purpose: to teach children to read, as a foundation to learning.

The work presented here by Thompson and Nicholson also avoids rigid stances: It ranges widely—from looks at family and societal context; to word identification, phonological awareness, and comprehension strategies; to literature-based instruction. The authors provide readers with an international viewpoint, centered in New Zealand. Controversial and provocative topics such as the role of phonemic awareness in beginning reading, how children learn words, and the nature of text structures and their influence on reading ability are addressed. The study and discussion questions at the end of each chapter help the reader to reflect on the chapter contents and act as a catalyst for questioning the authors and for further reading and discussion.

Thus the volume makes a significant contribution to the Language and Literacy series, which has typically been associated with holistic approaches—a narrower band of the spectrum of research and theory than that covered by Thompson and Nicholson. As importantly, we believe that volumes like this one push us to avoid the strident "either–or" positions that Dewey and Throne warn against and the ideological "opposition between the idea that education is development from within and that it is formation from without" (Dewey, 1938/1963, p. 17). The inclusion of *Learning to Read: Beyond Phonics and Whole Language* in this series is an invitation to readers concerned with language and literacy to engage in difficult and messy dialogues that acknowledge the possible roles of development from within and formation from without—with the goal of understanding better the complex processes of teaching and learning.

—Celia Genishi and Dorothy Strickland

REFERENCES

Adams, M. (1990). *Beginning to read: Thinking and learning about text*. Cambridge, MA: Harvard University Press.

Dewey, J. (1963). *Experience and education*. New York: Collier. (Original work published 1938)

Chall, J. (1983). *Learning to read: The great debate*. New York: McGraw-Hill.

Krashen, S. D. (1993). *The power of reading: Insights from the research*. Englewood, CO: Libraries Unlimited.

Throne, J. (1994). Living with the pendulum: The complex world of teaching. *Harvard Educational Review, 64*(2), 195–208.

Weaver, C. (1994). *Reading process and practice*. Portsmouth, NH: Heinemann.

Preface

Literacy has derived from the needs of human society for a recorded form of language. Human self-discovery about features of language enabled the invention of orthographies, which are the vehicle of literacy. But if literacy is to be maintained for all members of a society, then that society has to provide new generations with the means to learn and use the vehicle of literacy.

During the past 30 years a growing international body of quality research and theory has offered new understanding of how children learn to read. The processes of learning to read are complex, and they have diverse contexts and functions in society. It is little wonder then that there are few books available that bring together the diverse and complex research that informs professionals entrusted by society with passing on reading skills to new generations.

The plan of this book is to draw together a wide but integrated range of this research and theory. The contexts of society in which children learn the skills of literacy are discussed in Chapter 1. Consideration is given to the developing experiences within the family and society that move children onto and along the path of literacy learning. Next, in the chapters of Part I, a central place is given to research on how children learn to identify the print forms of words, examining not only these processes of learning but also the influence of instructional contexts on the processes. However, the identification of words is not usually an end in itself but a means to comprehension of a text. In Part II, the learning of comprehension aspects of reading is considered at different levels, including the role of word identification and of text structure. Part III places the skills of reading within a wider context, by an examination of how reading skills can be put to use in the context of literature, both literature as a vehicle of recreation and as an object of literary art.

This book principally considers the reading of English, although much of the content will be relevant to other languages with alphabetic orthographies. While there is reference to children who have difficulties in learning to read, the book is not intended to be a guide to research on the disabilities of learning. Nevertheless, it is relevant to important aspects of prevention of reading difficulties.

Learning to Read takes a research perspective that follows North American, British, and some European traditions. The contributing authors have been involved in research in New Zealand, where the approach to teaching reading has been influenced historically by selected English and U.S. practices and can be categorized as a version of the "whole-language" approach. As such, it has recently received much international attention. The research reviewed here includes some conducted within this New Zealand context as a contribution to the accumulating international research. Within this small country there has recently been a very wide range of high-quality research on the learning of reading. A sizable proportion of this work has come from talented young scholars offering their first research contributions. This book represents a pooling of diverse research knowledge. It brings together a range of important international research and theory, enlivened by the immediacy of the current research and special expertise of each author.

This volume is intended to inform student teachers, teachers, teacher educators, and remedial specialists, although it does not describe detailed procedures or lessons for teaching reading. It is intended to inform professionals about research and theory on learning to read and to provide them with an educated basis for their own selection or construction of programs of teaching. It is a book that equips the senior undergraduate and also provides a grounding for the more intensive study of the graduate student. It will be of interest not only to educators but also to psychologists and researchers.

We wish to acknowledge the patience of our contributors and their loyalty to the project. Credit is due also to Gundy Krumins for personal time given to making penetrating and helpful comments on earlier versions of the text.

G. Brian Thompson
Tom Nicholson
February 1998

Learning to Read

Beyond Phonics and Whole Language

Chapter 1

Literacy in the Family and Society

TOM NICHOLSON

a) Why is it that some children are early readers?

b) How does social background affect reading achievement?

c) What equity solutions are possible?

d) Do children from poorer backgrounds have more problems with some forms of linguistic awareness?

Nearly all children learn to talk at home, but hardly any children learn to read at home. The reason is that language development is to a large extent biologically determined. Unless some major life trauma occurs, the child will acquire language, no matter what language is spoken at home and no matter what home background the child comes from. Reading, however, is a cultural invention. The origins of speech go back 200,000 years, but the origins of writing go back only 5,000 years (Corballis, 1991). Language thus has an evolutionary base. It has emerged as part of the evolution of the human species, along with other abilities such as walking. So, while nearly everyone walks and talks, the relatively recent invention of writing has meant that reading and writing skills are not naturally acquired and thus have to be taught. They are not part of our evolutionary inheritance (Pinker, 1994).

EARLY READERS

This helps to explain why most children do not learn to read until they get to school. Durkin (1966) surveyed 9,568 school beginners in the United States and found that only 229 (2.4%) could read 18 words or more on a list she gave them to read. The list was made up of common words such as *mother, look,* and *funny.* How then did the 2.4% of early readers in Durkin's study learn to read? Durkin interviewed parents of the early readers in her study. She also interviewed parents whose children were not early readers. She wanted to find out what distinguished the early readers from the other readers. She found that parents of early readers tended to be proactive in reading. They spent more time with their children; read to them a lot; answered their questions; gave help with printing, spelling, sounds of letters, and identifying words. Parents of early readers reported that their children did a lot of writing. Durkin followed the early readers in her study during 6 years of school and found that they stayed ahead of their peers in reading through that period. This was a positive finding in the sense that parents sometimes worry about what will happen if their children learn to read before they go to school. Anbar (1986) mentions one concern that some parents have: "Am I creating a problem by helping her learn to read?" (p. 82). Anbar also raises a concern that preoccupies some teachers: "He [the early reader] is going to be bored in school" (p. 83). The results of Durkin's research suggest that parents and teachers should be relaxed about children knowing how to read before they begin school, since they will not be disadvantaged.

Other research on early readers has revealed that such children often come from home backgrounds where their parents have some special reason for teaching their children to read. In an English study of 32 children who could read before they started school, Clark (1976) noted that some of their parents wanted their children to do well and thus made special efforts to teach them to read. In one family, this was their first child after several attempts. The child was very special to them. In another family, the parents were not well educated but wanted their child to do better than themselves. Few of the mothers worked while their children were preschoolers. As a result, they were able to spend a lot of time with their children in literacy-related activities.

Anbar (1986), in the United States, studied six children who could read before they started school. Their home environments were not run-of-the-mill. In interviews, parents reported spending a great deal of time in reading and spelling activities. They read every day to their children, helped them with spelling, and played rhyming games: "'What rhymes with Mommy?' one of the mothers used to ask. (Her son's favorite response would be 'salami')" (p. 75). These parents had a huge range of materials: books, alphabet letters, flash cards, dictionaries, workbooks, electronic games, and so forth. Anbar reported that the motivation of the parents often stemmed from a special reason. Because these reasons were extremely interesting, they are quoted in detail here (Anbar, 1986):

Mark: Mark's parents' fears may have been the driving force behind their special interest in, and sensitivity toward, reading. The father remarked on his concern that Mark would become a poor reader like Mark's uncle. The mother was worried that, unless they did something specific about it, Mark would follow in his sister's footsteps, dropping out of school and "doing nothing" in spite of his talents. (p. 80)

Sean: In the case of Sean, it appears that reading development became something of a hobby for his parents. "Some parents build sand castles with their children; we made words with him," his mother explained. Perhaps because the father completed his formal education with only a high school diploma (and had a very high appreciation for education), Sean's parents derived much satisfaction from their work with the child and from his early reading development. (p. 80)

Betty: In the case of Betty, early reading development seemed to have justified for the mother the resignation from her 12-year-long career. (p. 81)

Victor: In the case of Victor, the parents related how reading activities were used by them at first as a means of keeping the child physically calm. This requirement was imposed on them by the child's pediatrician due to the child's asthmatic condition. (p. 80)

Marna: In Marna's case, reading activities seem to have been the lifeline between the child and her parents, who felt guilty about leaving her with a sitter so much of the time. Since she was a very tense and restless baby, they also read frequently to her in order to calm her. In addition, they had another, very personal, reason to encourage Marna's reading development: "It was good to see that the child was not retarded," the mother explained, in reference to her fears that her late pregnancy might have caused developmental problems. (pp. 80–81)

These results suggest that early readers get a great deal of instruction at home. But is it possible that children will learn to read naturally if parents focus their efforts on reading aloud to their children on a regular basis? Wells (1985), in a study of 32 children, found a positive relationship between parents' reading aloud to children at home and their children's later reading progress in school. Yet Scarborough and Dobrich (1994) reviewed 31 studies on the effect of parents' reading aloud to their children and found surprisingly little relationship between the amount of time parents spent reading to their children and their children's later reading development. Share, Jorm, Maclean, and Matthews (1984) gathered data on 500 kindergarten and 479 grade-1 Australian children. They also found little relationship. Phillips and McNaughton (1990) studied a group of 10 New Zealand parents who were recruited by placing notices in libraries and bookshops in two middle-class suburbs. These parents spent a phenomenal 3 hours each day interacting with their 3- and 4-year-old children in literacy activities. The families mostly comprised two adults, and one or two children. Mothers did most of the reading of books to their children. They read an average of four books a day to their preschoolers, usually at bedtime. They visited the library often. They each had, on average, 300 children's books in their homes (ranging from 50 to 500!). Yet none of the children could read. Tests showed that on average the children could identify 13 letters and two words. But that was all, despite the very rich print environments of their home backgrounds.

Although home-literacy experiences do not correspond directly with reading success in school, they may do so indirectly in that parents who read to their children at night and buy them books are more likely to be middle-class. A child from such a background may fail to read, but not because of lack of home support. Indicators such as the amount of time that parents spend reading to their children and the number of books that children have at home may reflect differences in income. Children from middle-class homes are likely to have a better chance of school success than children from low-income homes because they have more resources and parental know-how available to help them. The number of books in the home and the amount of reading parents engage in with their children may not be causal factors in learning to read. But they are an indirect measure of the extra benefits that come from being raised in a more affluent home environment.

SOCIAL CLASS AND READING

In Japan, where literacy levels are high, 36% of parents are already reading to their children when they are 12 months old (Sakamoto, 1976). In the United States, Adams (1990) has commented that reading to the very young is a middle-class phenomenon. It is very much what she did with her own child: "Since he was six weeks old, we have spent 30 to 45 minutes reading to him each day" (p. 85). Similar experiences have been recounted by others who have reported on the reading development of their children (Bissex, 1980; Lass, 1982, 1983).

In contrast, Teale (1986) surveyed 24 preschoolers in low-income families in the United States and found that their parents hardly ever read to them. He reported that they were read to on average five times a year. Feitelson and Goldstein (1986) studied 102 Israeli families. The researchers selected 51 families from schools where achievement was poor and 51 from schools where achievement was high. In the low-achieving schools, all parents in their sample had not progressed beyond primary school and were from Near Eastern or North African countries. In the high-achieving schools, all parents in the sample were high school graduates from European or English-speaking countries. The survey data showed that kindergartners attending schools with high achievement levels had an average of 54 books in the home and were read to for half-an-hour each day, even from an early age. In contrast, children from low-achieving schools did not own any books and were not read to at all.

In New Zealand, differences in home reading experiences were studied by Gibbons (1980) in a small sample of eight preschool children (4-year-olds). She categorized them as either 100-book kids or 1,000-book kids. She calculated the "1,000" by totaling the number of stories they would have been read by their parents if they had been read just one story each night from the time they were 12 months old, through to their fifth birthday. Gibbons found significant differences between the 100- and 1,000-book children in prereading skills, such as knowledge of the alphabet and ability to retell stories that had been read aloud to them.

Differences in home background experiences were also noted by Nicholson (1980) in a survey of 689 parents who participated in a course on helping their children to read. Questionnaire responses revealed that some parents were unable to provide the print environment that was possible in middle-class homes. The reasons were economic. To get to libraries, parents need transport; to buy children's books, parents need disposable income. Here are the written comments of a parent who had to use public transport to attend the reading course at her local play center:

> Leave home at 8.30 am with two toddlers to wait for school bus in frosts. Arrive at school. Wait in play center [at] which I had to light old-fashioned stove for heat. Meantime, baby is crying of cold. So I couldn't stand my children getting cold. So rather than face a freezing cold play center I dropped out as did other mothers without cars. (Nicholson, 1980, p. 19)

Some parents also felt lacking in information about what books to get for their children. Here is one written note from a parent:

> Yes I have two children how [sic] need books bad. They are very backwood [sic] in their readying [sic] at school. How do I get the right books for them? I am [sic] give you my name and address would you let me know about the books for my children I hope so. (Nicholson, 1980, p. 21)

Although many children from low-income backgrounds have low levels of reading achievement, some do not. There are well-known figures in history who were excellent readers and writers yet came from humble backgrounds. Abraham Lincoln, president of the United States during the Civil War, came from a background of rural poverty. D. H. Lawrence became a famous novelist, although his father was a coal miner.

My students recently conducted a case study of a 5-year-old early reader. He started school with a 7- to 8-year-old reading level and above-average intelligence as measured by a test of receptive vocabulary. Yet he had just been enrolled at a school in Otara, one of the poorest areas of Auckland. He came from a home in which Samoan, Maori, and English were all spoken. Our interviews with the parents revealed that they had not directly instructed their child in how to read. But like parents interviewed by Anbar (1986), they had provided him with a rich home environment. His mother had taken a child development course in which she learned about reading books to her baby while he was in the womb. She often left him in his crib while an audiotape of a book was playing. His mother recalled making flashcards to create words and sentences. He was sounding out words and reading words on signs when he was 4 years of age. Here is an extract from the parent interview:

> I was quite surprised. We'd be driving along the motorway and
> he'd start reading signs. He'd say something like, 'Dad, what's
> a furniture sale?' And I'd say, 'Where did you see that?' And
> he'd say, 'On the shop'. We'd stop at lights and he'd be reading
> things off. And I'd be sitting there all quiet just waiting for the
> lights to go green, and he'd start reading. (Nicholson, Lam,
> Van Kuyk, Brown, & Lemke, 1998)

Here was a 5-year-old boy, from a low-income suburb, who was still learning to tie his shoelaces but could read. He picked out his own books at the library, read the TV guide at the supermarket, and recited the Bible at Sunday School.

Yet the reality is that many children from low-income backgrounds are more likely to fail than to succeed. Not all children come from homes where there is the same level of support. Some children have parents who are nice to them, while others are not so lucky. In Duff's (1990) novel *Once Were Warriors*, the children of Jake Heke were raised in a violent home situation. All disposable income seemed to be spent on Jake's drinking habits. There were no books in the Heke home. As Jake's wife, Beth, considered it, "It occurred to Beth that her own house—no, not just her own house but every house she'd ever been in—was bookless. The thought struck her like one of Jake's punches" (Duff, 1990, p. 10).

There are children whose parents are neither helpful nor unhelpful. These children are neglected. The effects of neglect were noted in a case study by Morris (1984), in England, about a boy called Frank. At 11 years of age he was scarcely able to read elementary-level primers. His mother was illiterate. He and his mother lived in public housing that was scheduled for demolition. Frank was a neglected child, had a dirty ragged appearance, ate huge amounts of free school lunches, and roamed the streets late at night. In the case of Frank, the task of remediating his reading problems would have been extremely difficult because he lacked a caring home environment. Similar difficulties exist today, with many children from low-income homes coming to school hungry, or without any lunch (Turner, Connolly, & Devlin, 1992), or even not coming to school at all. In poor parts of Auckland, for example, there are more than a thousand children who have "disappeared" from school rolls. They have left school but not gone to another school. They move into extended families, but the families do not re-enroll them in another school ("Hundreds of school children missing," 1996). In contrast, children from middle-class homes are more likely to attend school regularly and be well fed (e.g., will bring lunch to school with them). As a result, they receive more consistent schooling and are able to give their school tasks more attention than children from low-income homes who are hungry or neglected or both, thus giving middle-class children an advantage in terms of learning to read.

Many children from low-income homes are well looked after, but they still experience difficulties. Their parents struggle to keep their children well fed and lack the financial resources needed to provide their children with school textbooks and other study materials. Orr (1995) reported the results of an interview survey of 500 Australian families who had children attending high school. The ages of the children ranged from 13 to 16 years. All families were receiving financial assistance from the Smith Family, a charity that provides emergency cash relief so that struggling families can buy food or pay outstanding bills necessary for their welfare (e.g., water, electricity). The Smith Family also provides a bursary for these children to assist with the purchase of school uniforms, books, and so forth. The researchers set their estimate of basic literacy at the 12-year level, since this is the approximate reading level required to read many newspapers, magazines, and books. The findings revealed that 60% of the children in the sample of 500 had not progressed beyond the 10-year level (grade 4), which meant that they would not be able to understand the novels and texts required for their high school studies. The pressures faced by these children are revealed in interviews. One comment was, "They say to me, 'Your family is poor and we don't want to hang around germs.'" Another comment was, "They would tease me because of the clothes I was wearing so then I got a uniform. . . . Now they just tease me because I wasn't born in Australia" (Orr, 1995, p. 21).

Poor academic achievement of pupils in rural areas also appears to be linked to income. People who live in the country, on average, tend to be poorer than people who live in the city. A recent ministerial inquiry in the state of Western Australia found that there were relatively more school-children from low-income backgrounds in rural schools than there were children from low-income backgrounds in city schools. A newspaper report of the findings of the ministerial inquiry stated, "Many more children in the country were from poor families and it was the poverty, rather than the resources, teaching or location of their schools, which explained their results" (Horin, 1995, p. 2).

HOME AND SCHOOL

Difficulties faced by high school children from low-income backgrounds have been studied in New Zealand. Wilson and Dupuis (1992) compared the home backgrounds and school experiences of 36 female students at an all-girls secondary school. Of the 36 students, 12 were low achievers from low-income backgrounds, 12 were high achievers also from low-income backgrounds, and 12 were high achievers from middle-class backgrounds. The researchers noted that the low-achieving female students from low-income backgrounds were worse off in terms of home facilities. As they put it, "In general the standard of housing was poor, lacking space and privacy. Most of the girls shared a bedroom and there was no quiet place for them to do their homework. . . . Half of the girls' families had no car, therefore activities that required a car were out of the question" (p. 3). These pupils were living in relatively large family situations, where the average number of children was four. They did a lot of chores (e.g., cleaning, ironing, cooking, baby-sitting). Time spent on chores averaged 12 hours per week. They all had reading difficulties and had experienced academic difficulties from the early grades on. Parents of seven of the pupils had visited the school, but only one had received help. Other parents had not gone to the school for help because they felt under stress; for example, "I was on a benefit in those days and there wasn't much extra money" (p. 5). Some felt that they were the ones to blame; for example, "I thought it was me at fault" (p. 5).

In contrast, the 12 pupils from low-income homes who were doing well at school had better home facilities. Parental incomes were low, but higher than those of pupils' parents in the low-achieving group. Most students had their own room at home, and most families had a car. Family size was smaller, with an average of three children, and students did fewer hours of chores, about 3 hours a week. These students were doing well, but this had not always been the case. All their parents had appproached the school, but with better results. For example, "Melissa had trouble with learning to read. I was told she was a trouble stirrer. Her teacher was very inadequate. After underachieving she [Melissa] was put into the bottom of Standard 1 [grade 2]. Luckily she had a teacher who put a lot of time into her and got her up to the top of the class within a year" (Wilson & Dupuis, 1992, p. 8).

In the middle-class group of 12 high-achieving females, the researchers found that home study facilities were better than those of the other two groups: "Every girl had her own room and a specific area in which to do her homework, including a desk with adequate lighting. The average family size was 2.75 [children], each family had a car, sometimes two" (Wilson & Dupuis, 1992, p. 9). These students also spent less time on chores, 1.5 hours a week. Five of the 12 high-achieving students had experienced difficulties at school, and their parents had visited the school for help. Two of the five parents had received a negative response but had the financial resources to obtain outside help (e.g., private tutoring). In all, these results suggest that children from low-income backgrounds can succeed in school, though the odds are stacked against those who live in families where there are financial and social stresses.

A longitudinal study in the United States of 32 children from low-income homes (Chall, Jacobs, & Baldwin, 1990) found that the academic problems of low-achieving students in their sample increased as they moved through the school grades. These problems were especially evident by grade 4, where the more academic content of the reading material led to a fall in reading achievement. A parallel study of the same children (Snow, Barnes, Chandler, Goodman, & Hemphill, 1991) found that parents were not aware that their children were having problems. When the children received report cards with grades of B and C, the parents assumed that their children were making adequate progress. But teachers at the school gave such grades to children who were performing badly. Also, teachers were giving children credit for extent of improvement during the year rather than for actual achievement. These results indicate problems in communication between low-income parents and schools.

A recent skills-test survey in Minnesota revealed a high failure rate for pupils from minority and low-income backgrounds ("Skills-test," 1996). In Minneapolis, the survey of eighth-grade pupils found that those from families with incomes below the state poverty line (these pupils received free lunches) had a much higher failure rate in reading (79%) than pupils who were not eligible for free lunches (44%). These statistics were similar to those obtained in a New Zealand survey of Form 3 pupils (13-year-olds) in eight secondary schools (Nicholson & Gallienne, 1995). Six of the schools were in low-income suburbs of Auckland and two were in middle-class suburbs. The survey found that pupils in the low-income schools were reading at an 11- to 12-year level (1 to 2 years below average). In one school, pupils were reading at a 10-year level (3 years below average). In contrast, pupils in the middle-class schools were reading at a 13- to 15-year level (up to 2 years above average).

Stanovich (1986) has summarized research showing that there are negative effects of attending schools where most pupils are from low-income backgrounds. Teacher expectations may be lower, classroom discipline may be more of a problem, teachers are harder to recruit, and those who are recruited tend to be less experienced. There are negative effects of being in a class where most of the children are low achievers. Pupils who need extra help with reading are less likely to get it if most of their classmates also need help with reading. Researchers have found that children who attend schools where the average level of achievement is high will make relatively better progress than children of similar abilities who attend schools where the average level of achievement is low (Nicholson & Gallienne, 1995; Rutter, 1983; Share et al., 1984).

If a parent has a low-achieving child in a school located in a low-income neighborhood, one solution would be to move the child to another school. A Minneapolis parent was quoted in a newspaper article ("Skills-test," 1996) as doing just that:

> Rabb and his wife recently transferred their 7-year-old son to another school after he had difficulty with reading, and teachers told them that the school was challenged by having many children from low-income families. Now the boy's reading has dramatically improved. "Our kid is a very bright kid," Rabb said. "We have a very rich environment in the home in terms of reading and writing. We are a professional family. And he still wasn't achieving." (p. A22)

But many parents may not be able to move their children to other schools. What other options are available to them? One option is to reduce class sizes in schools where there is a concentration of pupils from low-income backgrounds. Recent research in Tennessee (Finn & Achilles, 1990) revealed that reduced class sizes over a 2-year period led to significant benefits in reading as measured by standardized tests. In this longitudinal study, both pupils and teachers in each participating school were randomly assigned either to a small class (15–17), a regular class (22–25), or a regular class with a teacher aide (22–25). There were 76 schools in the study. Children were followed through kindergarten to the end of first grade. Results showed that children in small size classes had significantly better reading levels than children in regular size classes. The benefits of small classes were especially great for minority children.

POOR CHILDREN HAVE TROUBLE WITH PHONEMIC AWARENESS

Teachers may wish they could change children's home experiences. For example, they might wish that low-income parents would read more often to their children. But, as we have already noted, research indicates that this may not be the best wish for a teacher to make (Scarborough & Dobrich, 1994). Also, as Horin (1995) puts it, asking parents to read to their children "may not work for kids whose lives already lack structure and whose parents, coping with unemployment, desertion, violence or illness, may not feel like a cozy read every night" (p. 2). What else can teachers do? Perhaps one of the most important things teachers can do is focus on children's metalinguistic awareness skills, from the beginning of their schooling. Metalinguistic awareness refers to the ability to play with language and to think about it as a system. Metalinguistic awareness is knowing that talk can be broken into utterances, that utterances follow grammatical and pragmatic rules, that utterances can be broken into words, and that words can be broken into their component sounds, or phonemes (Tunmer & Bowey, 1984). Many children lack metalinguistic awareness skills when they start school. Such awareness is part of a general change in children's thinking, when children become able mentally to stand back from their own talk and reflect on it. Metalinguistic awareness emerges in middle childhood, from about 5 years of age, though it can appear earlier. Here is a remark from a 3-year-old who shows emerging metalinguistic awareness (Limber, 1973, cited in Hakes, 1980): "When I was a little girl I could go 'geek-geek' like that. But now I can go 'This is a chair'" (p. 164). In Piagetian terms, metalinguistic awareness coincides with the emergence of concrete operational thinking, whereby the child can think about a problem from two different perspectives (Foss & Hakes, 1978).

One form of metalinguistic awareness that is particularly important for learning to read is phonemic awareness, which refers to an awareness that spoken words are themselves made up of sounds. It may seem surprising that phonemic awareness is related to reading, since it is a skill that does not involve print. It just involves spoken language. Where it becomes important is in the early stages of learning to read, when children are

confronted with the problem of learning how to associate alphabetic characters with the "phonemes" they represent.

Children from different social backgrounds vary in phonemic awareness skills. Children from low-income backgrounds start school with significantly lower levels of phonemic awareness than do those from middle-
class backgrounds. Wallach, Wallach, Dozier, and Kaplan (1976), in a study
from the United States, found that 5-year-old children from low-income
backgrounds had difficulty with relatively easy phonemic awareness tests
(e.g., pointing to an illustration, the name for which started with a particular phoneme), much more so than middle-class children of the same
age. Dickenson and Snow (1987), also in the United States, found that 5-
year-old children from low-income backgrounds had more difficulty than
middle-class children with simple rime awareness tasks such as deciding
whether the spoken word "cat" rhymed with the spoken form "feet" or
"fat," or with onset awareness tasks such as being able to detect the first
sound (or, more precisely, phoneme) of a spoken word, as in /d/ for "dog."
Raz and Bryant (1990), in England, reported differences between low-
income and middle-class children in rime awareness tasks such as picking
the odd one out of a string of spoken words—such as "hug," "dig," "pig,"
and "wig," where "hug" is the odd one out. (Items in quotation marks
indicate spoken words that are heard by the child. Component sounds of
spoken words are indicated by slash marks, although not with International Phonetic Alphabet (IPA) symbols, to make the text easier to read.
For example, although the proper IPA form for the component sounds of
"cat" is /kæt/, it will be shown as /cat/. Print words or letters that are seen
by the child will be indicated by italics.)

The ability to separate onsets and rimes, which is necessary to understand nursery rhymes, seems to be a precursor to phonemic awareness.
Understanding nursery rhymes requires that the child break a heard syllable into its onset [the beginning consonant(s)] and its rime [a technical
word in linguistics, referring to the remainder of the syllable, which includes the vowel and optional consonant(s)]. For example, to work out
that the two words "fun" and "gun" rhyme with one another, the child
has to break each word into its onset ("fun":/f-/; "gun":/g-/) and then
compare their rimes ("fun":/-un/; "gun": /-un/). Since the rimes are the
same, the words rhyme, whereas the two words "fun" and "can" do not
rhyme. Bowey (1991) says that an understanding of onset-rime helps
children to notice similar letter-sound patterns in words that rhyme (e.g.,
"fat," "cat"). Onset-rime awareness is a midway skill between syllable
awareness (e.g., /pic-nic/ = "picnic") and complete phonemic awareness
(e.g., /c-a-t/ = "cat"). Children acquire more complex skills for segmenting heard sounds of words (e.g., they can tell you that there are three

phonemes in "fish"; they can tell you that "eat" is left if the first sound is taken from "meat"). They can use this knowledge to acquire single letter-sound correspondences, for example, the letters *sh* in *fish* represent the phoneme /sh/. Though onset-rime awareness is an intermediate step toward complete phonemic awareness, it may be the first step toward a more complex awareness of phonemes—and toward literacy.

Savin (1972) also reported that children from low-income backgrounds in inner-city schools in the United States had no trouble breaking heard words into syllables (e.g., "window" =/win/ + /dow/), but they lacked the ability to analyze syllables into phonemes. These children had teachers who could speak their dialect and who understood their needs, yet the children were still insensitive to rhyme. Savin cited one child who thought that the word "bicycle" rhymed with "hat," "cat," and "fat." Smith and Dixon (1995) surveyed 64 preschool children (4-year-olds) in the United States. Of the 64, 33 were from low-income backgrounds and attended Head Start preschools, while 31 were from middle-class backgrounds and attended preschools that charged tuition. All children were assessed in their first month of preschool. The researchers found significant differences in prereading skills, especially knowledge of letter names and sounds, ability to blend the heard sounds of syllables into words (e.g., /ta-ble/ = "table"; /el-bow/ = "elbow") and ability to blend onsets and rimes into words (e.g., What word is this? /t-ea/). Most low scorers were from low-income backgrounds, though 5 of the children from middle-class homes also scored very poorly on the alphabet and phoneme tasks. Most of the high scorers were from middle-class homes, but 3 of the children from low-income homes also scored very high. These findings suggest that problems with phonemic awareness are not unique to children from low-income backgrounds. They occur across a range of social strata, though they appear to be more pronounced among children from low-income families.

Thus we are likely to find children from a wide range of home backgrounds who have difficulty with phonemic awareness. They will focus exclusively on the meanings of words rather than also on their phonemic form. For example, if you ask a 5-year-old whether the spoken word "butterfly" is a long word or a short word, the child may answer correctly that it is a long word, but when you ask why, she might say something like, "It's got lots of colors." Or, if you ask a child whether the spoken word "spaghetti" is a long or short word, the child might respond wrongly that "spaghetti" is a short word. When asked why it is a short word, she may say, "Because my mommy cuts it up for me," which makes sense if we realize that the child is thinking of the meaning of "spaghetti" rather than about its phonological form. My students have asked 5-year-olds to say the sounds in the spoken word "cat." Some children will say "meow." All these examples illustrate the way in which many preschoolers focus on meaning rather than sounds in words. They do not yet know how to reflect on both the semantic and phonological structure of words.

Starting school with at least a minimal level of phonemic awareness seems very important. Share and colleagues (1984) assessed 500 Australian schoolchildren on 39 variables. They found that phonemic awareness at school entry was the best predictor of later reading success, even after taking account of many other variables including age, intelligence, and home background. Bryant, Bradley, MacLean, and Crossland (1989), in England, found that children's knowledge of nursery rhymes at 3 years of age strongly predicted their reading ability at 6 years of age. The 64 children (3-year-olds) in the city of Oxford were from a wide range of home backgrounds. They were asked to recite five rhymes: Humpty Dumpty, Baa-Baa Black Sheep, Hickory Dickory Dock, Jack and Jill, and Twinkle Twinkle Little Star. The researchers recorded whether or not the children knew the whole rhyme, part of it, or none at all. The children were later assessed at age 6 using a sentence reading completion task (e.g., *Lemons are: year, yet, yes, you, yellow*). Children who scored well on this 6-year-old reading test also had good knowledge of nursery rhymes at age 3. The predictive value of nursery rhymes held up even after taking account of factors such as intelligence and home background. Children from both low-income and middle-class home backgrounds who started school with good knowledge of nursery rhymes had a better chance of learning to read than those who did not know nursery rhymes.

The importance of starting school with at least a minimal level of phonemic awareness was supported in a longitudinal study by Juel (1988, 1994). She followed a group of 129 pupils from low-income home backgrounds in Austin, Texas, through grades 1 to 4. At the end of grade 4 only 54 pupils remained in the study. Many of the children's parents worked at a nearby Air Force base. Military personnel tend to move around a lot. Of the 54 children, 30 were average or good readers and 24 were poor readers. Juel found that the pupils who were poor readers in grade 4 had all entered school with low levels of phonemic awareness. For example, Juel (1994) reported data on one pupil, Javier, who had no awareness of phonemes even after 6 months of school: "When asked questions such as, 'What are the two sounds in 'up'?' in February Javier replied 'Climb up, fall down.'" (p. 52) Poor readers like Javier after 4 years in school had still not achieved reading levels attained by average and good readers after only 2 years at school. All 54 children lived in low-income housing, yet 30 of the 54 had achieved average or above-average reading levels at grade 4. These average and good readers had started school with much higher levels of phonemic awareness than had the children who became poor readers.

WHAT IS SO DIFFICULT ABOUT PHONEME AWARENESS?

Why is it that some preschoolers are phonemically aware and some are not? Tunmer, Herriman, and Nesdale (1988) found that the presence of Piagetian concrete operational thinking skills was associated with phonemic awareness. Also, some children's phonological differentiation of words in working memory may not be as well developed as other children's (Chomsky, 1970; Tunmer, 1997). Also, the task of isolating phonemes is difficult for children, due to the problem of parallel transmission in speech production. Speech sounds are not like beads on a string. They are glued together in the speech stream. For example, the phoneme /d/ can't be said in isolation. Instead, we say it as /duh/. This makes it difficult for the child to connect the letter *d* with the phoneme /d/. To isolate /d/ they mentally have to segment the syllable /duh/ into /d/ and /uh/ (Tunmer, 1997).

Whatever the causes of difficulties with phonemic awareness, many preschoolers do learn about phonemes. And researchers have had some success in teaching phonemic awareness to children from both middle-class and low-income backgrounds. Research on this topic is reviewed in Chapter 3, but we will briefly review some studies now that have focused on teaching children from low-income backgrounds. Phonemic awareness skills have been taught successfully in inner-city schools on Chicago's South Side to grade-1 children (Wallach & Wallach, 1979), in central and north Harlem to reading-disabled children aged 7 to 10 years (Williams, 1980), to preschool children attending Head Start programs (Whitehurst et al., 1994), and to kindergarten children (5-year-olds) in inner-city schools in upstate New York (Blachman, Ball, Black, & Tangel, 1994).

In my own work in New Zealand, I have had mixed success. In one study (see Chapter 3) we were very successfully able to teach phonemic awareness to school beginners (5-year-olds) from mostly middle-class backgrounds (Castle, Riach, & Nicholson, 1994; Nicholson, 1994). But I have had only modest success with 5-year-olds from low-income homes in South Auckland (Nicholson, 1997). In this study, 88 children in their first few months of school were divided into two matched groups (44 in each group). Children were matched on verbal ability, alphabet knowledge, and phonemic awareness. Each matched pair of children was of a similar age and from the same classroom. Children in the experimental group were taught in 12 small groups of three to five children. Each group received 12 weeks of daily 10-minute teaching sessions that focused on phonemic awareness, learning of the alphabet, and simple phonics. The matched control group was also taught in 12 small groups and received similar materials and attention to the alphabet, but without an emphasis on sounds or simple phonics. Only letter names were taught. We used *Sound Foundations* (Byrne & Fielding-Barnsley, 1991) and ideas from

Wallach and Wallach (1976) for much of the phonemic awareness instruction. The research materials concentrated mainly on beginning and ending sounds in words. When I compared the progress of the children trained in phonemic awareness (and simple letter-sound correspondences) with the matched control group of children who had not received the phonemic awareness instruction, the experimental group had made significant gains in phonemic spelling (e.g., *kt* for "cat"), reading of three-letter words (e.g., *cat*), and reading of pseudowords (e.g., *gac*). Like Whitehurst and colleagues (1994), who also used the *Sound Foundations* material with children from low-income backgrounds, I found that the experimental group gained only in ability to recognize the first sound in words. These results suggest that children from low-income backgrounds can benefit from phonemic awareness instruction but that they do not easily acquire phonemic awareness.

Training in phonemic awareness can be successful with low-income children, though they may need a lot of instruction over an extended period. There are still questions to be asked about how best to teach them. Some children will need more instruction than others. Some of the 5-year-olds in my study did not respond to phonemic awareness and simple phonics instruction. Blachman (1997) has reported that such children are "treatment resistors" who do benefit if given longer and more in-depth instruction. In my study, however, we were unable to provide the length and depth of instruction that they needed. At the end of the study, there were still some children who had made no progress. This was reflected in their test results and in their answers to our questionnaire about reading. We asked one child, "How often do you read at home?" The reply was, "Never. I hate reading now." This was from a 5-year-old still in his first year of school. We asked another child, "How do you feel when you come to a new word while reading?" The reply was, "I cry." We asked yet another child, "Would you rather clean up your room or read?" The child said, "Clean up my room, 'cause I *can* clean up my room, but I can't read." The wider classroom effects of not learning to read in the first year of school were already showing up. We asked one child, "How do you feel when it's your turn to read to the teacher?" The child said, "Sad, because the teacher gives you a growling." I am presently following up some of the children in the study. They are now 6 years old. A noticeable theme is the lack of resources at home for some of these children. We asked one child, "How do you feel when someone reads you a story at home?" The child said, "No one ever reads me a story at home." We asked another child, "How many children's books do you have at home?" The child said she had no books at all, and commented, "I never get to get any books." Another child said she had between five and ten books. When asked why, she said, "Because I've been good. My mum buys them, she's got the moneys [*sic*], she paid it." When the same child was asked whether she liked to read, she said, "No. Mum likes me to read, but I read ugly. 'Cause I don't know how to read." Such comments indicate the extent of the challenge that faces teachers who want (ideally) all their pupils to be able to read by the end of the first year of school. Early success in teaching reading, especially for children who come from struggling backgrounds, really is the most important contribution a teacher can make at that age level.

Teaching phonemic awareness is a first step to achieving the goal of teaching children to read. Some children will require lots of instruction; others, very little. We can easily start with children's prior knowledge of rhymes, such as traditional nursery rhymes. There may also be other rhymes that children know, for example, jump-rope rhymes such as "Cinderella, dressed in pink, went downstairs to the kitchen sink, the kitchen sink was full of ink, how many mouthfuls did she drink? One, two, three, four, . . . " (Turner, Factor, & Lowenstein, 1978). Teaching phonemic awareness can be a lot of fun, as well as being of real value. We can teach phonemic awareness successfully now, but the search for more and better ways of teaching phonemic awareness should continue.

REVIEW

Data from a number of studies indicate that children from low-income backgrounds do less well in school than children from middle-class backgrounds. There are many factors that militate against success for children from low-income homes, including the need to do lots of chores at home; lack of study facilities, books, and money for school materials; ostracism at school; attendance at schools with a preponderance of other pupils from low-income backgrounds; stress and feelings of inadequacy on the part of the parents of these children; and possible miscommunication between parents and schools about the academic progress of their children. In addition to these social disadvantages, there are linguistic disadvantages as well for children from low-income backgrounds. Compared with children from middle-class homes, they have less knowledge of the names and sounds of the letters of the alphabet, less knowledge of books, and less knowledge of the phonemic structure of spoken words.

Although children from low-income backgrounds are worse-off than middle-class children in terms of learning to read, it is also clear that many middle-class children also experience difficulty in learning to read. This has led researchers to believe that there may be a linguistic factor that makes learning to read a difficult task for children from all kinds of social backgrounds. The linguistic factor that seems responsible is phonemic awareness. Many children, from a wide range of social backgrounds, speaking many different languages, all over the world, experience difficulty in becoming phonemically aware. It is a difficulty that holds them back in learning letter-sound correspondences. This especially applies to alphabetic writing systems such as English, where there is a complex, indirect rule system of letter-to-sound correspondences, a rule system that is by no means transparent to the child.

Teachers may not be able to change the social realities of their pupils' home environments, but there is evidence to suggest that intensive early instruction in the skills of phonemic awareness and letter-sound relationships will enable children from all social backgrounds to get off to a better start in learning to read and spell.

STUDY AND DISCUSSION QUESTIONS

1. What is different about the home backgrounds of children who learn to read before they start school?
2. What kinds of social and linguistic differences are there between children from low-income and middle-class backgrounds?
3. What is phonemic awareness?
4. What evidence is there that phonemic awareness skills are important for learning to read and spell for all children, irrespective of family and social background?
5. Discuss the merits of the following proposals for getting children from low-income backgrounds off to a better start in reading and spelling:
   (a) Give them books so they can read at home, or be read to at home.
   (b) Teach them phonemic awareness skills.

FURTHER READING

Calfee, R. C., & Patrick, C. L. (1995). *Teach our children well: Bringing K–12 education into the 21st century.* Stanford, CA: Portable Stanford Series.

Chall, J. S., Jacobs, V. A., & Baldwin, L. E. (1990). *The reading crisis: Why poor children fall behind.* Cambridge, MA: Harvard University Press.

Juel, C. (1994). *Learning to read in one elementary school.* New York: Springer-Verlag.

Stanovich, K. E. (1986). Matthew effects in reading: Some consequences of individual differences in the acquisition of literacy. *Reading Research Quarterly, 21,* 360–407.

TEACHING MATERIALS

Byrne, B., & Fielding-Barnsley, R. (1991). *Sound foundations*. Sydney, Australia: Peter Leyden Educational.

Nicholson, T. (1994). *At the cutting edge: Recent research on learning to read and spell.* Wellington, New Zealand: New Zealand Council for Educational Research.

Nicholson, T. (1997). *Solving reading problems*. Wellington, New Zealand: New Zealand Council for Educational Research.

Wallach, M. A., & Wallach, L. (1976). *Teaching all children to read*. Chicago: University of Chicago Press.

REFERENCES

Adams, M. J. (1990). *Beginning to read: Thinking and learning about print.* Cambridge, MA: MIT Press.

Anbar, A. (1986). Reading acquisition of preschool children without systematic instruction. *Early Childhood Research Quarterly, 1*, 69–83.

Bissex, G. L. (1980). *GNYS AT WRK: A child learns to write and read.* Cambridge, MA: Harvard University Press.

Blachman, B. A. (1997). Early intervention and phonological awareness: A cautionary tale. In B. A. Blachman (Ed.), *Foundations of reading acquisition and dyslexia: Implications for early intervention* (pp. 409–430). Mahwah, NJ: Erlbaum.

Blachman, B. A., Ball, E. W., Black, R. S., & Tangel, D. M. (1994). Kindergarten teachers develop phonemic awareness in low-income, inner-city classrooms. *Reading and Writing, 6*, 1–18.

Bowey, J. (1991). Early reading: Rime and reason. *Australian Journal of Reading, 14*, 140–144.

Bryant, P. E., Bradley, L., MacLean, M., & Crossland, J. (1989). Nursery rhymes, phonological skills and reading. *Journal of Child Language, 16*, 407–428.

Byrne, B., & Fielding-Barnsley, R. (1991). *Sound foundations*. Sydney, Australia: Peter Leyden Educational.

Castle, J. M., Riach, J., & Nicholson, T. (1994). Getting off to a better start in reading and spelling: The effects of phonemic awareness instruction within a whole language program. *Journal of Educational Psychology, 86*, 350–359.

Chall, J. S., Jacobs, V. A., & Baldwin, L. E. (1990). *The reading crisis: Why poor children fall behind.* Cambridge, MA: Harvard University Press.

Chomsky, N. (1970). Phonology and reading. In H. Levin & J. P. Williams (Eds.), *Basic studies on reading* (pp. 3–18). New York: Basic Books.

Clark, M. M. (1976). *Young fluent readers: What can they tell us.* London: Heinemann.

Corballis, M. (1991). *The lopsided ape.* New York: Oxford University Press.

Dickenson, D. K., & Snow, C. E. (1987). Interrelationships among prereading and oral language skills in kindergartners from two social classes. *Early Childhood Research Quarterly, 2*, 1–25.

Duff, A. (1990). *Once were warriors.* Auckland, New Zealand: Tandem.

Durkin, D. (1966). *Children who read early*. New York: Teachers College Press.

Feitelson, D., & Goldstein, Z. (1986). Patterns of book ownership and reading to young children in Israeli school oriented and nonschool oriented families. *Reading Teacher, 39*, 924–930.

Finn, J. D., & Achilles, C. M. (1990). Answers to questions about class size: A statewide experiment. *American Educational Research Journal, 27*, 557–577.

Foss, D., & Hakes, D. (1978). *Psycholinguistics: An introduction to the psychology of language*. Englewood Cliffs, NJ: Prentice-Hall.

Gibbons, J. (1980). *The effects of book experience on the responses of four-year-olds to texts*. Unpublished master's thesis, University of Waikato, Hamilton, New Zealand.

Hakes, D. (1980). The development of metalinguistic abilities: What develops? In S. A. Kuczaj (Ed.), *Language acquisition: Language, cognition and culture* (pp. 163–210). Hillsdale, NJ: Erlbaum.

Horin, A. (1995, February 4). Poverty marks its victims in kindergarten. *Sydney Morning Herald*, p. 2.

Hundreds of school children missing. (1996, March 13). *East and Bays Courier* (Auckland, New Zealand), p. 17.

Juel, C. (1988). Learning to read and write: A longitudinal study of 54 children from first through fourth grades. *Journal of Educational Psychology, 80*, 437–447.

Juel, C. (1994). *Learning to read in one elementary school*. New York: Springer-Verlag.

Lass, B. (1982). Portrait of my son as an early reader. *Reading Teacher, 35*, 20–28.

Lass, B. (1983). Portrait of my son as an early reader II. *Reading Teacher, 36*, 508–515.

Morris, J. M. (1984). Children like Frank, deprived of literacy unless . . . In D. Dennis (Ed.), *Reading: Meeting children's special needs* (pp. 16–28). London: Heinemann.

Nicholson, T. (1980). *An evaluation study of the radio series "On the way to reading."* Report to the New Zealand Broadcasting Commission. Hamilton, New Zealand: University of Waikato.

Nicholson, T. (1994). *At the cutting edge: Recent research on learning to read and spell*. Wellington, New Zealand: New Zealand Council for Educational Research.

Nicholson, T. (1997). Closing the gap on reading failure: Social background, phonemic awareness, and learning to read. In B. A. Blachman (Ed.), *Foundations of reading acquisition and dyslexia: Implications for early intervention* (pp. 381–407). Mahwah, NJ: Erlbaum.

Nicholson, T., & Gallienne, G. (1995). Struggletown meets Middletown: A survey of reading achievement levels among 13-year-old pupils in two contrasting socioeconomic areas. *New Zealand Journal of Educational Studies, 30*, 15–24.

Nicholson, T., Lam, R., Van Kuyk, T., Brown, G. T., & Lemke, S. A. (1998). *Precocious readers: Two case studies*. Manuscript in preparation. University of Auckland.

Orr, E. (1995). *Australia's literacy challenge. The importance of education in breaking the poverty cycle for Australia's disadvantaged families*. Camperdown, Sydney: Smith Family.

Phillips, G., & McNaughton, S. (1990). The practice of storybook reading to pre-school children in mainstream New Zealand families. *Reading Research Quarterly, 25,* 196–212.

Pinker, S. (1994). *The language instinct.* New York: Morrow.

Raz, I. T., & Bryant, P. (1990). Social background, phonological awareness and children's reading. *British Journal of Developmental Psychology, 8,* 209–225.

Rutter, M. (1983). School effects on pupil progress: Research findings and policy implications. *Child Development, 54,* 1–29.

Sakamoto, T. (1976). Writing systems in Japan. In J. Merritt (Ed.), *New horizons in reading* (pp. 244–249). Newark, DE: International Reading Association.

Savin, H. B. (1972). What a child knows about speech when he starts to learn to read. In J. F. Kavanagh & I. Mattingly (Eds.), *Language by ear and eye* (pp. 319–326). Cambridge, MA: MIT Press.

Scarborough, H., & Dobrich, W. (1994). On the efficacy of reading to preschoolers. *Developmental Review, 14,* 245–302.

Share, D. L., Jorm, A. F., Maclean, R., & Matthews, R. (1984). Sources of individual differences in reading acquisition. *Journal of Educational Psychology, 76,* 1309–1324.

Skills-test failure rate high for minority, poor students. (1996, May 25). *Minneapolis Star Tribune,* pp. A1, A22.

Smith, S. S., & Dixon, R. G. (1995). Literacy concepts of low- and middle-class four-year-olds entering preschool. *Journal of Educational Research, 88,* 243–253.

Snow, C. E., Barnes, W. S., Chandler, J., Goodman, I. F., & Hemphill, L. (1991). *Unfulfilled expectations: Home and school influences on literacy.* Cambridge, MA: Harvard University Press.

Stanovich, K. E. (1986). Matthew effects in reading: Some consequences of individual differences in the acquisition of literacy. *Reading Research Quarterly, 21,* 360–407.

Teale, W. H. (1986). Home background and young children's literacy development. In W. H. Teale & E. Sulzby (Eds.), *Emergent literacy: Writing and reading* (pp. 173–206). Norwood, NJ: Ablex.

Tunmer, W. E. (1997). Metalinguistic skills in reading development. In V. Edwards & D. Corson (Eds.), *Encyclopedia of language and education: Vol. 2. Literacy* (pp. 27–36). Dordrecht, Netherlands: Kluwer.

Tunmer, W. E., & Bowey, J. (1984). Word awareness in children. In W. E. Tunmer, C. Pratt, & M. L. Herriman (Eds.), *Metalinguistic awareness in children* (pp. 73–91). Berlin: Springer-Verlag.

Tunmer, W. E., Herriman, M. L., & Nesdale, A. R. (1988). Metalinguistic abilities and beginning reading. *Reading Research Quarterly, 23,* 134–158.

Turner, A., Connolly, G., & Devlin, M. (1992). *Food related needs in a sample of Otara and Manurewa families.* Report for the Health Promotion Unit, Auckland Area Health Board. Auckland, New Zealand: Manukau City Council.

Turner, I., Factor, J., & Lowenstein, W. (1978). *Cinderella dressed in yella.* Richmond, Australia: Heinemann.

Wallach, L., Wallach, M. A., Dozier, M. G., & Kaplan, N. E. (1976). Poor children learning to read do not have trouble with auditory discrimination but do have trouble with phoneme recognition. *Journal of Educational Psychology, 69,* 36–39.

Wallach, M. A., & Wallach, L. (1976). *Teaching all children to read.* Chicago: University of Chicago Press.

Wallach, M. A., & Wallach, L. (1979). Helping disadvantaged children to learn to read by teaching them phoneme identification skills. In L. A. Resnick & P. A. Weaver (Eds.), *Theory and practice of early reading* (Vol. 3; pp. 227–259). Hillsdale, NJ: Erlbaum.

Wells, G. (1985). Preschool literacy-related activities and success in school. In D. R. Olson, N. Torrance, & A. Hildyard (Eds.), *Literacy, language and learning* (pp. 229–255). Cambridge, UK: Cambridge University Press.

Whitehurst, G. J., Epstein, J. N., Angell, A. L., Payne, A. C., Crone, D. A., & Fischel, J. E. (1994). Outcomes of an emergent literacy intervention in Head Start. *Journal of Educational Psychology, 86,* 542–555.

Williams, J. P. (1980). Teaching decoding with an emphasis on phoneme analysis and phoneme blending. *Journal of Educational Psychology, 72,* 1–15.

Wilson, C., & Dupuis, A. (1992). Poverty and performance. In *Set: Research information for teachers* (No. 1, Item 15). Wellington, New Zealand: New Zealand Council for Educational Research.

PART I

LEARNING WORD IDENTIFICATION

In Chapter 1 we looked at how the child's family and social experiences contribute to the learning of literacy skills. We now consider in Part I some specific ways in which these experiences, and the teaching received, contribute to the child's learning of reading skills in the initial years at school.

The central theme of Part I is the learning that enables the child to identify the print forms of words: to know which word is indicated by the letters seen on the page. In Chapter 2 Brian Thompson describes how the child learns the connection between the letters of the word and the meanings and sound of the word, in order to form in memory an orthographic representation of the word, as the print form of the word becomes familiar to the child. He also describes how the child is able to respond to many unfamiliar print words by generating a response. Four different ways in which the child may do this are described. In three of them the child relates letters of the word to component sounds of words. Learning and teaching about these component sounds is the topic of Chapter 3, by Jillian Castle. The assessment and teaching of phonemic awareness is examined. Particular attention is given to this teaching in the context of "whole-language" classroom programs.

Contrasting approaches to teaching reading are considered in Chapters 4 and 5. In Chapter 4 William Tunmer and James Chapman describe and critically examine several facets of the "whole-language" approach to teaching reading. They then offer an alternative set of teaching strategies that are intended to meet objections directed at both the whole-language approach and the contrasting "skill-and-drill" phonics approach. In Chapter 5 Vincent Connelly, Rhona Johnston, and Brian Thompson compare the learning effects of teaching approaches that include explicit phonics with those that don't. While in the past most such comparisons have been concerned exclusively with achievement-level outcomes, this chapter examines whether children's *ways* of learning differ under these different approaches to teaching, when the children in each instructional context have reached the same level of reading achievement. They conclude that the child will learn more than one way to identify words in reading but that contrasting instructional contexts influence the child to use some ways more than others.

Chapter 2

The Processes of Learning
to Identify Words

G. BRIAN THOMPSON

a) What knowledge do children acquire that enables them to read words?

b) What is there of this knowledge that can be taught?

c) Is there more than one way of learning to read words?

d) What are the current theories about learning to read words?

The reader's goal is usually the comprehension or understanding of a text, but this cannot be achieved without the reader identifying the words of the text. The purpose of this chapter is to introduce several important concepts about the processes the child uses to learn to identify print words. These concepts will be placed in the context of theoretical accounts of this learning, in particular the Knowledge Sources account and, at appropriate points, in the context of some important contrasting accounts. The processes of learning will also be related to contemporary theories of the adult reader's print-word identification. Normal reading development will be assumed. Consideration will be restricted to alphabetic orthographies (writing systems) and the examples to English orthography.

Print words, as stimuli in our environment, are patterns of lines on a two-dimensional surface, which may be paper, a computer screen, food packet, or graffiti-covered wall. Print or written words are used as signs for human language: the words heard and spoken. These have their use as carriers of meaning, and the child of 5 or 6 years has already learned such use. When being taught to read, that child begins to make use of the patterns of lines, which we call print words, for similar purposes. How does the child learn this? Does the beginner, for example, learn to read new words in a way different from the more experienced reader?

The first aspect of this new task to be mastered by the beginner (and still required for the adult reader) is to discriminate and categorize the print patterns to establish the identity of words, for example, to identify the print patterns *Bill* and **Bill** as the same word and *Mary* as a different word. The child has had prior experience in discriminating and identifying pictured objects. For example, the child is able to tell which of two pictures is a picture of a house and which is a picture of a tree. Can learning to identify print words make use of the same process? It can do so only for a very limited set of words. For example, it can work for discriminating and identifying the words *Bill* and *Mary*, where the picture-like characteristics of these two visual patterns differ. This is called primitive logographic responding. But for discriminating between *ball* and *bell*, which have picture-like characteristics that are so similar, logographic responding will not succeed. To discriminate these readily, the child would need to learn that each comprises four letters and that *a* and *e* are different letters. There is evidence to support the claim that normally developing children for a brief period, very early in learning to read, may make use of primitive logographic responding or pre-alphabetic visual features of words (Ehri, 1994, 1995; Ehri & Wilce, 1985). This may be for only a few days or weeks and may sometimes occur before school instruction in reading commences. It is clear that other means of identification of print words very soon become established.

ORTHOGRAPHIC MEMORY OF WORDS

The child soon learns to identify print words by storing knowledge of the component letters of the word as it becomes familiar. What does this procedure require? For the word *ball*, for example, the reader stores in memory information about which letter occupies each of the letter positions of the word: *b, a, l, l.* The storage of this orthographic representation of the word, as the reader becomes familiar with the print word, will enable the reader to identify the word, avoiding confusion with the print words *bell* and *doll,* as well as all the others that the child knows. This procedure will be called here identification by recall. It is sometimes also called sight word recognition. (The latter term can also refer to a type of teaching about words but is not the reference intended here.)

The orthographic representation of the word is connected in memory with the sound (phonology) and the meaning(s) of the word. Hence, for the reader the print word *ball* has the sound and meanings of "ball," not those of "bell," "doll," or any other word. As the child starts to learn to read, the teacher (or parent) will often provide the information for learning these connections. For example, the teacher says "ball" when the child sees the print word *ball*; or the teacher provides a correction when the child reads "doll" for the word *ball*. (There are other ways for learning the connections, but these will be considered later.)

The child will learn that each letter has a range of variants, for example, that the letter *b* can appear as any one of many visual shapes, such as b, *b*, ʙ, and so forth. The child will also learn that each letter has upper-case forms that also have their variants, for example, B, *B*, ʙ, and so forth. The child will soon learn that each of the 26 letters of our English alphabet does not have one particular visual shape but a range of various shapes. Hence the child learns that each of the 26 letters is an abstract category of variant shapes, called an *abstract letter unit* (ALU). There is no single visual shape that is the ALU, but a category of shapes. Any one of these various shapes of an ALU will enable the reader to distinguish it from all the other 25 ALUs of our alphabet. All this has to be learned and only becomes part of the child's implicit knowledge as the variant print forms of our English orthography become familiar to the child. As this occurs, the orthographic representation of a word gradually becomes a complete representation comprising ALUs, one for each letter position of the word.

If a child is identifying print words exclusively by primitive logographic means (i.e., by picture-like characteristics) and is able to identify the word *bag*, in lowercase print, then that child would have no way of knowing what *BAG* could be if this uppercase form of the word had never been seen before. For that child it would be an entirely strange picture-like pattern having no connection with *bag*. On the other hand, we would expect a different reading response if the child had the print word *bag* in memory as an orthographic representation that included storage of the letters and their letter positions in the word and if the child had already learned that *b* and *B* belong to one ALU, *a* and *A* to another, and *g* and *G* to yet another. A child with these representations in memory would have little difficulty identifying the previously unseen print form *BAG*. Such simple words in uppercase have been found to present no difficulties for children in the second year of reading instruction even when that instruction had emphasized whole words and did not include explicit phonics (Thompson & Johnston, 1998).

Not all the orthographic representation of a word will be learned at once. Some components will be acquired before others. For example, in learning the print word *crab* the letters *c* and *b* are likely to receive storage in memory before other components are fixed in memory. That is to say, the left and right boundary positions of the word are likely to take priority in this sequence of acquisition. There is evidence consistent with this claim about partial orthographic representation (Cassidy, 1992; Stuart & Coltheart, 1988). At the point of learning in which only *c* and *b* are represented in memory for the word *crab*, it may well be that the word *cab* has also been represented in memory with just the same two letters. Hence the child might respond "cab" to the print word *crab*. Similarly, the child may respond "got" for the print word *get* if only the two boundary ALUs for *g* and *t*, and not the medial ALUs, are stored in memory for these words.

During the child's initial experience with print words, the child has to learn the directional conventions of the orthography. For example, "got" is written in English as *got*, not with the ALUs in the reverse order, *tog*, or any other order. The child has to learn the left-to-right spatial convention of English orthography that corresponds to the order in time of the component sounds of the spoken word. The /g/ sound is the first in the spoken form and by the conventions of English orthography the corresponding ALU is printed (or written) in the position of the left, rather than the right, boundary of the word. Prior to learning this the child may well respond to the print stimulus *tog* with the response "got" or "get." As a general early aspect of this directional learning, the child will come to know the conventional order of reading print words. In English orthography this is left to right in every line and with the lines read from top to bottom of the page. See Clay (1970) for a study of children's learning of these directional conventions.

WORD IDENTIFICATION BY GENERATION

Letters of words systematically map onto sounds in words. This is the *alphabetic principle*. For example, the letter *b* maps onto the phoneme /b/, which is the sound common to the spoken words "job," "crab," "bell," "bit," and so forth. When the letter *b* appears in English orthography, it almost always has the same corresponding phoneme. Some letters often do not have such a simple correspondence with phonemes, especially the vowel phonemes. For example, the letter *i* in *find* has a different sound from that in *fish*. Nevertheless, the mapping is not capricious. It has systematic elements. The letter *i* will not correspond to the phoneme /b/ or /t/, for example. It will correspond to only a limited range of vowel sounds.

It should be noted that the alphabetic principle states that letters of words map onto *sounds in words*, not isolated sounds. Knowledge of instances of the alphabetic principle is more than knowledge of sound labels for isolated letters. For example, the child may learn that /buh/ is an appropriate sound label for the isolated letter *b*. However, if the child does not also know that the phoneme /b/ is common to the sounds of certain words, for example "job" and "crab," the child has not acquired an instance of the alphabetic principle. Knowledge of phoneme identities in the sound of words is necessary (Byrne & Fielding-Barnsley, 1990). The explicit form of this knowledge is demonstrated in the child's phonemic awareness, which is discussed in Chapter 3.

All the variant visual shapes of a letter, for example, b or *b* or B, and so forth, are related to the same phoneme (or limited range of phonemes in the case of letters for vowels). Hence it is the abstract letter units that are relevant when considering correspondences with phonemes. It is the abstract letter units or particular combinations of them that usually have a one-to-one correspondence with phonemes, for example, B, TH, NG, AI, EE, and so forth. These are called *graphemes*. For each there is usually only one corresponding phoneme, or in the case of vowels a small set of corresponding phonemes. Hence we have what are called *grapheme-phoneme correspondences* (GPCs).

If the child has knowledge of GPCs, the child can apply it in attempting to identify print words that are not familiar. For example, if *tag* is unfamiliar, and the child has available in memory the GPCs for the constituent graphemes, T, A, G, then the child can respond with a sound for each grapheme of *tag* and generate a pronunciation that approximates the pronunciation of "tag." This procedure sometimes includes "sounding out" the word but is commonly carried out by the child with no audible pronunciation and with the child having little or no awareness of the procedure. In either case, the procedure is an instance of what is often called *phonological recoding*, that is, converting a graphemic code into the corresponding phonological (phonemic) code in order to identify a word. Sometimes it is referred to as *decoding*, although this term can also be a synonym for word identification by any procedure. Sometimes, also, phonological recoding is described as the child's use of *graphophonic* or *graphophonemic* cues.

Phonological recoding can contribute to the child's generation, that is, working out of a response to an *unfamiliar* word. These and other sources of knowledge can contribute to the generation procedures for attempting to identify a print word (see Figure 2.1). Phonological recoding procedures are sometimes called *mediation* procedures because there is a working out process that mediates between the child's response to the letters of the word and the word identification response.

Generation procedures can be contrasted with the recall ("sight word") procedures that depend on the orthographic representation in memory of the *familiar* print word. In recall no such intermediary process is necessary, only memory connections between the orthographic representation of the familiar print word and the sound and meanings of the word. Now the reader has no way of knowing before attempting to identify a word

Figure 2.1 The Dynamics of Acquisition and Use of Knowledge Sources in the Procedures for the Child's Identification of Print Words

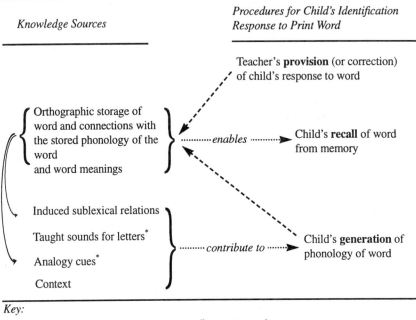

Knowledge Sources

Procedures for Child's Identification Response to Print Word

Teacher's **provision** (or correction) of child's response to word

Orthographic storage of word and connections with the stored phonology of the word and word meanings

.... *enables* ....➤ Child's **recall** of word from memory

Induced sublexical relations

Taught sounds for letters*

Analogy cues*

Context

.... *contribute to* ....➤ Child's **generation** of phonology of word

Key:

- - - ➤ Consistent repeated occurrences contribute to storage in memory

———➤ Connections in memory

*May not be available to the child.

whether the word will be one that is familiar or unfamiliar. This cannot be known until identification has taken place. Hence the reader will normally start to attempt identification with both generation and recall procedures. If the word is familiar enough to have an orthographic representation, then the recall procedure will enable the identification without it being necessary to complete the intermediary generation procedures. These will then have no direct part in the word identification made. If the print word is unfamiliar, generation procedures will be necessary to attempt a response to the word. These procedures will usually involve phonological recoding. They extend the reader's identification responses beyond those available by recall procedures, which will succeed only with familiar print words.

There are, however, some limitations in this extension. Phonological recoding will not work for a few English words, such as *eye, once, choir, yacht, does,* which exhibit little systematic correspondence between graphemes and phonemes. These words are in part exceptions to the alphabetic principle. Moreover, phonological recoding for the young child will be rather inaccurate for a much larger set of words, such as *bind, foot, steak*, which do follow the alphabetic principle and exhibit systematic GPCs but of a kind likely to be too complex for the beginner reader. In many dialects of English, pronunciation of the vowel in *bind* as in *fit*, the vowel in *foot* as in *zoo*, and the vowel in *steak* as in *weak* will result in identification errors (which are called regularization errors). Nevertheless, readers may treat such responses as only rough approximates that they can attempt to match against their existing hearing and speaking vocabulary and so self-correct the pronunciation. The simpler GPCs of words such as *lid, west,* and *trap* would present fewer difficulties for phonological recoding.

EVIDENCE FOR ORTHOGRAPHIC MEMORY OF WORDS

The orthographic representation of a word in memory, which we have described above, comprises the abstract letter units of the word but not correspondences between these units and phonemes. However, the orthographic representation of a word (e.g., *bat*), does have connections in memory to the stored representation of the sound of the whole word ("bat"), that is, the lexical phonology, which the child has already learned for hearing and speaking words. Connections to the stored meanings indicated by the word will also be available. The orthographic storage of words, that is, the lexical orthographic representations, enable the child to identify print words that have become familiar.

The memory storage of a word as a lexical orthographic representation means that the reader can, when required, identify a familiar word without using component sounds of the word such as phonemes. Nevertheless, it must be noted that the use of the lexical orthographic representation for identification by recall does not exclude the simultaneous processing of the component sounds of the word. Such processing may occur, although it has no direct part in the identification made on that occasion.

What evidence is there that as children learn to read they acquire a lexical orthographic representation that can be used to identify words by recall? A review of research on this question has given some support for a positive answer (Rayner & Pollatsek, 1989, pp. 377–382). Young children do store in memory the specific letters, or abstract letter units, of print words as they become familiar with them. Reitsma (1983a, 1983b) and Ehri and Saltmarsh (1995) have found that children in their first year of reading instruction did notice changes of only a single letter in words, although the sound for each word obtainable by phonological recoding was identical in the changed (e.g., *keap*) and original forms of the words (e.g., *keep*). So the children were apparently storing in memory the letter information about the specific words (which storage is not needed for identification of words by phonological recoding).

There is other recent evidence. Thompson and Fletcher-Flinn (1993, Experiment 8) found that 8-year-olds after two (corrected) readings of two-syllable target words (e.g., *pattern, wagon, carpet*) were able to recall, after 1 day, the first vowel letter of the words. In this recall task the children chose which of *a, e, i, o, u* completed the spelling of, for example, *p_ttern*. A control condition showed that this performance was in large part due to memory of letters of the specific words, not to general sound-to-letter correspondence knowledge applied to the sound of the words.

Yet other evidence comes from the child's ability to discriminate between homophones, for example, *brake* and *break*. If the child has no memory storage of the particular letters, or abstract letter units, of these two words, then there would be no way in which the child would know, for example, that the meaning conveyed by the phrase *slow down* was more appropriate to *brake* than *break*. They would have just as much difficulty as the child who heard (but did not see) the two words. The pronunciations of the words are identical and hence as a listening task it would be impossible to make a discrimination between them. It has been shown that 8-year-old children are able to distinguish between the meanings of the print forms of such homophones (Johnston, Thompson, Fletcher-Flinn, & Holligan, 1995, Experiment 1, word meaning control task, and Experiment 2, homophone semantic decision task). Moreover, this result applied to children who received systematic instruction about letter-sound correspondences (explicit phonics) as well as children who were taught without this instruction (Experiment 1).

However, the child's ability to distinguish such printed homophones might depend on a stored orthographic representation for spelling rather than reading, where these are considered distinct representations. The child may identify the sound of the print homophone, for example, *sun*, and through that sound identify *both* the meanings, for example, "male child" and "solar." Then the child could activate the stored knowledge of the *spellings* associated with each of these meanings, for example, SON and SUN. The child could mentally compare these two stored spellings with the stimulus print word, *sun*, and then select that meaning associated with the stored spelling that best matches the stimulus. There is evidence that 8-year-old readers use such an indirect spelling-check procedure (Johnston et al., 1995, Experiment 2). However, a subsequent series of experiments using a research design, in which children were trained over several weeks to improve their responses to homophones, shows that an orthographic representation for reading is available to 8- and 11-year-olds, as well as this spelling-check procedure (Thompson & Potts, 1998). It is plausible that the spelling-check procedure in fact uses a stored orthographic representation that may also sometimes be available for reading. Our conclusions here about reading, however, do not depend on making this assumption.

In view of these several results, it is apparent that as children learn to read, they do acquire lexical orthographic representations that enable them to identify familiar print words, that is, to identify the sound and meanings of a word by immediate recall. This is one source of knowledge children use for word identification, but there are also other sources that are used, especially for generation procedures (see Figure 2.1).

SOURCES OF KNOWLEDGE FOR GENERATION PROCEDURES

In contrast to the recall procedures, which will be successful for identification of familiar print words, there are the generation procedures that are needed for unfamiliar print words. Evidence for the child's use of these generation procedures requires examination of their diversity. There is more than one source of knowledge that the child may use to *generate* a word-identification response in reading. In fact, the child will usually use more than one source in attempting identification of a word. In the Knowledge Sources account of learning to read (Thompson, Cottrell, & Fletcher-Flinn, 1996), there are four such sources of knowledge (see Figure 2.1):

1. *Induced sublexical relations.* These are the relations, stored in memory, between orthographic (e.g., -*t*) and phonological (e.g., /-t/) components that are common to words (e.g., *bat, sit, cat, went, get*) that have become familiar as the child's reading vocabulary accumulates. These relations are acquired, largely through implicit learning, by *induction* from reading experience of the words. Induced sublexical relations are therefore a "lexical" source.
2. *Taught sounds for letters*, for example, /tuh/ for *t*. Because these do not necessarily depend on any prior accumulation of reading vocabulary, they can be regarded as an "alexical" source of knowledge.
3. *Analogy cues* (e.g., reading *hump* by analogy with *jump*) are another kind of lexical source.
4. *Context* of the word. This context may be a language context from the prior portion of text already read (e.g., *The bus will . . . ?*) or it may be a nonlinguistic context, such as an illustration.

Sources 1 and 2 are different uses of the alphabetic principle. They are different types of phonological recoding. Knowledge source 3 depends less directly on the alphabetic principle. The principle is irrelevant to source 4, as here the source of knowledge does not derive from the print word the child is attempting to read. While each of 1 and 2 will often be sufficient to make a successful identification of an unfamiliar word, each of 3 or 4 used alone will, in principle, not be sufficient. To give a reasonable chance of success, use of 3 or 4 will also require some contribution of either 1 or 2. The reasons will be clear as we fill in the details and evidence for each source.

Before considering these, it is important that the overall dynamics of the word-identification procedures be kept in mind (see Figure 2.1). Successful use of generation procedures will mean that learners are able to attempt new words on their own, thus acquiring independence from teaching assistance. The outcomes of generation procedures will be retained in memory. When the child has generated the same response to the same print word on several different occasions, orthographic memory of the word will become established, along with pathways between that stored orthographic representation and the child's other knowledge of the word, its phonology (sound) and meanings. The orthographic memory will then be the source of knowledge for identifying the print word by recall procedures. Generation procedures would then no longer be necessary for this relatively familiar print word.

Induced Sublexical Relations

Induced sublexical relations (ISRs) provide one type of phonological recoding, an application of implicit knowledge of the alphabetic principle. ISRs comprise relations between orthographic components of words and corresponding phonological components in memory, which the child learns largely implicitly and hence unconsciously. These relations are common to print words that have become part of the child's reading vocabulary. Children in the first year of reading instruction will have stored (at least partial) knowledge of the orthographic representations of several print words, such as *bat, sit, cat, went, get.* The child will learn, for example, that there is not only a final orthographic component, -*t*, in common among these print words but also a final-position phonological component, /-t/. The child will then (unconsciously) induce the implicit knowledge that -*t* relates to /-t/ and store this as an ISR. Similarly, there will be induction of the sublexical relation between *t*- and /t-/ from the accumulated knowledge of print words such as *to, take, tiger.* Other orthographic components, for example, *b-, g-, -g, th-, sh-, -sh,* and so forth, common to particular positions within known print words, will be similarly related by the child to sublexical phonological components. The child can then use these stored ISRs to attempt generation of an identification response to an unfamiliar word.

There is evidence that, very early in learning to read, children form such ISRs and are sensitive to position within words (Thompson, Cottrell, & Fletcher-Flinn, 1996). The incidence of the orthographic components -*t* and -*m*, of the right-boundary position of words, was relatively high among the words that a sample of 5- and 6-year-olds experienced in their reading books, but -*b* and -*th* were relatively rare. It was predicted therefore that it would be much more likely that these children had formed an ISR for -*t* and -*m* than for -*b* and -*th*. The results of the children's attempts to generate reading-identification responses for simple pseudowords such as *ot, om, ut, um,* and *ob, oth, ub, uth,* confirmed this prediction. Moreover, the print-word experience of some of the children was experimentally manipulated by introducing words ending with -*b*, for example, *crab, job, cab,* and so forth, in reading of meaningful sentences during 2 weeks of instruction. It was predicted that with this experience of words with -*b*, the children would form an ISR for -*b*. This was confirmed, as the children showed that they could then generate reading responses to simple pseudowords ending in *b*. No such generation was available from a pronunciation control group. All the children were taught in a "whole-language" school program that did not provide explicit instruction in the sounds of letters. In their reading it was rare for the children to attempt any overt "sounding out" of words. They did, however, have an alternative implicit means of phonological recoding available: sublexical relations induced by the children from their stored experience of print words and the related phonological components.

After a year or more of school instruction, the ISRs will be sensitive not only to position within the word but also to the context of other graphemes, and corresponding phonological components, within the word. For example, after 12 months of instruction the ISR for the grapheme *y* in final position of words such as *baby* and *happy* is distinguished by position from *y* in *yes* and *you*, where it corresponds to a different sound. It is also distinguished contextually from occurrences in words such as *by* or *my*, where it corresponds to yet another sound (Thompson & Fletcher-Flinn, 1993, Experiment 6). When the reading vocabulary begins to provide sufficient exemplars, ISRs will be formed and stored that take account of the contextual influence in *sequences* of graphemes and corresponding phonological components. Some ISRs will then be based on contextual dependencies in the mapping of grapheme-phoneme correspondences, such as the influence of consonant graphemes and associated phonemes on the mapping of the preceding vowel, for example, *hold* (versus *hot*), *fall* (versus *fat*), and sometimes on the following vowel, for example, *wand* (versus *hand*). ISRs based on contextual dependencies in sequences of graphemes would contribute to generation procedures for word identification *as well as* the simpler ISRs based on individual graphemes and corresponding phonemes.

Treiman, Goswami, and Bruck (1990) and Laxon, Masterson, and Moran (1994) report results from children aged 7 years that are consistent with the interpretation that the children were using ISRs that take account of such contextual dependencies in sequences of graphemes when they were responding to unfamiliar words (but not to familiar words). There is evidence (Coltheart & Leahy, 1992) that this commences as soon as 6½ years of age and is established by 8 years of age. However, earlier, in the initial months of instruction, with limited examples available in the child's reading vocabulary of familiar print words, they are not likely to acquire ISRs based on contextual dependencies in sequences of graphemes.

ISRs are implicitly induced by the reader from *all* relevant orthographic components and phonological components of words that have been experienced and sufficiently well established in memory by the reader. Although memory representations of phonological components are not required for recall from orthographic representations of print words, they receive activation at the time of recall. This contention is consistent with experimental evidence (Berent & Perfetti, 1995; Perfetti & Bell, 1991; Perfetti, Bell, & Delaney, 1988). This processed information about phonological components of words can then be related by the child to relevant orthographic components. These relations in memory are based on induction from print words that have become familiar to the child. As the reader's stored print-word experience accumulates, as more words are added to the learner's orthographic representations, so will the number of ISRs expand. Induction of these relations will be updated continuously and spontaneously by the reader and stored in the updated form. While the information for the simple grapheme-phoneme correspondences can be provided through direct teaching, this is not generally the case for ISRs. It would be implausible for a teacher to point out all new ISRs as the child's reading vocabulary expands. While the large number of these interrelationships is within the capacity of the child's nonconscious processing, explicit awareness of each of them would be overwhelming for both teacher and child. The child's implicit nonconscious processing copes with such a large collection of interrelationships. Conscious attention, however, is always limited to a focus on just a very few such relationships at any one time.

Because ISRs are formed largely implicitly, as part of the nonconscious mental processing of the child, they cannot be directly observed. Neither overt pronunciation of parts of words nor "sounding in the head" is required in using ISRs for generating a word-identification response.

Taught Sounds for Letters

This knowledge source comprises taught sounds for letters, for example, /tuh/ for the letter *t*. They are taught as sound labels or "phonic sounds." They may, for example, be taught by using a picture of a key word for the letter. The initial sound of the key word, for example, "tiger," is a prompt for the letter sound /tuh/. Sounds for letters provide the source of knowledge for this second type of phonological recoding that can contribute to the child's attempt to generate or "work out" an identification response to an unfamiliar word. Unlike the induced sublexical relations source of knowledge, this source depends directly on explicit teaching. Also, unlike the induced sublexical relations source, the sounds for letters are learned as items of knowledge that are not dependent on any pattern of letter-sound relations that children may induce from their accumulated reading vocabulary stored from prior print-word experience.

There are a range of procedures by which the child may make use of sound labels for letters in attempting to generate a word-identification response. At one end of the range are cuing procedures in which the sound label for the initial letter of the print word is used to cue words stored in the child's phonological lexicon, the child's existing vocabulary of heard/spoken words. For example, /tuh/ for the initial letter of the print word *tub* could cue "tub" but also "toy," "table," "tiger," and many other words, although the context may eliminate some of these as implausible. At the other end of the range of procedures, the child may engage in "sequential decoding" (Frith, 1985; Marsh, Friedman, Welch, & Desberg, 1981). In this procedure the child gives the sound label for each grapheme of the word in turn, in left-to-right sequence—for example, for *tub*: /tuh/, /uh/, /buh/ —and uses this information as an approximation to the closest matching word sound from the child's phonological lexicon. To facilitate this matching in these procedures, the child may engage in an explicit procedure of "blending" the sound for each grapheme into one word-like sound. This procedure is sometimes called assembly of sounds.

Often children receiving phonics instruction will engage in procedures that fall between these two extremes of initial sound cuing and full sequential decoding. Which procedures the child attempts, if any, will be influenced by the type of instruction the child receives. Some teachers who use phonics instruction expect their students to engage in full sequential decoding with explicit blending of the sounds. Other teachers using phonics include little, if any, explicit instruction on blending. Others may not emphasize complete left-to-right sequential "sounding out" and may accept partial sounding, for example, of the first two or three graphemes of the word, or of the first and last graphemes. The beginning reader will be likely to sound out aloud, but the child with more experience will carry out the conscious sounding "in the head" and later use the procedures without conscious awareness.

Analogy Cues

When using analogy cues to identify an unfamiliar print word—for example, *hump*—the child selects from memory the orthographic representation of a known print word, such as *jump*, to serve as an analogue of the unfamiliar word. The analogue is selected because it has a major orthographic component, -*ump*, in common with the unfamiliar word the child is attempting to identify. The phonological component, /-ump/, corresponding to the major orthographic component is then used to cue a pronunciation response for the unfamiliar print word. The reader would also have to generate the part of the response that is not a common element, the initial /h/ in this example. To do this, the reader would need to use one or another of the sources of knowledge 1 and 2 described above.

It should be noted carefully that in using an analogy cue the reader mentally *selects* from memory an analogue, the orthographic representation of a word with a major orthographic component in common with the unfamiliar stimulus word. This is a quite different process from that of using induced sublexical relations (ISRs), which process does not involve any selection of an analogue word. ISRs are relations between orthographic and phonological components that have been induced from *all* relevant common components of words that have been stored as a result of the reader's accumulated experience. Moreover, ISRs can be based on an orthographic component as small as a single letter or on larger components such as -*ook* or -*ent*. Larger components are required for analogy cues (Goswami, 1993). Evidence that children can use the larger components in identification of unfamiliar words (Bowey & Hansen, 1994; Leslie & Calhoon, 1995) does not in itself establish whether this use is based on analogy or on ISR knowledge sources.

There is evidence that, in children's developing phonological knowledge of the English language, by 5 years of age they are sensitive to phonological units at the level of onset and rime, for example, /s-/ and /-ent/ in "sent," /st-/ and /-ep/ in "step" (Bryant, MacLean, Bradley, & Crossland, 1990; Goswami & Bryant, 1990, 1992; Treiman, 1987, 1992). The "interactive analogy model" of acquisition of word identification (Goswami, 1993) proposes that the child starts to learn to read English by forming orthographic-phonological relationships based on these already available phonological units of onset and rime and that this learning is achieved by the formation of analogies. The claim is that these relationships are formed and used exclusively at first, and only later can the child also use other orthographic-phonological relationships, in particular those that require access to phonemic segments within either rime or onset. In contrast, in the Knowledge Sources theoretical account presented here, the formation of orthographic-phonological relations based on such phoneme segments can take place during the initial months of instruction (Thompson, Cottrell, & Fletcher-Flinn, 1996).

Prompted analogy cues can be used by children as young as 6 years. In prompted cues the selection of the analogue is made by the teacher (or researcher), who shows and pronounces this analogue word as a cue that is either continuously present (Goswami, 1986, 1991, 1993) or available shortly beforehand (Goswami, 1988, Experiment 3). Does such prompted use of analogy cues have a permanent influence sufficient to produce learning of word identification in beginning readers that is superior to the use of grapheme-phoneme correspondences? This would be the expectation of the interactive analogy model (Goswami, 1993). Such an expectation has not been confirmed in published studies that make a comparison of these types of teaching during the first year of instruction (Haskell, Foorman, & Swank, 1992; Sullivan, Okada, & Niedermeyer, 1971). Prompted analogy teaching did not produce better reading progress for beginning readers than teaching of grapheme-phoneme correspondences of the words. In fact, Sullivan and colleagues (1971) found that the children at an early level of reading attainment were disadvantaged by prompted analogy teaching, although those at a higher reading level did show an advantage. This result is the converse of the expectation from the Goswami interactive analogy model. Nevertheless, prompted analogy teaching may have a place as a remedial teaching strategy for older children. Some evidence on this is presented in Chapter 4.

Are children able to *spontaneously* use analogy cues, that is, without any teacher prompt? Apparently normal-progress children aged 7 years and older do sometimes make spontaneous use of analogy cues for generating an identification response to unfamiliar words. This was shown by presenting pseudowords, for example, *inswer*. Some of the children's reading responses to these were pronunciations that were analogous to a word, for example, *answer*, that has an exceptional letter-sound correspondence not obtainable by phonological recoding (Manis, Szeszulski, Howell, & Horn, 1986). The available studies do not show spontaneous use of analogy by average-progress children younger than 7 years. If the child cannot use analogy cues spontaneously and has to rely on teacher provision of analogy prompts, then this source of knowledge is not adequate for the child's independent generation of a reading response. The other three sources of knowledge described here can all be used spontaneously and independently by the child within the first few months of reading instruction.

Context

This knowledge source for generating a word-identification response is different from the other three described above, in that it is the only one that does not make use of information from the word the child is attempting to read. For example, suppose the child is attempting to identify the unfamiliar word *turn* in this sentence: *The bus will turn here.* The other words of the sentence will activate the child's knowledge of syntax and meanings, indicating that the unfamiliar word will say something that is plausible to say about a bus. This information reduces the range of likely candidate responses for the word. Nevertheless, as the context of the word is not information from the word itself, it would be expected that, on its own, the context would be an inadequate knowledge source for generating an accurate identification response to an unfamiliar print word. This is so, but when used along with information from the word, the context does contribute to generation of a word-identification response (Chapter 4; Tunmer & Chapman, 1998).

Our concern here has been the child's generation of an identification response to unfamiliar print words. In contrast, when identifying familiar words by recall procedures under normal reading conditions, context has very little influence on performance for either mature adult readers (Mitchell, 1982; Rayner & Pollatsek, 1989) or children (Perfetti, 1995; Stanovich, 1986). These conclusions are for word identification in reading. They do not hold for the reader's processing of syntax and meaning of the text. In this, the context is indispensable for both child and adult readers. The identified words of a sentence have to be related to the other words of the sentence for the reader to process the syntax and meaning. That is a matter of reading comprehension, not word identification.

USE OF THE SOURCES OF KNOWLEDGE AND
READING DEVELOPMENT

In the Knowledge Sources theoretical account of word identification we have described, there are (1) orthographic word storage, a knowledge source which enables the child to identify familiar print words by recall, and (2) another four knowledge sources that may contribute to the child's generation of identification responses to unfamiliar print words (see Figure 2.1). By this account, children in the first few weeks of reading instruction will start forming orthographic storage of words, although these representations in memory at first will only be partial (incomplete). Initial information about the identity of the word may be provided by a teacher or parent. Also, such information may be provided by the teacher's or parent's correction of the child's erroneous reading response. When sufficient orthographic representations of words are available to provide examples of common letter-sound relations, the child will implicitly induce these sublexical relations. Such are, in turn, a source of knowledge for generating responses to unfamiliar print words. The children will also make use of context of the word as a source of knowledge to contribute to their generation attempts. It is expected that children provided with explicit phonics instruction will use their taught knowledge of sound labels for letters. Prompted use of analogy cues may contribute as a source of knowledge, if analogy words are provided by the teacher.

Without a teacher providing the responses to new words, the child can, in these ways, generate identification responses to new words. When successful with further instances of the word, an orthographic representation of the word will be established in memory along with connections to the previously existing memory storage of the spoken and heard form of the word (phonology of the word) and the stored meanings of the word. Then recall from orthographic word storage, along with memory connections to stored sound and meanings, will be sufficient for the child's identification of the word in reading. Orthographic word storage is not the operation of highly practiced generation procedures. These are no longer required for those words that have orthographic storage established. Orthographic word storage advances the child toward greater efficiency and subsequent automaticity in identification of the word (see Chapter 7).

There are alternative theoretical accounts which claim that orthographic storage of words will occur only after a period of development in which the child has been able to generate word-identification responses by phonological recoding from taught sounds for letters. By such theoretical accounts, orthographic storage of words is subsequently formed and is a way to "bypass" the phonological recoding. This *developmental bypass hypothesis*, as it has been called by Van Orden, Pennington, and Stone (1990), is a feature of some developmental accounts of reading acquisition (e.g., Frith, 1985).

There are several pieces of evidence, however, inconsistent with such a developmental bypass hypothesis (Rack, Hulme, Snowling, & Wightman, 1994; Thompson, Cottrell, & Fletcher-Flinn, 1996; Thompson, Fletcher-Flinn, & Cottrell, in press). Moreover, the use of an orthographic word representation, or any of the four knowledge sources for generation of a word-identification response, does not imply a particular developmental stage for the child. The mature skilled reader, as well as the child in the first few months of reading instruction, will both use orthographic representations for the familiar words they come across and also several of the sources of knowledge for generation procedures that are needed for unfamiliar words. However, analogy cues may not be used spontaneously until the child is older. Whether or not the child uses knowledge of taught sound labels for letters, and how that is used in generation procedures, will depend on the type of reading instruction the child receives.

Ehri (1991, 1994) has presented accounts of the acquisition of print-word identification that are based on developmental phases. Rather than fitting the evidence into successive developmental phases, our emphasis is on the sources of knowledge for learning and procedures for using these sources. We have described learning progressions, but those apply in large part to the individual print words as the child accumulates experience of them rather than to overall periods of development. For example, a learning progression has been described as the reader, becoming more familiar with a word, moves from only a partial orthographic representation of a word to a complete representation in memory. This will occur while some other words already have a complete representation and yet others have no orthographic representation at all. Some such progression would apply to the mature reader learning a new word as well as the young child to whom most print words are new. Other learning progressions have been described. The extent of the reader's accumulated word-identification vocabulary will be a major governing factor in the range and kind of induced sublexical relations formed by the reader. The view taken here is that each such factor should be considered directly, rather than as part of a classification into three or four developmental phases intended to describe the overall progression of all major aspects of the acquisition of word identification.

RELATIONSHIPS TO OTHER CONTEMPORARY ACCOUNTS

Several contemporary influential theoretical accounts of word identification in reading have been worked out in fine detail for reading of isolated words by adult readers, those who have already learned the skill. The account given in this chapter does not attempt to provide such fine detail, and it is intended to be applicable to children learning identification of words in text rather than only skilled readers' responses to words in isolation.

"Dual-route" theories of mature reading of isolated words have been very influential since the 1970s (Baron, 1977; Besner & Smith, 1992; Coltheart, 1978, 1980; Coltheart, Curtis, Atkins, & Haller, 1993; McCusker, Hillinger, & Bias, 1981; Meyer, Schvaneveldt, & Ruddy, 1974; Paap & Noel, 1991). These theories have a direct word look-up procedure ("lexical route"), which will be successful only for familiar print words, and a phonological recoding procedure ("phonological route"), which can generate responses to unfamiliar words, including regular pseudowords, for example, *blup, besof*. In most dual-route theories the generation procedure comprises grapheme-to-phoneme correspondence rules such as $b \rightarrow /b/$, along with more complex versions of such rules. Words that cannot be generated by these rules because they have exceptional grapheme-phoneme relations, for example, *yacht*, will be identifiable only by the direct word look-up procedure.

Dual-route theories traditionally have been static accounts of retrieval of the reading response from the existing knowledge bases of the already skilled reader. However, more recently there have been computational dual-route theoretical models (Coltheart et al., 1993; Reggia, Marsland, & Berndt, 1988) that give some account of how word identification in reading is learned. In dual-route theories this is an account of how readers learn generalizations (implicit rules) for grapheme-phoneme correspondences that are inherent in their accumulated print-word experience. This generation procedure differs qualitatively from the direct look-up procedure that is available for familiar print words. In dual-route theories this direct look-up procedure is necessary for words with exceptional grapheme-phoneme relationships but not for words with regular grapheme-phoneme correspondences. In contrast, "connectionist" accounts have broken with the tradition of the dual-route theories. In the connectionist accounts (Plaut, McClelland, Seidenberg, & Patterson, 1996; Seidenberg & McClelland, 1989) a single process for learning to identify the sounds of words handles both exception words and words with regular grapheme-phoneme correspondences.

The Knowledge Sources account described here also differs in some important respects from the tradition of dual-route theories. For example, the implicitly learned rules of grapheme-phoneme correspondences in dual-route theories do not contain information on the frequency of the reader's experience of print-word instances from which the rules were acquired (apart from a lower-bound criterion for acceptance as a rule). In contrast, the induced sublexical relations in the present account are sensitive to the frequency and recency of the instances of the print words from which they were induced. This means the generation procedures that depend on induced sublexical relations are sensitive to features of the reader's print-word vocabulary. These features would include the recency and frequency of the word instances that originally provided the experiences for formation of the induced sublexical relations. The source of knowledge that is the taught sounds for letters will not be influenced in this way, but by the exposure of the reader to explicit teaching about the letter-sound correspondences.

Moreover, in the present account there are four possible sources of knowledge for generation procedures for responding to unfamiliar words. Any one source will quite often provide only partial, rather than complete, information for successful generation of a word-identification response. Often two or more sources will contribute information for a response. This will be seen, for example, in the contribution of induced sublexical relations to phonological recoding, which enables generation procedures to succeed with some words that are exceptions in letter-sound relationships if information from context is also available. This is an aspect considered in further detail in Chapter 4. In the dual-route accounts there is usually only one source of knowledge for generating a response, namely, the implicit grapheme-phoneme correspondence rules. In the major connectionist accounts, the orthographic-phonological connections, acquired by readers from their print-word experience, comprise the only source of knowledge for responding to unfamiliar words. Very recently, however, some recognition has been given to taught letter-sound correspondences (Plaut et al., 1996, p. 67).

The extent to which phonological recoding is used by the reader to achieve identification of *familiar* print words is currently a matter of controversy. Although the standard account, which fits dual-route theories, has been that familiar print words are normally identified without use of phonological recoding, this account has been challenged by Van Orden and colleagues (1990), who claim that phonological recoding is often used to achieve identification of familiar print words in silent reading. However, others would argue that phonological recoding is usually too slow to achieve the rapid automatic identification of familiar words. Berent and Perfetti (1995) have reported a series of studies supporting the view that phonological recoding of the component consonant letters of a word is in fact very fast and that only for the vowel letters is it relatively slow. This raises the possibility that phonological recoding of the consonants, but not the vowels, normally takes place in the rapid identification of familiar words.

TEACHING AND LEARNING IMPLICATIONS

Will our account of how children learn to read words be adequate for children taught in widely different ways? For example, it may be argued that neither of the knowledge sources for phonological recoding is relevant if the child is taught by a whole-language approach with the emphasis on responding to whole words in the context of whole stories. This argument is not convincing, however, considering two lines of evidence from New Zealand, where teaching is of this kind (Thompson, 1993). One line of evidence shows that the better progress readers at 6½ years of age are much more likely to engage in phonological recoding of unfamiliar words than those children making slower progress (Thompson, 1986). The other line of evidence shows that induced sublexical relations are spontaneously formed by average-progress readers within the first year of reading instruction of this kind (Thompson, Cottrell, & Fletcher-Flinn, 1996).

It may be expected that children taught from the beginning with sound labels for letters would have some initial advantage over children without such teaching. These other children would be likely to acquire induced sublexical relations for phonological recoding, but these can only be acquired after the child has some orthographic storage of words. Hence the children who from the beginning are taught sound labels for letters and how to use them for generating a word-identification response would be expected to engage in more phonological recoding earlier than the children without this teaching. Such use of sound labels for letters would be expected to be successful with unfamiliar words, provided they have regular letter-sound correspondences. In Chapter 5 there is a report of evidence from 5- and 6-year-olds that supports this expectation. This evidence also indicates that children taught to read by a whole-language approach showed some differences in other respects compared to children whose teaching included explicit phonics, with its emphasis on using taught sounds of letters. Both groups of children were selected as having reached the same overall level of word-reading attainment, but the whole-language–taught children were more accurate in identification of words with exceptional letter-sound correspondences. They also read text faster than the phonics-taught children, although with a little less accuracy in comprehension. The reason for these differences was considered to be the whole-language–taught children's relatively greater reliance on orthographic word storage as a source of information for word identification (see Figure 2.1).

Whether or not children are taught explicit phonics, they will acquire orthographic word storage. Those without the phonics instruction will apparently rely on this source of knowledge more than those with phonics (Johnston & Thompson, 1989; Thompson & Johnston, 1998). Successful acquisition of orthographic word storage requires that the child experience the print word a number of times and that the correct associations with meaning and sound of the word be available. These associations may be provided by a teacher, peer, or parent, or self-generated by the child. Extensive reading of meaningful text at a level of difficulty low enough to meet these conditions will usually be the principal means for the child to acquire orthographic storage for print words as they become familiar after repeated occurrence in varying contexts.

At the same time, children need to learn ways of generating their own responses to unfamiliar print words so that they become less dependent on other people to supply the response. In the account of the learning of word identification given here, all normal-progress children within the first year of receiving reading instruction will have available at least two sources of knowledge for generating identification responses to unfamiliar words: induced sublexical relations and context of the word. In addition, from the beginning of instruction children may be explicitly taught sounds for letters, which provides a further knowledge source. Subsequently, analogy cues may provide yet another source of knowledge. Context of the word, when used along with one or more of the other three sources, can contribute to generation of a word-identification response. Teaching should enable the child to make use of as many of the four sources of knowledge as would be effective when words are new or unfamiliar to the child. At the same time, teaching should give opportunity for extensive experience and practice in reading texts, which is needed for the child to become familiar with the print words and acquire orthographic storage of them.

The extent to which the child's learning of phonological recoding can be facilitated by direct teaching has for a long time in many countries been a matter of controversy (Thompson, 1997). Some direct teaching is required if the child is to learn the sounds for letters and how to apply them in attempting responses to unfamiliar words. However, unlike taught sounds for letters, it is clear that most of the induced sublexical relations cannot be directly taught. There are too many and some are too complex for that. This large collection of interrelationships is acquired mainly through the nonconscious processing that constitutes implicit learning. Nevertheless, it is important that the teacher assist the beginning reader to acquire as soon as possible some knowledge of the alphabetic principle—that letters of words systematically map onto sounds in words. The teacher will be able to assist by directing the child's attention to listen to selected individual sounds in words and by demonstrating how these sounds correspond to particular letters in words. With this kind of preliminary knowledge and the appropriate experience of print words, children will be able to proceed on their own to acquire and use induced sublexical relations for phonological recoding.

CONCLUSIONS

Phonological recoding is often regarded as the critical procedure for enabling progress in learning to read words. For example, Share (1995) and Share and Stanovich (1995) apply the metaphor of "self-teaching" to phonological recoding. This metaphor draws attention to the idea that successful phonological recoding of a word, carried out by the child without teacher assistance, will enable the child to acquire orthographic storage of that word.

In the present account of learning word reading, a distinction is made between two sources of knowledge for phonological recoding: (1) induced sublexical relations and (2) taught sounds for letters. In Share's account of the learning of beginning readers, the focus is on the readers' use of taught sounds for letters. That is to say, children are taught how to use each one of a set of instances of the alphabetic principle, which enables some "self-teaching" of new reading vocabulary (orthographic word storage) through phonological recoding. In contrast, the account given here goes beyond that, to the beginning readers' use of their implicit knowledge of the alphabetic principle to self-discover *untaught* instances of this principle. The children do this by inducing patterns of sublexical relations between print and sounds, from those that are common in the child's accumulating reading vocabulary. Evidence cited in this chapter indicates that this form of "self-teaching" can take place for beginning readers with only very small reading vocabularies.

What this means is that very early in learning to read the child is not only starting to engage in "self-teaching" of reading vocabulary, by phonological recoding, but also engaging in "self-teaching" of new instances of the alphabetic principle, which is the basis for phonological recoding itself. These two kinds of "self-teaching" certainly do not eliminate the role of the teacher. They require a teacher who is active in several important ways, as outlined in the previous section.

REVIEW

In this chapter we have described how the child learns to read words and make connections in memory between the letters seen on the page and the stored sound and meanings of the word. On becoming familiar with a print word, the child forms an orthographic representation of the word in memory. This representation comprises the sequence of abstract letter units for that word. The representation has connections in memory with the stored sound and meanings of the word and is used by the child to recall those aspects when responding to the word seen on the page. We have described some research evidence which shows that the young child does in fact learn such orthographic representations of words.

There are two types of knowledge sources for the child's learning of orthographic representations of words and the associated connections in memory. The first source is a teacher's provision of the sound of the word when the child sees the print form of the word. The second source is the child's own generation of a response to the print word. Consistent repeated experiences of either type of knowledge source will contribute to learning of appropriate orthographic representations and memory connections for the words.

In the Knowledge Sources account of learning word identification that was described, the child's generation of a response to an unfamiliar print word depends on one or more of four sources of knowledge: (1) induced sublexical relations, (2) taught sounds for letters, (3) analogy cues, and (4) context of the word. Induced sublexical relations and taught sounds for letters are two different sources of knowledge for phonological recoding. They are two different ways of using the alphabetic principle that letters of words systematically map onto sounds in words. Teaching the sound labels for letters is the teaching of a specific set of instances of the alphabetic principle and how the child can use these instances to attempt generation of responses to unfamiliar print words. In contrast, the numerous induced sublexical relations are formed by the child on the basis of implicit knowledge of the alphabetic principle, *as a principle*, and not as a specific set of explicitly taught instances. The sublexical relations are self-discovered (induced) by the child as instances of the principle that are applicable to his or her accumulated reading vocabulary. The induced sublexical relations provide "self-teaching" of *untaught* instances of the alphabetic principle.

Induced sublexical relations are formed by the child from the relations between orthographic and phonological components that are common to those print words familiar to the child. These sublexical relations are formed mainly by implicit learning based on the child's accumulating reading vocabulary, which means the child is usually unaware that the learning is occurring. In contrast, there can be explicit teaching and learning of the sounds of letters and their use for identification of unfamiliar words. Moreover, taught sound labels for letters do not have to depend upon the child's prior accumulation of reading vocabulary (orthographic word storage). The child's use of analogy cues as a source of knowledge is dependent on the child's accumulated reading vocabulary, although the procedure is different from induction of sublexical relations. The context of the word is not information from the print word itself and in this respect is different from the other three sources of knowledge, which do provide information from the word. When used along with one or more of these sources, however, context can contribute to generation of a word-identification response.

The ideas presented here on learning to read words differ in several ways from developmental stage theories of reading. These differences were discussed. Some of the relationships of the present ideas to the main contemporary theories of word identification in the mature reading skill of adults were also discussed.

Several teaching and learning implications of the main ideas of this chapter were considered. The child needs extensive reading of meaningful texts at a level of difficulty low enough to meet the conditions for acquiring effective orthographic storage for print words, as they become familiar on repeated occurrences in varying contexts. The teacher's provision of reading responses for the child, and correction of the child's responses, are important early in the child's learning. However, it is also important that the child start to learn ways to generate a response to unfamiliar words so that the child becomes less dependent on other people to supply a response. Thus early in the child's learning, teaching should guide the child to use as many as possible of the sources of knowledge that can effectively contribute to generation of a response. Four such sources have been described in this chapter.

STUDY AND DISCUSSION QUESTIONS

1. (a) What is an orthographic representation of a word in memory, and how is it used by a reader? Include examples in your answer.
   (b) What are the sources of knowledge for the child's acquisition of orthographic representations of words?
   (c) How does the child's orthographic representation in memory change as the child becomes increasingly familiar with a print word?

2. "The sounds of words are irrelevant to the child learning to read, as skilled reading is only a matter of making connections between the print and the text meaning." Make a criticism of this statement. Use illustrative examples. Include research evidence in your answer.

3. (a) Explain the *alphabetic principle*.
   (b) Describe how children may (i) learn a specific set of instances of the principle and (ii) learn how to discover by themselves numerous untaught instances of the principle.
   (c) What are the implications of (b) above for the learner's development of independence from the support of a teacher.
   (d) What are the advantages and disadvantages of the early learning of (i) in (b) above. Include research evidence in your answer.

4. Describe how the Knowledge Sources account of learning to read words differs from developmental stage theories of reading acquisition.

FURTHER READING

Adams, M. J. (1990). *Beginning to read: Thinking and learning about print.* Cambridge, MA: MIT Press.

Ehri, L. C. (1994). Development of the ability to read words: Update. In R. B. Ruddell, M. R. Ruddell, & H. Singer (Eds.), *Theoretical models and processes of reading* (4th ed.; pp. 323–358). Newark, DE: International Reading Association.

Gough, P. B., Ehri, L. C., & Treiman, R. (Eds.). (1992). *Reading acquisition.* Hillsdale, NJ: Erlbaum. Chapters 5 and 6.

Perfetti, C. A. (1995). Cognitive research can inform reading education. *Journal of Research in Reading, 18,* 106–115.

Rayner, K., & Pollatsek, A. (1989). *The psychology of reading.* Englewood Cliffs, NJ: Prentice-Hall. Chapter 9.

Thompson, G. B., Tunmer, W. E., & Nicholson, T. (Eds.). (1993). *Reading acquisition processes.* Clevedon, UK: Multilingual Matters.

REFERENCES

Baron, J. (1977). Mechanisms for pronouncing printed words: Use and acquisition. In D. LaBerge & S. J. Samuels (Eds.), *Basic processes in reading: Perception and comprehension* (pp. 175–216). Hillsdale, NJ: Erlbaum.

Berent, I., & Perfetti, C. A. (1995). A rose is a REEZ: The two-cycles model of phonology assembly in reading English. *Psychological Review, 102,* 146–184.

Besner, D., & Smith, M. C. (1992). Models of visual word recognition: When obscuring the stimulus yields a clear view. *Journal of Experimental Psychology: Learning, Memory, and Cognition, 18,* 468–482.

Bowey, J. A., & Hansen, J. (1994). The development of orthographic rimes as units of word recognition. *Journal of Experimental Child Psychology, 58,* 465–488.

Bryant, P. E., MacLean, M., Bradley, L., & Crossland, J. (1990). Rhyme and alliteration, phoneme detection, and learning to read. *Developmental Psychology, 26,* 429–438.

Byrne, B., & Fielding-Barnsley, R. (1990). Acquiring the alphabetic principle: A case for teaching recognition of phoneme identity. *Journal of Educational Psychology, 82,* 805–812.

Cassidy, S. (1992). *A computer model of reading development.* Unpublished doctoral dissertation, Victoria University of Wellington, New Zealand.

Clay, M. M. (1970). An increasing effect of disorientation on the discrimination of print: A developmental study. *Journal of Experimental Child Psychology, 9,* 297–306.

Coltheart, M. (1978). Lexical access in simple reading tasks. In G. Underwood (Ed.), *Strategies of information processing* (pp. 151–216). London: Academic Press.

Coltheart, M. (1980). Reading, phonological recoding, and deep dyslexia. In M. Coltheart, K. Patterson, & J. C. Marshall (Eds.), *Deep dyslexia* (pp. 197–226). London: Routledge & Kegan Paul.

Coltheart, M., Curtis, B., Atkins, P., & Haller, M. (1993). Models of reading aloud: Dual-route and parallel-distributed processing approaches. *Psychological Review, 100,* 589–608.

Coltheart, M., & Leahy, J. (1992). Children's and adults' reading of nonwords: Effects of regularity and consistency. *Journal of Experimental Psychology: Learning, Memory, and Cognition, 18,* 718–729.

Ehri, L. C. (1991). Development of the ability to read words. In R. Barr, M. L. Kamil, P. B. Mosenthal, & P. D. Pearson (Eds.), *Handbook of reading research* (Vol. 2; pp. 385–419). White Plains, NY: Longman.

Ehri, L. C. (1994). Development of the ability to read words: Update. In R. B. Ruddell, M. R. Ruddell, & H. Singer (Eds.), *Theoretical models and processes of reading* (4th ed.; pp. 323–358). Newark, DE: International Reading Association.

Ehri, L. C. (1995). Phases of development in learning to read words by sight. *Journal of Research in Reading, 18,* 116–125.

Ehri, L. C., & Saltmarsh, J. (1995). Beginning readers outperform older disabled readers in learning to read words by sight. *Reading and Writing, 7,* 295–326.

Ehri, L. C., & Wilce, L. S. (1985). Movement into reading: Is the first stage of printed word learning visual or phonetic? *Reading Research Quarterly, 20,* 163–179.

Frith, U. (1985). Beneath the surface of developmental dyslexia. In K. E. Patterson, J. C. Marshall, & M. Coltheart (Eds.), *Surface dyslexia: Neuropsychological and cognitive studies of phonological reading* (pp. 301–330). London: Erlbaum.

Goswami, U. (1986). Children's use of analogy in learning to read: A developmental study. *Journal of Experimental Child Psychology, 42,* 73–83.

Goswami, U. (1988). Orthographic analogies and reading development. *Quarterly Journal of Experimental Psychology, 40A,* 239–268.

Goswami, U. (1991). Learning about spelling sequences: The role of onsets and rimes in analogies in reading. *Child Development, 62,* 1110–1123.

Goswami, U. (1993). Toward an interactive analogy model of reading development: Decoding vowel graphemes in beginning reading. *Journal of Experimental Child Psychology, 56,* 443–475.

Goswami, U., & Bryant, P. E. (1990). *Phonological skills and learning to read.* Hove, UK: Erlbaum.

Goswami, U., & Bryant, P. E. (1992). In P. B. Gough, L. C. Ehri, & R. Treiman (Eds.), *Reading acquisition* (pp. 49–63). Hillsdale, NJ: Erlbaum.

Haskell, D. W., Foorman, B. R., & Swank, P. R. (1992). Effects of three orthographic/phonological units on first-grade reading. *Remedial and Special Education, 13,* 40–49.

Johnston, R. S., & Thompson, G. B. (1989). Is dependence on phonological information in children's reading a product of instructional approach? *Journal of Experimental Child Psychology, 48,* 131–145.

Johnston, R. S., Thompson, G. B., Fletcher-Flinn, C. M., & Holligan, C. (1995). The functions of phonology in the acquisition of reading: Lexical and sentence processing. *Memory & Cognition, 23,* 749–766.

Laxon, V., Masterson, J., & Moran, R. (1994). Are children's representations of words distributed? Effects of orthographic neighbourhood size, consistency and regularity of naming. *Language and Cognitive Processes, 9,* 1–27.

Leslie, L., & Calhoon, A. (1995). Factors affecting children's reading of rimes: Reading ability, word frequency, and rime-neighbourhood size. *Journal of Educational Psychology, 87,* 576–586.

Manis, F. R., Szeszulski, P. A., Howell, M. J., & Horn, C. C. (1986). A comparison of analogy- and rule-based decoding strategies in normal and dyslexic children. *Journal of Reading Behavior, 18,* 203–218.

Marsh, G., Friedman, M., Welch, V., & Desberg, P. (1981). A cognitive-developmental theory of reading acquisition. In G. E. MacKinnon & T. G. Waller (Eds.), *Reading research: Advances in theory and practice* (Vol. 3; pp. 199–221). New York: Academic Press.

McCusker, L. X., Hillinger, M. L., & Bias, R. G. (1981). Phonological recoding and reading. *Psychological Bulletin, 89,* 217–245.

Meyer, D. E., Schvaneveldt, R. W., & Ruddy, M. G. (1974). Functions of graphemic and phonemic codes in visual word-recognition. *Memory & Cognition, 2,* 309–321.

Mitchell, D. C. (1982). *The process of reading: A cognitive analysis of fluent reading and learning to read.* Chichester, UK: Wiley.

Paap, K. R., & Noel, R. W. (1991). Dual-route models of print to sound: Still a good horse race. *Psychological Research, 53,* 13–24.

Perfetti, C. A. (1995). Cognitive research can inform reading education. *Journal of Research in Reading, 18,* 106–115.

Perfetti, C. A., & Bell, L. (1991). Phonemic activation during the first 40 ms of word identification: Evidence from backward masking and priming. *Journal of Memory and Language, 30,* 473–485.

Perfetti, C. A., Bell, L., & Delaney, S. (1988). Automatic phonetic activation in silent word reading: Evidence from backward masking. *Journal of Memory and Language, 27,* 59–70.

Plaut, D. C., McClelland, J. L., Seidenberg, M. S., & Patterson, K. (1996). Understanding normal and impaired word reading: Computational principles in quasi-regular domains. *Psychological Review, 103,* 56–115.

Rack, J., Hulme, C., Snowling, M., & Wightman, J. (1994). The role of phonology in young children learning to read words: The direct-mapping hypothesis. *Journal of Experimental Child Psychology, 57,* 42–71.

Rayner, K., & Pollatsek, A. (1989). *The psychology of reading.* Englewood Cliffs, NJ: Prentice-Hall.

Reggia, J. A., Marsland, P. M., & Berndt, R. S. (1988). Competitive dynamics in a dual-route connectionist model of print-to-sound transformation. *Complex Systems, 2,* 509–547.

Reitsma, P. (1983a). Word-specific knowledge in beginning reading. *Journal of Research in Reading, 6,* 41–55.

Reitsma, P. (1983b). Printed word learning in beginning readers. *Journal of Experimental Child Psychology, 36,* 321–339.

Seidenberg, M. S., & McClelland, J. L. (1989). A distributed, developmental model of word recognition and naming. *Psychological Review, 96,* 523–568.

Share, D. L. (1995). Phonological recoding and self-teaching: *Sine qua non* of reading acquisition. *Cognition, 55,* 151–218.

Share, D. L., & Stanovich, K. E. (1995). Cognitive processes in early reading development: Accommodating individual differences into a model of acquisition. *Issues in Education: Contributions from Educational Psychology, 1*(1), 1–57.

Stanovich, K. E. (1986). Matthew effects in reading: Some consequences of individual differences in the acquisition of literacy. *Reading Research Quarterly, 11,* 360–406.

Stuart, M., & Coltheart, M. (1988). Does reading develop in a sequence of stages? *Cognition, 30,* 139–181.

Sullivan, H. J., Okada, M., & Niedermeyer, F. C. (1971). Learning and transfer under two methods of word-attack instruction. *American Educational Research Journal, 8,* 227–239.

Thompson, G. B. (1986). When nonsense is better than sense: Nonlexical errors to word reading tests. *British Journal of Educational Psychology, 56,* 216–219.

Thompson, G. B. (1993). Reading instruction for the initial years in New Zealand schools. In G. B. Thompson, W. E. Tunmer, & T. Nicholson (Eds.), *Reading acquisition processes* (pp. 148–154). Clevedon, UK: Multilingual Matters.

Thompson, G. B. (1997). The teaching of reading. In V. Edwards & D. Corson (Ed.), *Encyclopedia of language and education; Vol. 2. Literacy* (pp. 9–17). Dordrecht, The Netherlands: Kluwer.

Thompson, G. B., Cottrell, D. S., & Fletcher-Flinn, C. M. (1996). Sublexical orthographic-phonological relations early in the acquisition of reading: The Knowledge Sources account. *Journal of Experimental Child Psychology, 62,* 190–222.

Thompson, G. B., & Fletcher-Flinn, C. M. (1993). A theory of knowledge sources and procedures for reading accquisition. In G. B. Thompson, W. E. Tunmer, & T. Nichlson (Eds.), *Reading acquisition processes* (pp. 20–73). Clevedon, UK: Multilingual Matters.

Thompson, G. B., Fletcher-Flinn, C. M., & Cottrell, D. S. (in press). Learning correspondences between letters and phonemes without explicit instruction. *Applied Psycholinguistics.*

Thompson, G. B., & Johnston, R. S. (1998). *Orthographic representation of words early in learning to read.* Manuscript prepared for publication.

Thompson, G. B., & Potts, D. M. (1998). *The function of phonology in accessing meaning from print during the transition to skilled reading.* Manuscript prepared for publication.

Treiman, R. (1987). On the relationship between phonological awareness and literacy. *Cahiers de Psychologie Cognitive, 7,* 524–529.

Treiman, R. (1992). The role of intrasyllabic units in learning to read and spell. In P. B. Gough, L. C. Ehri, & R. Treiman (Eds.), *Reading acquisition* (pp. 65–106). Hillsdale, NJ: Erlbaum.

Treiman, R., Goswami, U., & Bruck, M. (1990). Not all nonwords are alike: Implications for reading development and theory. *Memory & Cognition, 18,* 559–567.

Tunmer, W. E., & Chapman, J. W. (1998). Language prediction skill, phonological recoding ability, and beginning reading. In C. Hulme & R. M. Joshi (Eds.), *Reading and spelling: Development and disorder* (pp. 33–67). Hove, UK: Erlbaum.

Van Orden, G. C., Pennington, B. F., & Stone, G. O. (1990). Word identification in reading and the promise of subsymbolic psycholinguistics. *Psychological Review, 97,* 488–522.

Chapter 3

Learning and Teaching
Phonological Awareness

JILLIAN M. CASTLE

a) What is phonological awareness?

b) What contribution does it make to learning to read?

c) Can phonological awareness be assessed and taught?

d) How can phonological awareness teaching be incorporated into whole-language programs?

Phonological awareness as a precursor to reading achievement has been widely researched over the past 25 years. It is considered one of the several metalinguistic abilities necessary for beginning readers to make progress in reading an alphabetic orthography (Tunmer & Rohl, 1991). These abilities enable children to put the function of language in the background and to focus attention on different properties of language. Phonological awareness allows children to focus on the constituent sounds or the phonemic structure of a word as divorced from its meaning.

Phonemic awareness has been defined as "conscious access to the phonemic level of the speech stream and some ability to cognitively manipulate representations at this level" (Stanovich, 1986, p. 362). The phonemic level of speech refers to those units of sound of the language that the alphabet letters can represent (and sometimes combinations of letters such as *th* or *ea*). Phonemes are inherently abstract because many of them cannot be sounded accurately in isolation. The phenomenon of parallel transmission of phonological information means that a phoneme in a spoken word may overlap with the succeeding phoneme. Trying to pronounce separately the three phonemes of "bag," for instance, results in the nonsense word /buh-ah-guh/, yet the phonemes are able to be identified at the abstract level in that the spoken word "bag" differs from "rag" in the first phoneme, "big" in the second, and "bat" in the third (Liberman, Shankweiler, Fischer, & Carter, 1974).

Phonological awareness and phonemic awareness are terms that are sometimes used interchangeably in the literature. Phonological awareness can refer to the whole spectrum of awareness from primitive awareness of the sounds and intonation of speech to rhyme awareness and sound similarities through to syllable and phoneme awareness. Phonemic awareness refers more specifically to the awareness of sound structure at the phoneme level.

PHONEMIC AWARENESS AND READING ACQUISITION

In order to become a skilled reader, a child must master correspondences between letters and phonemes, but this usually requires instruction (Gough & Hillinger, 1980), and even with instruction some children fail to learn. Correlational studies over many years have shown that children who possess high levels of phonemic awareness before beginning to read do better at reading than children with low levels of this skill. Phonemic awareness has been shown to be a more potent predictor of reading success than intelligence, vocabulary, or listening comprehension (Adams, 1990). So how exactly is it related to reading acquisition?

The exact relationship of phonemic awareness to reading acquisition has been the subject of much research. There are three views about this relationship. The first view states that phonemic awareness develops as a result of learning to read an alphabetic script. Ehri (1989), for example, argues that knowledge of letters and their corresponding sounds may be necessary for children to be able to manipulate the phonemic aspects of speech. In a cross-linguistic study Mann (1986) compared beginning readers in Japan learning a syllabary with American beginning readers learning an alphabetic script. She found that in the very early reading years, absence of an alphabetic script does result in lack of awareness of phonemes. Mann noted that phonemic awareness did develop in Japanese readers later, whether they had begun reading an alphabetic script or not. Some researchers, however, have suggested that young preliterate children can perform some of the more complex phoneme manipulation tasks if the tasks are presented with corrective feedback (Content, Kolinsky, Morais, & Bertleson, 1986). Arguments against the first view also include evidence that phonemic awareness has been developed in prereaders without the use of written materials in some training studies (e.g., Lundberg, Frost, & Petersen, 1988).

The second view states that phonemic awareness precedes and predicts later reading success. The strong version of this view states that this awareness is necessary, while the weak version suggests it only facilitates reading acquisition. Correlational studies cannot tell us whether a third factor may be impacting on both reading and phonemic awareness. It is through carefully controlled training studies that we get some evidence on this second view. When children trained in phonemic awareness outperform their untrained peers in subsequent reading tasks, we see evidence that this skill is a precursor to reading rather than the result of reading. See Goswami and Bryant (1990) for a full discussion of an adequate test for this second view.

The third and most commonly adopted view states that reading and phonemic awareness are mutually facilitating, and that reciprocal influences exist between them. Some researchers have found that simple levels of phonemic awareness exist before learning to read while more complex phoneme manipulation tasks are not performed well by nonreaders. Stanovich (1986, 1992) has stated, for example, that some minimal level of phonemic awareness may be necessary for reading acquisition, but these and other metalinguistic abilities develop in a boot-strapping fashion as reading skills are acquired.

Tunmer and Nesdale (1985) demonstrated that phonemic awareness was necessary, but not sufficient on its own, for reading acquisition, and this view is well supported. The many training studies that have been conducted to show that phonemic awareness is necessary for success in later reading are reviewed extensively in texts such as Goswami and Bryant (1990). One study worthy of note is that of Bradley and Bryant (1983). These researchers pretested and retested for a 4-year period a large group of beginning readers (368 children). Longitudinal evidence supported earlier findings that children low in phonemic awareness did not perform as well in reading and spelling. In addition, the researchers selected children low in phoneme awareness and trained them in 40 sessions spread over 2 years. One group of children learned to select pictures of objects with names having common initial (e.g., "hen," "hat"), final (e.g., "hen," "man"), and medial (e.g., "hen," "pet") phonemes. There was training only on sounds of words; no letters or print words were presented. Another matched group of children made similar comparisons of the component sounds of words but in doing so used plastic letters to represent the sounds. The training resulted in some significant positive effects for spelling and reading, though this occurred only for the second group, who were also taught to construct words with letters and associate these with the component sounds. Bradley (1988) later sought to clarify the use of letters with a further training study and concluded that phonemic awareness training combined with letter-sound training was more effective than either type of training alone. However, both letter-sound training on its own and the combined training improved reading ability.

Phonemic Awareness and Reading Difficulties

Many studies have shown that children with poor reading ability are also low in phonemic awareness. Stanovich (1986) points out that both dyslexic readers and poor readers ("garden variety") with below-average intellectual abilities are deficient in this skill. A recent study (Hurford, Schauf, Bunce, Blaich, & Moore, 1994), which was designed to find out whether "at-risk" children could be identified early, gave reading, intelligence, and phonological processing tests to preschoolers and followed them up for 2 years. These children were later assessed as either nondisabled, reading-disabled, or "garden-variety" poor readers. The preschool tests of intelligence and phonemic awareness had predicted membership of these groups for all but 3 of the 171 children. Consistent with other literature, the results confirmed that intelligence scores by themselves did not differentiate good and poor readers. Hurford and colleagues suggest that early identification of at-risk children will allow remediation of phonological processing deficits. The two poor reading groups were both inferior in real-word and pseudoword reading after 2 years of reading instruction in relation to the nondisabled group.

Juel, Griffith, and Gough (1986) and Juel (1988) reported findings of a longitudinal correlational study that followed beginning readers for 4 years. According to Juel (1988), the children who became poor readers were all low in phonemic awareness at school entry. By the end of fourth grade, the children who became poor readers had still not achieved the level of ability for decoding words that the good readers had at the end of second grade. In the study of Juel and colleagues (1986), it was found that children did not benefit from instruction in letter-sound relationships if they did not possess adequate levels of phonemic awareness. It seems that low phonemic awareness contributes to lower word-decoding ability, which sets up a vicious cycle culminating in poor readers reading far less text than good readers.

If the correlational link between phonemic awareness and reading progress is such a strong one, and if at-risk children can be identified early as shown in the study by Hurford and colleagues (1994), then it is essential that children be identified as early as possible and remediation begun before the adverse effects of failure can set in. Some children require explicit instruction in phonemic awareness in order to benefit from instruction in letter-sound relationships. In a whole-language program where letter-sound correspondences are only learned incidentally, such children may be at even greater risk.

Levels of Phonological Awareness

Before considering how phonological awareness is assessed and taught, it is important to clarify what is meant by "levels" of phonological awareness. Stanovich (1992) talks about a continuum of phonological sensitivity ranging from deep to shallow sensitivity. At a deeper level of sensitivity, a child would be able to explicitly report on small sound units such as phonemes, while at a shallower level of sensitivity the child may be able to recognize only larger sound units such as syllables, or onsets and rimes (which make up syllables). Treiman (1991) suggests a hierarchical structure in levels of phonological awareness, with an intermediate level between syllables and phonemes. At this intermediate level there is onset-rime awareness in which the child recognizes alliteration (the onset or initial consonant portion of a syllable) and rhyme (the rime portion of a syllable). This awareness may then allow the child to develop a self-teaching strategy for decoding words by analogy (e.g., *mean* begins like *man* but has the same rime pattern as *bean*). For a full development of this argument, see Goswami and Bryant (1990); for counterarguments, see Gough (1993) and Chapter 2.

Assessing Phonological Awareness

The variety of tasks used to assess phonological awareness reflects the levels described above. To date there are no standardized measures that assess all levels. Various researchers have devised tests that suit the research or training experiments they wish to conduct. The Lindamood and Lindamood (1975) auditory discrimination task includes segmentation tasks and manipulation tasks and is used by some clinicians to determine phonemic awareness. The odd-one-out test used in research by Bryant and Bradley in their various studies is available in a text by Bradley (1980). Other tests include tapping tasks requiring the counting of phonemes in segmented words (e.g., Tunmer & Nesdale, 1985).

When considering the task difficulty of these measures, one must take account of the size of the unit of sound to be segmented, blended, or manipulated, and the actual skill involved in performing such a task. For instance, recognition of rhyme (e.g., Do these rhyme? "cat," "rat") is easier than substituting phonemes to create a rhyme (e.g., Give a rhyme for "cat" beginning with /r/).

Adams (1990) identified various measures used to assess phonological awareness and predict reading acquisition, according to the level of awareness being tapped. The six levels she identified were:

1. A primitive ear for sounds of words, assessed with knowledge of nursery rhymes.
2. Rhyme and alliteration recognition, assessed by an odd-one-out task such as that used by Bradley and Bryant (1983), for example, the child hears four words—"bat," "rag," "fat," "sat"—and must identify the nonrhyming one.
3. Blending tasks in which the tester provides the segmented sounds of a word and the child must recompose the word, for example, "What does /b/ /a/ /g/ say?"
4. Onset-rime syllable splitting, where the child must remove the initial sound and say what is left, for example, "cat" without the /c/ says /at/.
5. Segmentation or phoneme counting tasks, for example, the child says the sounds of a word, /c/ /a/ /t/ for the heard word "cat."
6. Manipulation of phonemes: reversing the sounds of words, for example, "pot" is "top" said backwards; or deleting a medial sound from a word, for example, "splat" without the /l/ is "spat," as in the Bruce (1964) deletion task.

Onset-rime tasks tap a shallower level of phonological sensitivity than phoneme manipulation tasks, so it is necessary to look carefully at assessment devices to determine just what level of skill is being assessed. A child who can say there are two sounds in "no" may in reality be only identifying the onset /n/ and the rime /o/. Some tasks will be more cognitively demanding and require higher levels of abstract thinking and even some letter-sound knowledge to perform. Such tasks may not be appropriate to use for prereaders, for example, the Bruce (1964) deletion task. There is some evidence, also, that rhyme awareness in preschoolers and phonemic awareness may make independent contributions to later reading and spelling (Bryant, Bradley, MacLean, & Crossland, 1989). While early rhyme awareness does predict reading success quite well, rhyme tests do not always correlate highly with other phonological awareness tests (Stanovich, Cunningham, & Cramer, 1984). Likewise, Yopp (1988) found that two factors were present when she used a wide range of measures of phonological awareness on the same children. One factor she called simple awareness, which included rhyme awareness and phoneme segmentation, and the other, comprising phoneme deletion and manipulation, she called compound awareness. It is likely that rhyme awareness develops through exposure to poetry and word games.

Teaching Phonemic Awareness

The tasks outlined above are also the basis for many teaching programs. Segmentation and blending are the most commonly taught skills. Lewkowicz (1980) reviewed the tasks used both to assess and to train phonemic awareness. The ten most commonly used tasks were:

1. Word-sound to sound matching: Does "fish" (spoken word) start with /f/?
2. Word-sound to word-sound matching: Does "dog" end like "pig"?
3. Recognition of rhyme: Does "fish" rhyme with "dish"?
4. Isolation of initial, medial, or final sound: What is the first sound in "fish"?
5. Phonemic segmentation, that is, isolating the sounds of a word in correct sequence: What are the three sounds in "fish"?
6. Counting phonemes in a word: How many sounds are in the word "fish"?
7. Blending isolated speech sounds to recompose a word: What word is this, /f/ /i/ /sh/ ?
8. Deleting a phoneme: Say "fish." Now say it without the /f/.
9. Specifying which phoneme has been left out: Say "meat." Now say "eat." Which sound was left out?
10. Phoneme substitution: Say "meet." Now say it with /f/ instead of /m/.

The most commonly used tasks for teaching phonemic awareness are segmentation tasks and blending tasks. Segmentation or the slow, stretched pronunciation of words allows a child to perceive the separate sounds. It is important that the child listen to these articulated sounds to identify all the auditory cues. This has been done in a technique devised by Elkonin (1973) in which the child pushes counters (or tokens) into boxes of a diagram that mark each successive phoneme of the spoken word, for example, one counter for each of the three successive phonemes /d-o-g/. The early intervention program, Reading Recovery (Clay, 1985), uses this procedure to teach phonemic awareness in a writing exercise. Lie (1991) also suggests that articulation cues, for example, /p/ the "lip-popper," help children learn segmentation and blending skills. For sounds that do not stretch well (i.e., stops), some educators (Lie, 1991; Lundberg et al., 1988) suggest using an iteration technique, for example, /p-p-p-pumpkin/, to help children identify a target sound (based on the work of Zhurova [1963]).

Segmentation is also learned better by young children if syllable segmenting is trained first, for example, /el-e-phant/, and then onset-rime, for example, /p-ig/ (Liberman et al., 1974). The most difficult level of segmentation is individual phonemes. A variety of games and songs and movement exercises can help children acquire these skills. Picture cards and matching games help children to identify words that begin with or end with the same phoneme.

Blending is usually taught when children are familiar with rhyme and alliteration and can segment phonemes. The program devised by Williams (1980) teaches only a small range of consonant and vowel sounds initially and introduces more sounds later, when segmentation skills are well developed. Manipulation of phonemes is the most difficult skill for children to acquire, but in Scandinavia Lundberg and colleagues (1988) found that preschool abilities in this skill predicted later reading success. Children who are able to manipulate phonemes can eventually play complex games with invented languages, for example, "pig Latin," in which the first consonant is transferred to the end of the word and followed by /ay/; thus "good morning" would be "oodgay orningmay."

Stanovich (1992) has pointed out that only shallow phonological sensitivities are required for reading acquisition to be facilitated, so it is questionable whether teachers would be prepared to invest time in teaching more complex levels of awareness to beginning readers. *Sound Foundations*, a program developed for teacher use by Byrne and Fielding-Barnsley (1991) as a result of their research work, concentrates on teaching several consonant and vowel sounds in initial and final positions. Picture cards, posters, and rhyme tapes make up the basis for this preschool/early reading skills program. The training program has some similarity to that in the research study to be presented in detail below. Byrne and Fielding-Barnsley (1991) have shown that phoneme awareness and letter-sound associations together facilitate reading acquisition.

Another factor that has been significant in successful acquisition of both phonemic awareness and reading skills is the method of teaching the tasks. Cunningham (1990) showed that a skill-and-drill approach to teaching phonemic awareness was not as successful as a metalevel approach that taught children how to relate these skills to other reading and writing tasks and to verbalize the aims of the tasks performed. Some of the activities would not transfer to classroom reading that did not reinforce segmenting and blending skills. Cunningham also gradually introduced the use of letters as phonemic analysis skills were acquired.

To summarize, training programs designed to remediate children with low levels of phonemic awareness prior to, or in conjunction with, early reading instruction should incorporate identification of initial and final sounds (positional analysis), segmenting (or sequential analysis) skills, and blending (or synthesis) skills. This is best achieved using a selected group of consonants and vowels, the gradual introduction of letters for sounds, and explicit instruction in how these skills relate to actual reading and writing activities.

A STUDY OF TEACHING PHONEME AWARENESS

A training study was conducted with beginning readers to determine whether a short course of phonemic awareness training would impact on their reading acquisition (Castle, Riach, & Nicholson, 1994, Experiment 2). The children were 5 years of age and selected because they had low phonemic awareness. They were being taught to read in a whole-language classroom program. This type of program emphasizes the use of context for identifying words in reading and avoids both explicit phonics instruction and isolated word reading. This program has been used for more than 30 years in New Zealand, where the study was conducted.

Method

Design. A group of 17 children were trained in phonemic awareness skills, while a matched control group of 17 children received an alternative training program based on whole-language activities. Where possible both groups used the same learning materials but in the second group they were used with an emphasis on meaning rather than on the sounds of the words. A third group of 17 children were pre- and posttested but not trained. The children were spread across five schools, so within each school there were three or four children in each of the three groups. Two children from the trained control group left during the study, so the final data comprised 15 children for each group, with pretest matching across the three groups. This matching was on the basis of two variables, phonemic awareness and verbal ability.

Pretest Measures. Phonemic awareness was assessed by using a test constructed by Roper-Schneider (1984), which covers segmentation, blending, deleting initial or final phoneme, and substituting initial or final phoneme. Other measures included the Peabody Picture Vocabulary Test, PPVT-R (Dunn & Dunn, 1981), which was administered as an indicator of verbal ability. A concrete operativity test (based on Arlin [1981]) was also used as a Piagetian measure of cognitive development.

The Bryant Test of Basic Decoding Skills (Bryant, 1975) was administered, but at pretest none of the children were able to read any of the items, which comprised pseudowords such as *kib* and *groat*. The revised Burt word reading test (Gilmore, Croft, & Reid, 1981) and Clay word reading test

(Clay, 1985) were administered, together with a letter identification task (Clay, 1985). All children in the study were at the emergent level of reading, levels 1–2 in a 22-level system of graded readers for beginners (Department of Education, 1985).

Posttest Measures. All pretests other than the PPVT-R and the operativity test were repeated as posttests. In addition, other tests included a test of concepts about print and two writing tests (all from Clay, 1985). The first writing test required children to write as many words as they could within a 10-minute span, and the second test, dictation, required the children to write a dictated sentence that gave an indication of how well they could analyze words phonemically and represent those words in written form.

The ability to read aloud connected text was also assessed using an informally graded set of stories (Clay, 1985). The cutoff for determining each child's "book level" was when accuracy dropped below 93%.

Training. The two training groups in each school were taught for one session of 20 minutes each week for a total period of 15 weeks. This added up to a total training time for each group of 5 hours. Since a metalevel approach to teaching was taken, each lesson opened with an overview and a review of previous learning. The aims for each lesson were also reviewed at the close of the lesson, and children were asked how the skills they were learning might aid reading and writing.

The phonemic awareness skills trained included alliteration ("big," "bad," "bug") and rhyme ("fat," "bat"). Segmentation activities involved using the Elkonin technique (Clay, 1985) whereby children placed tokens into squares that represented each successive phoneme of the word. Other activities involved games in which children had to decide what picture cards started with the same sound or had the same end or middle sound. In addition to these segmenting and positional analysis tasks, children were also asked to blend sounds given by the teacher (e.g., /mmmm-oooo/ = /moo/) and to identify which of several pictures represented the sounds given. When segmenting skills were well learned, the children were able to supply the segmented word for other children to blend.

The program was adapted in part from that described by Williams (1979, 1980), with seven consonant sounds (/b/, /c/, /g/, /m/, /p/, /s/, /t/) and two short vowel sounds (/a/, /o/) selected for initial training. These were selected so as to avoid auditory confusion (and visual confusion of the corresponding letters). They also produced a high number of consonant-vowel-consonant real words, and they showed regularity of phonemes (e.g., "pot," "cat," and "map"). A second set of phonemes was introduced when segmenting and blending skills were well established with the first. Activities were adapted from the list of tasks recommended in Lewkowicz (1980). Later in the training, letters replaced counters in the sound games and plastic letters were used in substitution exercises (based on Bradley & Bryant, 1983). Hence the children received some letter-sound correspondence training as well as phonemic awareness training. Table 3.1 shows an analysis of the types of tasks used in instruction and the frequency of each type across the 15 sessions. Some examples of the types of activities used are included in this table.

Table 3.1 Type and Frequency of Tasks Used in the 15 Sessions of Phonemic Awareness Instruction

Phonemic awareness task (with example)	Number of times task presented	Activities used to present task (examples)
Segment, /cat/→/c-a-t/	15	Target word from poem, using Elkonin technique with counters to say the word slowly. Using picture cards, count the phonemes in the word pictured.
Blend, /c-a-t/→/cat/	9	Bingo—teacher says a word slowly, child covers that picture if it appears on their Bingo card.
Rhyme, /cat, hat/	11	Finding pictures that rhyme with a target picture. Identifying a missing rhyme word in a poem.
Identify initial phoneme, /cat/→/c/	8	Identifying picture cards that start with the same sound.
Identify medial phoneme, /cat/→/a/	9	Using a contrasting color counter for medial sound, use Elkonin boxes to represent word pairs such as /bag, big/, /cat, cot/.
Identify final phoneme, /cat/→/t/	4	Grouping picture cards with the same end sound.
Manipulate initial phoneme		Puppet who talks funny. Make the puppet say a word with the first
-delete: /cat/→/at/	2	sound missing. What is the puppet saying? (To introduce the
-add: /at/→/cat/	3	activity, teacher says child's name without first phoneme.)

The alternative training control group received the same training format and was exposed to the same materials wherever possible but with an emphasis on meanings of the words or letter names rather than the sounds. Picture cards were used to play categorization games, and target words in poems were identified using semantic rather than sound cues. The same experimenter trained all groups.

Results

Each group improved over time on the measures that were pretested and posttested, but the trained group performed significantly better than the controls on the phonemic awareness test, although not significantly better on the word-reading tests. Figure 3.1 shows the pretest and posttest (adjusted) mean scores in phonemic awareness for the three groups. The no-training control group had performed better than the trained control group, but a significant difference in favor of the no-training group had been found for concrete operativity, which had not been matched between groups. To counter the effects of this cognitive advantage, the data were analyzed with this factor as a covariate and adjusted means were used for the final analysis (see Figure 3.1). This was done because operativity has been shown to be a predictor of reading progress and also highly correlated with phonemic awareness (Tunmer, Herriman, & Nesdale, 1988).

Figure 3.1 Adjusted Mean Pretest and Posttest Scores for Phonemic Awareness

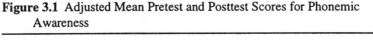

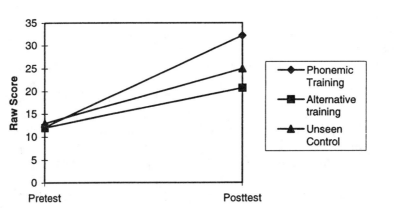

Among the other tests for which posttest results were available, there was a significant difference in favor of the phonemic awareness training group for dictation and the Bryant pseudoword reading (Figure 3.2). Both of these tasks require phonological recoding skills. For all other tests there were no significant differences between the groups. The letter-identification test had almost reached ceiling for all groups.

These results indicate that phonemic awareness training can have significant effects on skills related to reading. The training, which also included teaching of letter-sound knowledge, allowed the phonemic group to do a better job of reading pseudowords, a skill highly correlated with reading success (Juel et al., 1986; Tunmer & Nesdale, 1985). The dictation test, on which the trained children also performed significantly better, measures phonemic spelling skills. That phonemic awareness training can have a significant effect on spelling acquisition (in particular pseudoword spelling) has been shown in another New Zealand study (Castle et al., 1994, Experiment 1). Further, pseudoword reading has been found to be correlated with reading success more than verbal IQ (Felton & Wood, 1992). Phonemic awareness training appears to have enabled the children to acquire letter-phoneme correspondences, which were realized most clearly in the pseudoword reading and spelling dictation tests.

The fact that the knowledge of letter-phoneme correspondences did not appear to impact on text reading or real-word reading may have been due to the context-driven nature of the class reading instruction program.

Figure 3.2 Adjusted Mean Pretest and Posttest Scores for the Bryant
Pseudoword Reading Test

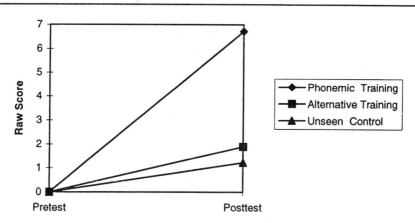

In whole-language classrooms, children are taught to use context as a main strategy and to make minimal use of letter-sound knowledge (Department of Education, 1985). In this way the positive effects of the phonemic awareness training may have been obscured.

INCORPORATING THE TEACHING OF PHONEMIC AWARENESS SKILLS WITHIN A WHOLE-LANGUAGE PROGRAM

The study outlined above adds further evidence to support previous findings that phonemic awareness training, particularly when provided in conjunction with letter-sound correspondence training, is beneficial for children who enter school with low levels of this skill. If phonemic awareness levels at school entry can predict reading success 1 year later and if children with low levels can benefit from acquiring these skills, it is important that the subsequent impact of this type of training at the start of reading instruction be considered. As Stanovich (1986) points out, small initial gains in phonemic awareness may have a snowball effect on reading progress. In practical terms, the results of my study suggest that those who arrive at school with low levels of this skill may not be well equipped to take advantage of letter-sound instruction and may in fact be unable to grasp the alphabetic principle (that letters map onto sounds in words in a systematic way). Such children are more likely to come from disadvantaged backgrounds (Wallach, Wallach, Dozier, & Kaplan, 1977) and are more likely to require remedial assistance (see Chapter 1). The children of my study were followed up 1 year after school entry, and of the trained group ($n = 17$) only 23% required Reading Recovery (a remedial procedure that approximately 30% of 6-year-old New Zealand children are exposed to), while 43% of the 32 children remaining in the control groups required this remediation.

Further relevant evidence comes from the research of Iverson and Tunmer (1992), who found that modified Reading Recovery lessons with an added emphasis on phonemic awareness allowed children to move through to program completion much faster than the ordinary Reading Recovery program. All these findings suggest that extra phonemic awareness training at the beginning of reading instruction can reduce the need for subsequent remedial tuition.

CONCLUSIONS

My study found that phonemic awareness training, with some letter-sound correspondence instruction, added to the whole-language classroom approach to reading did have a positive effect on children's phonological recoding skills. Tests showed that basic recoding and spelling skills were improved for children who began with low levels of phonemic awareness and who were at risk of reading failure.

Adams (1990) stresses that children need to achieve appropriate levels of phonological awareness, and this should not be left to chance. Schools can ensure that such training is provided by assessing children's school-entry level in this skill and ensuring that the daily literacy program, from school entry, includes phoneme segmentation and synthesis training combined with letter-sound training. Yopp (1992) suggests that this should be for at least 5 to 10 minutes each day and has made some interesting suggestions for incorporating the learning of these skills into games and songs.

REVIEW

This chapter has looked at phonemic awareness and its possible links to reading acquisition and reading difficulty in alphabetic orthographies. It was suggested that the ability to segment, blend, and manipulate the phonemic structure of words is a necessary, but not sufficient, precursor to reading acquisition. Three possible connections between phonemic awareness and reading were presented. The first states that phonemic awareness develops as a result of learning to read. The second states that phonemic awareness precedes and predicts reading. The third states that reciprocal influences exist; that some rudimentary levels of phonemic awareness are required for the alphabetic principle to be acquired, but other deeper levels of phonemic awareness develop as a result of learning to read. Stanovich (1992), who supports this third view, suggests that phonological awareness exists along a continuum from shallow to deeper sensitivity.

Various methods of assessing and teaching phonological awareness were outlined. Some are more difficult than others. Some phonemic manipulation tasks are not likely to be helpful in aiding children to develop reading skills until prior (simpler) levels of phonological awareness have been developed. The various training tasks reviewed included identification of rhyme and alliteration, phoneme segmentation, blending, and manipulation tasks. These skills allow children to acquire letter-phoneme knowledge that they can use in phonological recoding to read words (see Chapter 2). Phonological recoding is often assessed using pseudoword reading and sometimes using spelling tasks, and it is significantly correlated with reading ability.

My research on this topic was presented. The results, along with those from many other studies, demonstrate that phonemic awareness training can have an impact for potentially at-risk children who are taught in a whole-language classroom reading program. While the positive effects of the training were only small, they were significant. As Stanovich (1986) points out, even small initial gains in phonemic awareness may have a snowball effect on later reading progress. My own study certainly suggests that children who enter school low in these skills will benefit from the addition of explicit instruction to their classroom work, in that they more easily acquire the alphabetic principle. Once this is achieved, they are equipped with the self-teaching mechanisms of phonological recoding for reading new words.

STUDY AND DISCUSSION QUESTIONS

1. What do the terms *phonological* and *phonemic awareness* refer to?
2. What contribution does phonemic awareness make to learning to read in an alphabetic orthography?
3. How is phonemic awareness linked with reading difficulties?
4. How is phonological awareness usually assessed?
5. What are the skills commonly taught for phonemic awareness?
6. How can phonemic awareness instruction and assessment be incorporated into whole-language reading programs?

FURTHER READING

Adams, M. J. (1990). *Beginning to read: Thinking and learning about print*. Cambridge, MA: MIT Press.
Goswami, U., & Bryant, P. (1990). *Phonological skills and learning to read*. Hove, UK: Erlbaum.
Juel, C. (1994). *Learning to read in one elementary school*. New York: Springer-Verlag.
Nicholson, T. (1994). *At the cutting edge: Recent research on learning to read and spell*. Wellington, New Zealand: New Zealand Council for Educational Research.

REFERENCES

Adams, M. J. (1990). *Beginning to read: Thinking and learning about print*. Cambridge, MA: MIT Press.
Arlin, P. K. (1981). Piagetian tasks as predictors of reading and math readiness in grades K–1. *Journal of Educational Psychology, 73,* 712–721.
Bradley, L. (1980). *Assessing learning difficulties: A diagnostic and remedial approach*. Houndsmill, UK: Macmillan Education.

Bradley, L. (1988). Making connections in learning to read and to spell. *Applied Cognitive Psychology, 2*, 3–18.

Bradley, L., & Bryant, P. E. (1983). Categorising sounds and learning to read—a causal connection. *Nature, 301*, 419–421.

Bruce, D. J. (1964). The analysis of word sounds by young children. *British Journal of Educational Psychology, 34*, 158–170.

Bryant, N. D. (1975). *Bryant Test of Basic Decoding Skills.* New York: Teachers College Press.

Bryant, P. E., Bradley, L., MacLean, M., & Crossland, J. (1989). Nursey rhymes, phonological skills and reading. *Journal of Child Language, 16*, 407–428.

Byrne, B., & Fielding-Barnsley, R. (1991). Evaluation of a program to teach phonemic awareness to young children. *Journal of Educational Psychology, 83*, 451–455.

Castle, J. M., Riach, J., & Nicholson, T. (1994). Getting off to a better start in reading and spelling: The effects of phonemic awareness instruction within a whole language program. *Journal of Educational Psychology, 86*, 350–359.

Clay, M. M. (1985). *The early detection of reading difficulties* (3rd ed.). Auckland, New Zealand: Heinemann.

Content, A., Kolinsky, R., Morais, J., & Bertleson, P. (1986). Phonetic segmentation in prereaders: Effect of corrective information. *Journal of Experimental Child Psychology, 42*, 49–72.

Cunningham, A. E. (1990). Explicit versus implicit instruction in phonemic awareness. *Journal of Experimental Child Psychology, 50*, 429–444.

Department of Education. (1985). *Reading in junior classes.* Wellington, New Zealand: Author.

Dunn, L. M., & Dunn, L. M. (1981). *Peabody Picture Vocabulary Test—Revised.* Circle Pines, MN: American Guidance Service.

Ehri, L. C. (1989). The development of spelling knowledge and its role in reading acquisition and reading disability. *Journal of Learning Disabilities, 22*, 356–365.

Elkonin, D. B. (1973). U.S.S.R. In J. Downing (Ed.), *Comparative reading* (pp. 551–579). New York: Macmillan.

Felton, R. H., & Wood, F. B. (1992). A reading level match study of nonword reading skills in poor readers with varying IQ. *Journal of Learning Disabilities, 25*, 318–326.

Gilmore, A., Croft, C., & Reid, N. (1981). *Burt Word Reading Test: New Zealand Revision.* Wellington, New Zealand: New Zealand Council for Educational Research.

Goswami, U., & Bryant, P. (1990). *Phonological skills and learning to read.* Hove, UK: Erlbaum.

Gough, P. B. (1993). The beginning of decoding. *Reading and Writing, 5*, 181–192.

Gough, P. B., & Hillinger, M. L. (1980). Learning to read: An unnatural act. *Bulletin of the Orton Society, 30*, 179–196.

Hurford, D. P., Schauf, J. D., Bunce, L., Blaich, T., & Moore, K. (1994). Early identification of children at risk for reading disabilities. *Journal of Learning Disabilities, 27*, 371–382.

Iverson, S., & Tunmer, W. E. (1992). Phonological processing skills and the Reading Recovery program. *Journal of Educational Psychology, 85,* 112–126.

Juel, C. (1988). Learning to read and write: A longitudinal study of 54 children from first through fourth grades. *Journal of Educational Psychology, 80,* 437–447.

Juel, C., Griffith, P. L., & Gough, P. B. (1986). Acquisition of literacy: A longitudinal study of children in first and second grade. *Journal of Educational Psychology, 78,* 243–255.

Lewkowicz, N. K. (1980). Phonemic awareness training: What to teach and how to teach it. *Journal of Educational Psychology, 72,* 686–700.

Liberman, I. Y., Shankweiler, D., Fischer, F. W., & Carter, B. (1974). Syllable and phoneme segmentation in the young child. *Journal of Experimental Child Psychology, 18,* 201–212.

Lie, A. (1991). Effects of a training program for stimulating skills in word analysis in first grade children. *Reading Research Quarterly, 26,* 234–250.

Lindamood, C. H., & Lindamood, P. C. (1975). *The A.D.D. Program, Auditory Discrimination in Depth.* Hingham, MA: Teaching Resources.

Lundberg, I., Frost, J., & Petersen, O. (1988). Effects of an extensive program for stimulating phonological awareness in preschool children. *Reading Research Quarterly, 23,* 263–284.

Mann, V. A. (1986). Phonological awareness: The role of reading experience. *Cognition, 24,* 65–92.

Roper-Schneider, H. D. W. (1984). *Spelling, word recognition and phonemic awareness among first grade children.* Unpublished doctoral dissertation, University of Texas, Austin.

Stanovich, K. E. (1986). Matthew effects in reading: Some consequences of individual differences in the acquisition of literacy. *Reading Research Quarterly, 21,* 360–406.

Stanovich, K. E. (1992). Speculations on the causes and consequences of individual differences in early reading acquisition. In P. B. Gough, L. C. Ehri, & R. Treiman (Eds.), *Reading acquisition* (pp. 307–342). Hillsdale, NJ: Erlbaum.

Stanovich, K. E., Cunningham, A. E., & Cramer, B. B. (1984). Assessing phonological awareness in kindergarten children: Issues of task comparability. *Journal of Experimental Child Psychology, 38,* 175–190.

Treiman, R. (1991). Phonological awareness and its roles in learning to read and spell. In D. Sawyer & B. Fox (Eds.), *Phonological awareness in reading: The evolution of current perspectives* (pp. 159–190). New York: Springer-Verlag.

Tunmer, W. E., Herriman, M. L., & Nesdale, A. R. (1988). Metalinguistic abilities and beginning reading. *Reading Research Quarterly, 23,* 134–158.

Tunmer, W. E., & Nesdale, A. R. (1985). Phonemic segmentation skill and beginning reading. *Journal of Educational Psychology, 77,* 417–427.

Tunmer, W. E., & Rohl, M. (1991). Phonological awareness and reading acquisition. In D. Sawyer & B. Fox (Eds.), *Phonological awareness in reading: The evolution of current perspectives* (pp. 1–30). New York: Springer-Verlag.

Wallach, L., Wallach, M. A., Dozier, M. G., & Kaplan, N. E. (1977). Poor children learning to read do not have trouble with auditory discrimination but do have trouble with phoneme recognition. *Journal of Educational Psychology, 69,* 36–39.

Williams, J. P. (1979). The ABD's of reading: A program for the learning disabled. In L. B. Resnick & P. A. Weavers (Eds.), *Theory and practice of early reading* (Vol. 3; pp. 179–195). Hillsdale, NJ: Erlbaum.

Williams, J. P. (1980). Teaching decoding with an emphasis on phoneme analysis and phoneme blending. *Journal of Educational Psychology, 72,* 1–15.

Yopp, H. K. (1988). The validity and reliability of phonemic awareness tests. *Reading Research Quarterly, 23,* 159–177.

Yopp, H. K. (1992). Developing phonemic awareness in young children. *Reading Teacher, 45,* 696–703.

Zhurova, L. E. (1963). The development of analysis of words into their sounds by preschool children. *Soviet Psychology and Psychiatry, 2,* 17–27.

Chapter 4

Teaching Strategies for Word Identification

WILLIAM E. TUNMER AND JAMES W. CHAPMAN

a) What are the key features of the whole-language approach to teaching literacy?

b) What are the alternative views?

c) What are the instructional dimensions for teaching word identification?

d) What are the recent research findings on these instructional dimensions?

The major aim of this chapter is to provide an overview of the theoretical arguments and empirical evidence in support of different approaches to facilitating the development of word-identification skills in beginning readers. The chapter is divided into four sections. The first presents a discussion of the key defining features and underlying theoretical assumptions of the "whole-language" approach to literacy instruction. The second provides an alternative conceptual framework of beginning literacy development that draws attention to several shortcomings of the whole-language approach. The third describes a continuum of approaches to beginning reading instruction and suggests that reading programs designed to facilitate the development of word-identification skills differ on several instructional dimensions, four of which may be particularly important. And the fourth section briefly describes two studies in which aspects of these four dimensions were investigated.

THE WHOLE-LANGUAGE APPROACH TO LITERACY INSTRUCTION

The whole-language movement has attracted an enormous amount of attention in recent years (Adams, 1990, 1991; Adams & Bruck, 1993; Edelsky, 1990; Gersten & Dimino, 1993; K. S. Goodman, 1989; Y. M. Goodman, 1989; Liberman & Liberman, 1992; McKenna, Robinson, &

Miller, 1990; Nicholson, 1992; Perfetti, 1991; Stahl & Miller, 1989; Stanovich, 1990, 1991; R. A. Thompson, 1992; Vellutino, 1991). While educational movements come and go, many observers believe that there has
never been anything quite like the whole-language movement. It has
certainly polarized the reading community, both practitioners and researchers alike. However, whole language means different things to different people (Bergeron, 1990), and people seem to like or dislike it for
different reasons. In the subsections that follow we describe what we believe are the four key defining features of the whole-language approach
to literacy instruction. Because the New Zealand literacy program is often
cited by whole-language advocates as a success story for the whole-
language orientation to literacy instruction (e.g., Y. M. Goodman, 1989),
illustrative examples will be drawn from the New Zealand version of whole
language.

Literature-Based Approach

Proponents of whole language espouse a *literature-based* approach to
beginning reading instruction in which the use of graded reading materials based on controlled vocabulary and sentence structure is greatly de-
emphasized or eliminated altogether. Programs involving such controls,
which are often referred to as *basal* reading programs, have been severely
criticized by whole-language advocates because the application of readability formulas often results in unnatural language (e.g., *See Spot run*).
These programs have also been attacked for their use of overly explicit
instruction involving scope-and-sequence charts, a heavy emphasis on
teaching skills in isolation, the use of workbook activities, and an overall
lockstep approach to literacy instruction.

In place of basal readers, whole-language proponents strongly recom-
mend the use of so-called real books (also referred to as "little books," story
books, or trade books) that contain stories (usually one per book) that can
be read in a single sitting. In such "natural" language texts, the language
of print is as close as possible to the spoken language of children (J. W.
Smith & Elley, 1994). It is worth mentioning that in New Zealand basals
were not abandoned for any of the reasons mentioned above. Rather, the
reasons were primarily economic (Nicholson, 1992). In the postwar period New Zealand used a basal series from Britain that had originally been
adapted from an American basal series. However, the latest printing of the
series was regarded as too expensive. Also, there was a desire to use reading materials that reflected the experiences of New Zealand children.

The first set of graded story books, called *Ready to Read*, was adopted
in the early 1960s. After extensive trials in schools, the books selected for

use were graded into a sequence of difficulty levels based on teacher judgments of children's responses to each story as a whole rather than to the vocabulary items within the story (G. B. Thompson, 1993). As a consequence of this shift in emphasis to the story level, there was very little deliberate control of either the degree of difficulty or rate of introduction of new words in the latest version of the *Ready to Read* series.

Hundreds of story books have been graded in difficulty against the latest version of the *Ready to Read* series, which was adopted in the early 1980s. The difficulty level of a new book is based on teachers' judgments of how children respond to the book. To be assigned to a particular level for instructional purposes, a child must be able to read the books at that level with a word-recognition accuracy rate above 90%. In support of this feature of New Zealand reading instruction, research indicates that beginning readers derive the greatest benefit from instruction when their error rate is kept fairly low. At all reading levels low error rates are positively correlated with reading growth, while high error rates are negatively correlated with reading growth (Rosenshine & Stevens, 1984).

Because no readability formulas are used in assessing text level in this approach, children reading at a particular level are exposed to a wider range of vocabulary and a greater variety of language forms than they would be when reading at a particular level in most basal reading series. However, it is precisely for this reason, in our view, that even greater emphasis needs to be placed on directly teaching children word-recognition strategies, especially children who may be at risk for failure. Because such a high proportion of the words used in school reading materials appear infrequently (Adams, 1991), beginning readers are continually encountering words that they have not seen before and may not set eyes on again for some time. Reliance on contextual guessing will be of little help because research has demonstrated that the average predictability of content words in running text is about 10%, compared to about 40% for function words (e.g., *on*, *the*, *to*), which are typically short, high-frequency sight words that the child can already recognize (Gough, 1983). The meaning of text therefore depends disproportionately on the meanings of its least familiar and least predictable words. Consequently, unless a child is reading a very low-level text with repeated sentence structures, a high degree of predictability, and a large amount of picture support, he or she will have a one in ten chance of correctly guessing unfamiliar words.

Child-Centered Instruction

Another key feature of the whole-language approach is its emphasis on child-centered instruction. This is not a particularly unique characteristic of the whole-language approach, as it has been known for some time that children should be viewed as active rather than as passive learners and that teachers should build on what children know.

A major advantage of the child-centered approach to literacy instruction is that it recognizes the enormous variation in literacy-related skills and experiences that children bring to school. For example, in New Zealand the phrase "1,000-book children" is often used to refer to new entrants who have been read an average of one or more stories every day by their caregivers during the 2 to 3 years prior to school entry. Some obvious benefits of listening to read stories include learning about decontextualized language (i.e., language that is not embedded in familiar perceptual and social contexts) and gaining insights into the nature and functions of print. However, there are children in New Zealand and elsewhere who arrive at school without ever having listened to read stories or engaged in other relevant literacy-related activities. The latter include looking at books and playing games that increase knowledge of letter names and their relation to sounds in words (e.g., "z is for zebra"), playing rhyming and sound analysis games that increase phonological sensitivity (e.g., pig Latin, I spy, nursery rhymes, Dr Seuss books), and manipulating movable letters to form preconventional spellings of words (e.g., KLR for *color*). Children who have not had these experiences may begin school at a disadvantage, especially if responding to the individual needs of children is not a prominent feature of the beginning literacy program at their school.

Integration of Reading and Writing

The integration of reading and writing is another commonly cited feature of whole-language programs. Children are introduced to writing instruction at the same time they begin receiving reading instruction, as it is thought that there is a reciprocally facilitating relationship between the two (J. W. Smith & Elley, 1994). Normally children are asked to draw a picture relating to a personal or shared experience, and then to write a one- or two-sentence "story" directly beneath the drawing.

Preconventional spellings are encouraged if the child has adequate knowledge of letter names and/or sounds. In general, so-called risk taking is strongly promoted in both reading and writing, which means that not all errors are corrected. Rather, the child is praised for attempts that make sense, such as spelling the word *fairy* as FRE. A possible advantage of an early emphasis on writing that includes the use of preconventional spellings is that children are encouraged from the outset to make use of the alphabetic code while communicating in print meaningful messages based on their personal experiences.

However, a major shortcoming of this approach, in our view, occurs somewhat later when the teacher begins placing increasing emphasis on learning the *conventional* spellings of words. In New Zealand schools, for example, the words that children are asked to study in their personal spelling lists are based almost entirely on misspellings that occurred in each child's own writings. There is little or no systematic study of common spelling patterns across groups of words. Instead, words are studied in groups only if they relate to a particular theme or shared classroom experience, or form meaningful categories, such as the word groupings presented at the end of *Spell-Write* (Croft, 1983), the most widely used spelling book in New Zealand. For example, listed under the general category of *nature* are 10 subcategories (*animals, body parts, colors, matter, places*, etc), and listed under the *places* subcategory are the words *beach, cave, ground, hill, hole, island, land,* and *mountain.*

This approach to learning the conventional spellings of words reflects the guiding principle of the whole-language philosophy, which is "no meaning, no gain." This brings us to the most important defining feature of whole language, the emphasis on meaning construction.

Emphasis on Meaning Construction

At one level the emphasis on meaning construction is not a particularly noteworthy characteristic of whole language, as the goal of any literacy program must be to help children derive meaning *from* print and express meaning *in* print. The question is how best to do it.

A central belief held by whole-language advocates is that learning to read is essentially like learning to speak. However, this belief is clearly false, as written language is a culturally transmitted artifact whereas spoken language is part of the biological heritage of the human species (Liberman & Liberman, 1992). As Perfetti (1991) points out:

> Learning to read is not like acquiring one's native language, no matter how much someone wishes it were so. Natural language is acquired quickly with a large biological contribution. Its forms are reinvented by every child exposed to a speech community in the first years of life. It is universal among human communities. By contrast literacy is a cultural invention. It is far from universal. And the biological contribution to the process has already been accounted for, once it is acknowledged that it depends on language rather than parallels it. (p. 75)

From the incorrect assumption that the ability to read evolves naturally and spontaneously out of children's prereading experiences in much the same way that their oral language develops, whole-language theorists concluded that reading instruction should be modeled on first-language acquisition, where the focus is on meaning construction, not the abstract structural units by which meaning is conveyed. It therefore followed that language should be kept "whole" during instruction. K. S. Goodman (1986), a leading proponent of the whole-language view of literacy acquisition, argued that teachers make learning to read difficult "by breaking whole (natural) language into bitesize abstract little pieces" (p. 7), and that this postpones the natural purpose of language, which is the communication of meaning. Word-study activities should therefore emphasize the process of "making meaning," not the mechanics of reading words in isolation or translating written words into sounds. If children are immersed in a print-rich environment in which the focus is on the meaning of print, they will readily acquire reading skills, according to this view.

In New Zealand, and in other school systems that use whole-language programs, children are urged to use sentence context as the primary strategy for recognizing words in text. They are taught to monitor for meaningfulness and to make corrections only when necessary to make sense. When children encounter a difficult word, they are encouraged to guess what the word might be and often receive praise if the response fits the context, even if the response is incorrect. Children are also taught to use graphophonemic cues, but only very sparingly and mostly to confirm language predictions. As a consequence, instruction in letter-sound correspondences almost always arises *incidentally* in the context of reading text, not in isolation.

In New Zealand this approach to reading instruction has been strongly influenced by Marie Clay, who, like K. S. Goodman (1967) and F. Smith (1978), describes fluent reading as a process in which minimal word-level information is used to confirm language predictions:

> In efficient rapid word perception the reader relies mostly on the sentence and its meaning and some selected features of the forms of words. Awareness of the sentence context (and often the general context of the text as a whole) and a glance at the word enables the reader to respond instantly. (Clay, 1991, p. 8)

If this statement were true (and the available evidence indicates that it almost certainly is not; see Stanovich [1986] for a review of research), then it would follow that reading instruction should focus primarily on teaching beginning readers to use sentence context to predict the words of text.

AN ALTERNATIVE CONCEPTUAL FRAMEWORK
OF BEGINNING LITERACY DEVELOPMENT

The major question arising from our brief overview of the defining features of whole language is whether it is the most effective way to teach children literacy skills, especially children at risk of failure in reading. The available research suggests that it is not (Adams, 1990; Adams & Bruck, 1993). Nevertheless, there is widespread enthusiasm for whole language. For example, with respect to the New Zealand version of whole language, Y. M. Goodman (Adams et al., 1991) from the United States recently claimed that the Reading Recovery program was developed in New Zealand "for a small percentage of children selected from holistic instructional settings where the vast majority of children learn to read without direct intensive phonics" (p. 377). However, as Nicholson (1992) points out, this begs the question of what constitutes a "small percentage." Statistics reported by the Ministry of Education in New Zealand indicate that every year since 1990 a staggering 25% of all 6-year-olds participated in the Reading Recovery program. That is, after a full year in school, one out of every four children in New Zealand undergoes special tutoring in reading. Many of these children have made little or no progress toward gaining independence in reading during their first year of schooling.

Presented in Figure 4.1 is an alternative conceptual framework that specifies the relationships among the major learning tasks, learning strategies, and cognitive prerequisites of beginning literacy development. *Learning tasks* refer to the procedural ("how-to") knowledge that children must acquire in a given problem-solving domain; *learning strategies* are the cognitive plans of action that children must develop or be taught in order to achieve success in performing specified learning tasks; and *cognitive prerequisites* are the cognitive skills that are necessary for acquiring the learning strategies. According to the framework, children are faced with two major learning tasks. They must learn to read unfamiliar words in meaningful texts, and they must learn to write unfamiliar words in meaningful messages. In learning to read unfamiliar words, children are normally taught two general learning strategies: to use sentence context cues and to use mappings between the subcomponents of written and spoken words (or graphophonemic cues). The latter strategy is also used to produce conventional and preconventional spellings of words. The framework further proposes that two cognitive prerequisites are required. The ability to use sentence context cues to identify unfamiliar words requires sensitivity to the semantic and syntactic constraints of sentence context (called *syntactic awareness*). Syntactic awareness provides children with immediate feedback when their attempted responses to unfamiliar words fail to conform

Figure 4.1 Relationships Among Learning Tasks, Learning Strategies, and Cognitive Prerequisites of Beginning Literacy Development

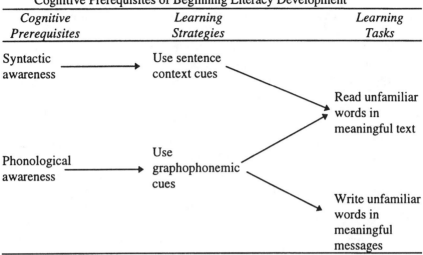

to the surrounding grammatical context (e.g., "The boy *slept* the bed," "The shirt *ran*"). The ability to use mappings between letters and sounds (e.g., that the letter *b* maps onto the sound /b/, and vice versa) to read and write unfamiliar words requires sensitivity to the subcomponents of spoken words (e.g., that the spoken word "bag" begins with the /b/ sound). This sensitivity is often referred to as *phonological awareness*.

This framework draws attention to three important issues in relation to the whole-language view of beginning literacy development. First, what are the relative contributions of language prediction skill (i.e., the ability to use the constraints of sentence context) and letter-sound knowledge (i.e., the ability to use mappings between letters and sounds) to the development of word-identification ability. Second, do some children require extra help in acquiring the cognitive prerequisites necessary for learning to read? And third, what is the best way to facilitate the development of letter-sound knowledge in beginning readers?

Contributions of Language Prediction Skill and Letter-Sound Knowledge

With regard to the first issue, although most practitioners and researchers would agree that beginning readers should be encouraged to make use of both sentence context cues and letter-sound cues in recognizing unfamiliar words, the critical question is this: What relative emphasis should be placed on each? Put simply, if a child is reading aloud and comes across a word that he or she does not know, what is the first thing that the teacher should tell the child to do? As noted earlier, whole-language advocates would argue that children should predict meaning from sentence context cues at the outset and use their knowledge of letter-sound correspondences for confirmation. For example, if a child cannot identify the word *away* in the sentence *The boy ran away from the wasp*, he or she would be encouraged to use prior sentence context to guess what the word might be, or, if necessary, to skip the word and read to the end of the sentence, and then reread the sentence and put in a word that makes sense. The child would then be encouraged to "check on language predictions by looking at some letters" (Clay, 1985, p. 22). The opposite view, which we support, is that children should be encouraged to look for familiar spelling patterns first and to use context only as back-up support to confirm hypotheses about what the word might be (Tunmer & Chapman, 1993). For example, in the sentence given above, the child would be encouraged to look for and pronounce known words and word parts (e.g., *a, way, ay*) in the unfamiliar word and then to use sentence context to check whether the attempted response makes sense.

In support of the latter view is a considerable amount of convergent evidence indicating that with very rare exceptions progress in learning to read can occur only if the child achieves a fairly advanced level of *phonological recoding* ability, which is the ability to translate letters and letter patterns into phonological forms (Adams & Bruck, 1993; Ehri, 1991, 1992; Tunmer & Hoover, 1992, 1993). A commonly used measure of phonological recoding ability is the ability to pronounce correctly pseudowords such as *dut, sark, toin,* and *thrain*. Another commonly used measure is the ability to judge which of two pseudowords sounds like a real word (e.g., *rane* versus *sark*, where *rane* is pronounced like the real word *rain*). The reason that the ability to use phonological information is so critical is that sublexical analyses involving phonological information result in positive learning trials (i.e., correct word identifications), which in turn lead to the amalgamation of orthographic (i.e., the specific letter sequence) and phonological representations in semantic memory (Ehri, 1992). These amalgamated representations provide the basis for rapid and efficient access to the mental lexicon, which in turn frees up cognitive resources for allocation to comprehension and text integration processes. More specifically, as words are recognized their phonological representations are stored in working memory until sufficient information has accumulated to permit assembly of the lexical entries into larger units of relational meaning called *propositions*. Because proposition encoding takes place within the limits of working memory, lexical access that is inefficient and capacity draining will disrupt the temporary representation of text in working memory, and comprehension will suffer as a result. In short, children who are having trouble identifying the individual words of text quickly and accurately will also encounter difficulty in *comprehending* what they are reading.

Children who rely mostly on visual cues at the expense of phonological information will experience progressive deterioration in the rate of reading development as they grow older (Bruck, 1992; Byrne, Freebody, & Gates, 1992). As Adams and Bruck (1993) point out, "without the mnemonic support of the spelling-to-sound connections, the visual system must eventually become overwhelmed: the situation in which [these children] are left is roughly analogous to learning 50,000 telephone numbers to the point of perfect recall and instant recognition" (p. 130). Because there is little interaction between orthographic and phonological codes in the word processing of poor readers who rely mostly on nonphonological strategies (such as partial visual cues and contextual guessing), the development of awareness of individual phonemes and knowledge of correspondences between graphemes and phonemes is not promoted (Bruck, 1992). Consequently, the word-identification skills of these children remain relatively weak because they do not develop as rich a network of sublexical connections between orthographic and phonological representations in semantic memory as normally developing readers (for a discussion of connectionist models of reading, see Adams [1990] and Adams & Bruck [1993]).

Despite this evidence, however, whole-language advocates continue to argue that explicit and systematic instruction in letter-sound correspondences is unnecessary for three reasons: first, concentrating too heavily on learning letter-sound correspondences will result in children losing the natural insight that print is meaningful; second, the small amount of letter-sound knowledge that beginning readers need can, in any event, be acquired through writing activities; and third, English orthography contains so many irregularities anyway that focusing too much attention on teaching letter-sound correspondences will not only waste valuable time but possibly even confuse children and impede progress (F. Smith, 1978).

Against the latter claim, Gough and colleagues (Gough & Hillinger, 1980; Gough & Walsh, 1991) have argued that because no word in English is completely phonologically opaque, even irregularly spelled "exception" words (e.g., *stomach, castle, money, glove*) provide accurate phonological cues to the word's identity. When beginning readers apply their developing knowledge of grapheme-phoneme correspondences to unfamiliar exception words, the result will often be close enough to the correct phonological form that sentence context cues can be used to arrive at a correct identification (e.g., He couldn't find his *money*). In support of Gough's claim that phonological recoding skill is essential for acquiring word-specific knowledge (i.e., amalgamated representations) are the results of two experiments that we recently carried out as part of a larger study (Tunmer & Chapman, 1991).

In the first experiment, 67 year-2 and year-3 children (with mean ages of 6 years, 8 months and 7 years, 7 months, respectively) were individually administered a mispronunciation correction task. The children were introduced to a hand-held puppet named Peter and told that when Peter tried to say a word, he said it the "wrong way." The child's task was to try to figure out what word Peter was trying to say. The "words" presented to the children were all formed from the regularized pronunciations of irregularly spelled words. For example, the word *stomach* was pronounced "stow-match." The children were presented with a total of 80 regularized pronunciations and managed to figure out many of them (more than 25% on average). When these same mispronounced words were presented in context in another test session, the children performed even better, averaging 66% correct. For example, when Peter said, "The football hit him in the stow-match," most children immediately said that Peter was trying to say the word "stomach." It is important to note that the contexts we used in the task were deliberately underdetermining ones, which research indicates is the more naturally occurring situation. As noted earlier, the average predictability of content words in running text is about 10%. When the 80 sentence contexts were presented as an oral cloze task to a separate sample of children, the average predictability of the target words was 8%. The results of the experiment clearly demonstrate that the graphophonemic information contained in irregularly spelled words can be very useful, especially when combined with sentence context cues.

In the second experiment, 289 year-2 and year-3 children (with mean ages of 6 years, 6 months and 7 years, 6 months, respectively) were individually administered the Burt Word Reading Test, an oral cloze task, a pseudoword naming task (which comprised nonwords like *med, dut, sath,* and *pake*), and a contextual facilitation task. In the latter task the children were asked to read aloud 80 irregular words, first in isolation and then, on another occasion, in context (the words and contexts were the same as those used in the first experiment). The children were asked to read along silently as the experimenter read aloud the prior sentence context. When the target word was reached, the experimenter pointed to the word and asked the child to read it aloud. As expected, there was a strong positive correlation between the ability to pronounce pseudowords and the ability to identify exception words presented in isolation ($r = 0.78$). Of greater interest, a scatterplot of the data revealed that there were many children who performed reasonably well on the pseudoword naming test but recognized few irregular words. However, there were no children who performed poorly on the pseudoword naming test and well on the irregular-word naming test. These findings suggest that phonological recoding skill (as measured by the pseudoword naming task) is necessary but not sufficient for the development of word-specific knowledge (see also Gough & Walsh, 1991).

The results of the contextual facilitation task indicated that accuracy in recognizing irregular words improved with context. Of particular interest was the finding that children with moderate or emerging phonological recoding skills showed the largest gains when the words were presented in context. It appears that the ability of these children to take advantage of the available graphophonemic cues in irregular words was not sufficiently advanced for them to identify many of the words in isolation. However, when the same words were presented in underdetermining contexts, the performance of these children greatly improved. In contrast, the contextual facilitation scores of the poor decoders were relatively low, suggesting that if beginning readers are unable to make use of the graphophonemic information provided in irregular words, context will be of little or no benefit to them. A scatterplot of the relation of phonological recoding ability to reading unfamiliar words primed by context (as assessed by the number of words that the children were able to read correctly when the first 15 words that they missed in isolation were presented in context) supported this interpretation. Only children who had begun to acquire phonological recoding ability were able to use context to identify unfamiliar words. Consistent with this finding, a multiple regression analysis of the data indicated that, although the ability to use sentence context cues (as measured by the oral cloze task) made an independent contribution to variance in recognizing unfamiliar exception words primed by underdetermining contexts, phonological recoding skill accounted for a much greater amount of independent variance. That is, even in the extreme case of learning to recognize irregularly spelled words, phonological recoding skill was much more important than language prediction skill.

The Development of Phonological Awareness and Phonological Recoding

The second issue raised by the conceptual framework presented in Figure 4.1 concerns the cognitive prerequisites required to take advantage of sentence context cues and graphophonemic cues in identifying unfamiliar words. Given the evidence indicating that the ability to use letter-sound mappings is much more important than the ability to use the constraints of sentence context, the development of phonological awareness is especially important. To discover mappings between spelling patterns and sound patterns, children must be able to segment spoken words into subcomponents. However, as Marie Clay observed many years ago, some beginning readers find it extraordinarily difficult to detect sound sequences in words. It was for this reason that Clay (1985) incorporated a phonological awareness training procedure into her Reading Recovery program. Children who are experiencing difficulties in detecting sound sequences in words need explicit instruction in the development of phonological awareness skills, a claim supported by a considerable amount of research (Lundberg, 1994).

The third issue raised by the general framework that we have proposed is how best to facilitate the development of phonological recoding ability, given that such ability appears to be so crucial for the development of word-recognition skills. This issue will be addressed in the remaining sections of the chapter. The point we wish to emphasize here is that children experiencing phonological-processing difficulties will not be able to derive maximum benefit from reading instruction and as a consequence will be prevented from taking advantage of the reciprocally facilitating (i.e., "boot-strapping") relationships between reading achievement and other aspects of development, such as vocabulary growth, ability to comprehend more syntactically complex sentences, and development of richer and more elaborated knowledge bases, all of which facilitate *further* growth in reading by enabling readers to cope with more difficult textual materials (Stanovich, 1986). As a result of repeated learning failures, many problem readers will also develop negative self-perceptions of ability and therefore not try as hard as other children because of their low expectations of success and poor reading-related self-efficacy (Chapman & Tunmer, 1995). *Self-efficacy* refers to personal beliefs about one's ability to carry out a designated task, such as learning to read.

The latter considerations have caused us to modify our original framework and draws attention to another difference between our view and the whole-language approach. Proponents of whole language place particular emphasis on developing within beginning readers a positive attitude toward reading, as if this were a major contributing factor to the acquisition of basic reading skills. Much attention is therefore devoted to exposing beginning readers to beautifully illustrated and written children's literature. While agreeing that the inclusion of good children's literature is an important component of any literacy program, our view is that poor attitude toward reading is primarily a *consequence* of reading failure, not a cause of it (see Figure 4.2). It is the lack of appropriate skills (such as the ability to use graphophonemic cues and sentence context cues) and associated cognitive prerequisites (i.e., phonological awareness and syntactic

Figure 4.2 Relationships Among Learning Tasks, Cognitive Motivational
Factors, Learning Strategies, and Cognitive Prerequisites of Beginning
Literacy Development

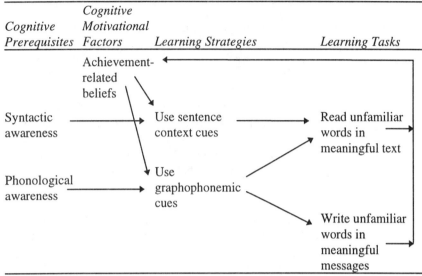

awareness), and/or the use of inappropriate or ineffective learning strategies (such as relying on contextual guessing and/or partial visual cues), that give rise to negative achievement-related beliefs in the first place. These beliefs may in turn impact negatively on children's willingness to exert much effort in acquiring more effective learning strategies, as shown in Figure 4.2. Exposure to good children's literature alone will be of little or no benefit to children experiencing reading difficulties.

CONTINUUM OF VIEWS ON APPROACHES
TO BEGINNING READING INSTRUCTION

A continuum of approaches to beginning reading instruction is presented in Table 4.1. As noted earlier, the whole-language approach developed in part as a rejection of the behavioristically oriented "skill-and-drill" approach common to many basal reading programs. An important feature of the skill-and-drill approach is the strong tendency to break reading performance down into several subskills (e.g., letter identification) and/ or rules (especially phonics rules) that are taught in isolation and in a particular sequence. The metacognitive strategy teaching approach, which

Table 4.1 Continuum of Approaches to Beginning Reading Instruction

Isolated skill-and-drill approach	Metacognitive strategy teaching approach	Whole-language approach
• Atomistic view of reading acquisition; reading broken down into several subskills	• Dynamic view of reading acquisition; child seen as active learner	• Reading acquisition seen as natural process that is meaning-driven; "no meaning, no gain"
• Heavy emphasis on teaching subskills in isolation; much seatwork and use of workbooks	• Emphasis on developing self-improving strategies for recognizing words and on how and when to use such strategies	• Minimal emphasis on word analysis activities; should only arise *incidentally* in context of reading connected text

we favor, also rejects aspects of the skill-and-drill approach but without accepting the unsupported claims of whole language. Moreover, unlike the whole-language approach, the metacognitive strategy teaching approach *does* advocate explicit and systematic training in phonological recoding skill. However, unlike the skill-and-drill approach, the metacognitive strategy teaching approach places greater emphasis on developing self-improving strategies for *acquiring* letter-sound correspondences rather than on teaching individual letter-sound correspondences per se. As Juel (1991) argues, a little explicit phonics instruction may go "a long way" in facilitating the process by which children induce untaught spelling-sound relationships (p. 783). That is, when children are made aware of the importance of letter-sound information, they may begin using incomplete graphophonemic information (possibly in combination with sentence context cues, see above) to identify unfamiliar words from which additional spelling-sound relationships can be (unconsciously) induced without explicit instruction (see Chapter 2).

The issue we wish to address now is what can be done to help beginning readers acquire letter-sound knowledge. Beginning reading programs designed to facilitate the development of phonological recoding skills may differ on several instructional dimensions (see Adams [1990] for a comprehensive review of the literature). Four dimensions that appear to be particularly important are skill-and-drill versus metacognitive approaches to instruction in phonological recoding skills, systematic versus incidental instruction in alphabetic coding, the degree of reliance on writing as a means of teaching recoding skills, and the use of individual letter-to-sound correspondences versus the inclusion of phonograms (the common elements in word families) in beginning code instruction.

Metacognition refers to knowledge about one's own thinking processes and learning strategies, including knowledge about when particular strategies are appropriate. Metacognitive approaches to instruction in phonological recoding skills place particular emphasis on making beginning readers conceptually aware of the interrelatedness of the visual patterns and sounds shared by different words. Gough and Juel (1991) refer to this awareness as *cryptanalytic intent*: The child "must grasp that there is a system of correspondences to be mastered" (p. 51). For example, children may be taught the strategy of reading unfamiliar words by detecting and pronouncing known words and word parts in unfamiliar words (Gaskins et al., 1988; Goswami & Bryant, 1990). This may include making beginning readers aware that some unfamiliar words contain spelling patterns that are associated with more than one pronunciation (e.g., *o-w-n* as in *down* and *blown*) and that they may need to generate alternative pronunciations until one matches a word in their listening vocabulary. Gaskins and colleagues (1988) refer to this as a "set for diversity" (p. 38). Instruction that places emphasis on metacognitive aspects of learning may also be useful in facilitating the development of phonological awareness in children (Cunningham, 1990). In general, metacognitive approaches to instruction are in sharp contrast to skill-and-drill approaches in which word-level skills are taught in an isolated, piecemeal fashion with little or no emphasis placed on developing within beginning readers an understanding of how and when to apply such knowledge.

A second important dimension concerns the question of whether instruction in the alphabetic code should arise incidentally in the context of reading connected text, or whether such instruction should be more explicit and systematic. As noted previously, advocates of the whole-language approach to reading instruction argue that word analysis skills should only be taught in context and only as back-up support to confirm language predictions. Strickland and Cullinan (1990), for example, claim that "phonics is best learned in the context of reading and writing" (p. 429) and that "the evidence supports a whole language and integrated language arts approach with some direct instruction, in context, on spelling-to-sound correspondences" (p. 433). Research indicates, however, that compared to normally achieving children, at-risk beginning readers are less able to discover grapheme-phoneme correspondences as a by-product of more general reading, suggesting that these children require more explicit instruction in alphabetic coding (Calfee & Drum, 1986). Although a "naturalistic," informal, whole-language approach to reading instruction (in which word analysis activities arise *incidentally* from the child's responses during text reading) may be suitable for many children, at-risk children appear to require a more highly structured, systematic, strategies-based approach with particular emphasis on the development of phonological recoding skills. As Adams and Bruck (1993) argue, "Wherever children who cannot discover the alphabetic principle independently are denied explicit instruction on the regularities and conventions of the letter strings, reading disability may well be the eventual consequence" (p. 131).

Another instructional dimension concerns the extent to which the development of phonological recoding skills can occur through writing activities. Whole-language advocates argue that instruction in the use of letter-sound correspondences to identify unfamiliar words is largely unnecessary because children can acquire knowledge of the alphabetic code through their experiences of attempting to spell words (Clay, 1991). Research has shown, however, that children initially use different strategies in reading and spelling (Goswami & Bryant, 1990). In early spelling the strategies are phonologically based. Analyses of children's early ("invented") spellings indicate that from the very beginning most children attempt to figure out the sounds in words and then represent the sounds with alphabetic letters (e.g., *HKN* for "chicken," *KLR* for "color") (Read, 1986; Treiman, 1993). However, Treiman (1993) found little evidence in these early spellings for the use of visual knowledge of spelling patterns gained through reading (e.g., *HLPT*, where the morpheme for past tense was represented by *t* instead of *ed*, as in *helped*). In contrast, the strategies used by children in early reading are visually based. Children learn to recognize their first words by relying on partial visual cues (Gough, 1993). To advance beyond an initial stage of reading in which words are recognized by selective association, beginning readers must eventually learn to make use of the systematic correspondences between elements of written and spoken language (see earlier discussion). However, simply exposing children to spelling instruction may not be adequate. In a study of word-identification skills in beginning readers, G. B. Thompson and Fletcher-Flinn (1993) found that knowledge of phoneme-to-letter correspondences acquired through spelling did not automatically transfer as a source of knowledge for letter-to-phoneme correspondences in reading. Consistent with these findings, Foorman, Francis, Novy, and Liberman (1991) found that direct instruction in phonological recoding skills supported reading growth better than did spelling instruction combined with incidental instruction in phonological recoding skills.

A fourth instructional dimension concerns the issue of exploiting phonograms in beginning reading programs as opposed to relying solely on individual letter-to-sound correspondences. Phonograms are the common elements in "word families" (e.g., the letter sequence *an* in *ran, man,* and *can*). There appear to be three advantages in using phonograms in the beginning stages of reading instruction. First, the use of phonograms enables children to take advantage of the intrasyllabic phonological units of onset and rime, where *onset* is the initial consonant or consonant cluster and *rime* is the vowel and any following consonants (Treiman, 1992). Research indicates that phonological awareness of onsets and rimes precedes the development of full-blown phonemic segmentation ability (Goswami & Bryant, 1990). Because onsets and rimes are more accessible to young children and because onsets often comprise single phonemes (e.g., /f/-/un/), an initial focus on word families may greatly facilitate the process of learning to isolate and recognize individual phonemes (Treiman, 1992). A second advantage in using phonograms in beginning reading instruction is that the complexity of vowel generalizations is greatly reduced (Adams, 1990). Vowel sounds are generally quite stable in the rime segments of words that appear in beginning reading materials. For example, the letter *a* has a consistent pronunciation when it precedes *ng* (e.g., *bang, hang, rang, sang*) but has many different pronunciations when it follows *c* (e.g., *cat, call, cake*). Wylie and Durrell (1970) showed that knowledge of only 37 phonograms enabled beginning readers to recognize 500 of the most frequently occurring words in beginning reading materials. A third possible advantage of initially focusing on teaching phonograms is that it temporarily delays the need for acquiring the ability to blend individual phonemes within onset and rime spelling units (Ehri & Robbins, 1992), the latter being a difficult operation to perform because of the large amount of processing required (Perfetti, Beck, Bell, & Hughes, 1987). In support of this claim is recent research by Wise (1992) indicating that blending onset and rime units into words (e.g., /bl/-/ast/ to "blast") is much easier for beginning readers than blending phonemic units into words (e.g., /b/-/l/-/a/-/s/-/t/ to "blast").

RECENT RESEARCH

Aspects of the four instructional dimensions that we have discussed were investigated in two recent studies (Greaney & Tunmer, 1996; Iversen & Tunmer, 1993).

Teaching the Child Strategies for Phonological Recoding

The first study (Iversen & Tunmer, 1993) examined the instructional strategies used in Reading Recovery, a remedial reading program that was developed in New Zealand by Marie Clay (1985) to reduce the number of children with reading and writing difficulties. The program, which is essentially a more intense version of what occurs in the regular New Zealand classroom, focuses on 6-year-old children who, after 1 year in school, are identified by teachers as not making good progress. The children are assessed with a battery of tests and observational procedures constituting the Diagnostic Survey (Clay, 1985). The children selected for assistance are provided with 30 to 40 minutes of individual instruction per day by a specially trained Reading Recovery teacher. The aim of the instruction, which supplements the children's regular classroom literacy program, is to help children to achieve a reasonable degree of independence in reading and to reach a level of reading performance that is at or above the class average (determined by performance on the full Diagnostic Survey, see below), in as little time as possible. This process usually takes between 12 and 20 weeks, at which time the child's Reading Recovery program is discontinued.

Research indicates that Reading Recovery is much more effective than remedial instruction in small groups (Pinnell, De Ford, & Lyons, 1988). However, similar findings have been reported for other remedial programs involving one-to-one tutoring but employing altogether different approaches than that used in Reading Recovery (e.g., Slavin, Madden, Karweit, Dolan, & Wasik, 1991), which suggests that it may be the intensive, one-to-one nature of these programs that is primarily responsible for their superiority over small-group instruction. A major aim of the study, therefore, was to determine whether the specific procedures and instructional strategies of Reading Recovery are more effective than other remedial approaches when the basic parameters of the program are held constant. We were particularly interested in determining whether the inclusion of more explicit and systematic instruction in phonological recoding skills would increase the effectiveness of the Reading Recovery program. Clay (1985) argues that instruction in alphabetic coding (i.e., the use of graphophonemic information) should only arise incidentally in the context of reading connected text and that explicit instruction in the use of letter-to-phoneme correspondences is largely unnecessary because children can acquire knowledge of the alphabetic code through spelling.

Three carefully matched groups of 32 children each were formed: a modified Reading Recovery group, a standard Reading Recovery group, and a standard intervention group that involved small-group instruction. The children were all first-graders in the United States who had been identified as at risk for failure on the basis of their performance on the Diagnostic Survey (Clay, 1985) and the Dolch Word Recognition Test. The Diagnostic Survey comprises a letter-identification task, a word-recognition task, a concepts-about-print task, a writing-vocabulary task, a dictation task, and an assessment of text level. In addition to the Diagnostic Survey and Dolch Word Recognition Test, the children were given three phonological-processing measures: a phoneme-segmentation test, a phoneme-deletion test, and a pseudoword-decoding test.

The children in the standard Reading Recovery group received regular Reading Recovery lessons in which word analysis activities arose incidentally from children's responses during text reading. This reflects the view that graphophonemic cues should only be used very sparingly and mostly to confirm language predictions (see earlier discussion). In contrast, the children in the modified Reading Recovery group received *explicit* training in phonological recoding skills as part of their lesson. The aim of the instruction incorporated into the modified Reading Recovery program was to make the children more aware that words with common sounds often share the same spelling patterns (e.g., b*at*, r*at*, p*at*; h*a*s, h*a*d, h*a*t). The procedures were similar to those developed by Bryant and Bradley (1985), and they included an initial focus on phonograms. The children were asked to manipulate magnetic letters to make, break, and build new words that had similar visual and phonological elements. Beginning with the manipulation of initial sounds/letters, the teacher modeled the task and then within each lesson gradually passed control over to the child. This procedure was then repeated daily with different words until the child demonstrated that he or she knew how to manipulate initial sounds/letters/clusters. The teacher then moved to final and then medial sounds/letters/clusters. The instruction focused not only on making children aware that certain words are visually and phonologically similar but also, in the context of the surrounding lessons, on developing strategies for knowing how and when to apply such knowledge. Whenever possible the teacher required the children to use their newly gained strategic knowledge to help them identify unfamiliar words in text. In short, the emphasis was on developing metacognitive knowledge and strategies for identifying unfamiliar words, not on "knowing" a particular list of words.

An analysis of the pre-treatment data confirmed that there were no significant differences between the means of the three comparison groups for all pre-treatment measures. The pre-treatment data also revealed that the children in the three intervention groups performed extremely poorly on the three phonological-processing measures. An analysis of the same measures at discontinuation showed that the two Reading Recovery groups performed at very similar levels and that both groups performed much better on all measures than the standard intervention group.

The most significant finding of the study is presented in Table 4.2. Although the two Reading Recovery groups performed at very similar levels

Table 4.2 Mean Number of Lessons to Discontinuation as a Function of Type of Reading Recovery Program

Type of Reading Recovery program	n	Mean	Standard deviation	$t(62)$
Modified	32	41.75	10.62	5.70*
Standard	32	57.31	11.22	

*$p < .001$

on all measures at discontinuation, the results shown in Table 4.2 indicate that it took the children receiving the standard Reading Recovery program much longer to reach the same point. The difference in the mean number of lessons to reach the discontinuation criterion was highly statistically significant and indicates that the standard Reading Recovery program was 37% less efficient than the modified Reading Recovery program. To rule out the possibility that the extra lessons received by the standard Reading Recovery group children enabled them to eventually overtake the children in the modified Reading Recovery group, an analysis of measures taken at the end of the year revealed no differences between the two groups.

A statistical path analysis of the data was carried out to determine the structure of relationships between measures at discontinuation and measures at the end of the year. The results suggest that phonological awareness is primarily responsible for the development of phonological recoding ability, that phonological recoding ability is in turn primarily responsible for the development of context-free word-recognition ability, and that context-free word-recognition ability is in turn primarily responsible for the development of the ability to read connected text. Unlike the predictive correlations for the phonological-processing measures, the predictive correlations between spelling measures and end-of-year reading measures failed to reach significance, suggesting that letter-to-phoneme knowledge, not phoneme-to-letter knowledge as claimed by Clay (1991), is primarily responsible for "driving" the development of word-recognition skills.

In summary, the results of the study indicated the following: that systematic instruction in phonological recoding skill was much more effective than incidental instruction; that the inclusion of direct instruction in phonological recoding skill yielded better results than relying on writing activities as the primary means of developing knowledge of the alphabetic code; and that a metacognitive approach to code instruction that included the use of phonograms could be a very effective intervention strategy for at-risk readers. The results further indicated that the children selected for Reading Recovery were particularly deficient in phonological-processing skills and that their progress in the program was strongly related to the development of these skills.

Teaching Analogy Strategies

The second study that we wish to describe was carried out by Greaney and Tunmer (1996) and focused on older poor readers from 9 to 11 years of age. The study was motivated by three questions. First, do poor readers *spontaneously* use orthographic analogies to identify unfamiliar words to the same extent as normal readers? That is, do they use the strategy of reading unfamiliar words by detecting and pronouncing known word parts in unfamiliar words without being prompted to do so? Second, if not, why not? Is it because they lack a sufficient level of onset-rime sensitivity to take advantage of (large-unit) analogies; that is, a level of sensitivity that would, for example, enable them to read *peak* by analogy to *beak*? Or is it because they possess the requisite knowledge but do not make use of such knowledge when confronted with unfamiliar words, relying instead on ineffective or inappropriate learning strategies? Third, if poor readers do not take full advantage of orthographic analogies, can procedures be developed to help them do so when they encounter unfamiliar words in connected text?

Using a reading-age match design, Greaney and Tunmer found that younger normal readers performed as well as or better than older poor readers (of the same reading age) on four measures of onset-rime sensitivity (i.e., rhyme awareness), and performed better on a task that measured children's ability to take advantage of analogical units when reading lists of words that varied in whether the words containing the common unit were presented contiguously (e.g., *book, took, look, shook, hook; sheep, peep, sleep, steep, deep*) or noncontiguously (where order of presentation of all the words was randomized), and in whether the unit constituted the rime portion of the words (e.g., *b-all, t-all, w-all, h-all, f-all*) or was embedded in the rime portion of the words (e.g., *f-ar-m, h-ar-d, st-art-t, c-ar-d, p-ar-t*).

A follow-up intervention study was carried out to determine whether poor readers could be taught to use analogies when they encountered unfamiliar words while reading connected text. The poor readers were divided into two carefully matched groups. The treatment group received instruction in the use of orthographic analogies, whereas the comparison group received remedial instruction emphasizing context-cue usage.

The children in both training groups were asked to read one of four prose passages twice, once before and once after the training procedures. As the children read a passage, their errors were underlined by the experimenter on a copy of the passage. The children were informed prior to the reading that any errors they made would be underlined by the experimenter, but the experimenter provided no prompting or feedback during the reading.

For the children in the analogy-training group, the following procedure was then carried out. On the experimenter's copy of the passage (and adjacent to the actual text), the children were asked to spell a frequently occurring word provided by the experimenter that contained an analogical unit identical to one that appeared in the misread word. If the spelling was incorrect, other examples were selected by the experimenter. If all spelling attempts were incorrect (which was rare), the experimenter wrote down a word for the child that contained the relevant orthographic unit. The child was then asked to locate the common analogical unit, to say the sound, and then to copy it in a separate column. For example, a child who could not read the word *gently* was asked to spell the words "went," "bent," and "tent," and then to identify, say, and write down the common sound unit /ent/. This procedure was repeated for as many of the reading errors as possible (some of the errors did not contain suitable analogical units from which example spellings could be based). As with the previous study by Iversen and Tunmer (1993), the purpose of the procedure was to develop metacognitive knowledge and strategies for identifying unfamiliar words, not to learn a particular list of words.

The children in the control group were encouraged to make use of context cues to identify unfamiliar words. The experimenter taught the children a variety of meaning-based strategies and used prompts to encourage them to make use of these strategies. For example, if the strategy of using the prior sentence context did not result in the correct identification of an unfamiliar word, the child was encouraged to skip the word and read to the end of the sentence, and then reread the sentence and put in a word that makes sense.

Following the completion of the training procedure, the children in both groups were asked to read the passage a second time. The children in the analogy group were asked to attend to the spellings and common sound units of the words previously misread, whereas the children in the context-cue group were encouraged to make use of context cues to identify the unfamiliar words encountered during the first reading of the text.

The mean number of reading errors made by each training group before and after training are presented in Table 4.3. Although both groups showed significant reductions in the mean number of post-treatment errors, the children in the analogy-training group made considerably fewer post-treatment errors. This finding suggests that poor readers can be taught to use analogies to identify unfamiliar words and that analogy training is more effective in increasing the error corrections of poor readers than train-

Table 4.3 Mean Number of Reading Errors as a Function of Group and Time of Testing

		Time of testing	
		Pretreatment	Posttreatment
Group	n	reader errors	reader errors
Analogical transfer	15	20.20	7.13
		(6.17)[a]	(5.60)
Context cue usage	15	21.00	13.20
		(4.52)	(3.88)

[a] Standard deviations in parentheses

ing in context-cue usage. The results of this study and the Iversen and Tunmer (1993) study provide convergent evidence in support of a metacognitive strategy teaching approach to beginning reading instruction in which particular emphasis is placed on developing within beginning readers self-improving strategies for identifying unfamiliar words and on how and when to use such strategies.

REVIEW

In summary, we began this chapter by describing the key defining features of the whole-language approach to literacy instruction. We argued that whole-language programs place particular emphasis on literature-based and child-centered approaches to instruction that include the integration of reading and spelling and a major focus on the construction of meaning. We then presented an alternative conceptual framework that specified the relationships among the learning tasks, learning strategies, and cognitive prerequisites of beginning literacy development. The framework drew attention to major shortcomings of the whole-language view of literacy development, in particular, the failure to recognize the central role played by phonological recoding ability in learning to read. This led to a discussion of how best to facilitate the development of phonological recoding ability. A continuum of approaches to beginning reading instruction was presented, and it was suggested that reading programs designed to facilitate the development of word-identification skills differ on several instructional dimensions, four of which may be particularly important. These are skill-and-drill versus metacognitive approaches to instruction in phonological recoding skills, systematic versus incidental instruction in alphabetic coding, the degree of reliance on writing as a means of teaching recoding skills, and the use of individual letter-to-sound correspondences versus the inclusion of phonograms in beginning code instruction. In the final section two studies were described in which aspects of these four dimensions were investigated. The results of both studies suggest that a metacognitive approach to alphabetic code instruction that exploits the use of orthographic analogies can be a very effective intervention strategy for children experiencing reading difficulties.

STUDY AND DISCUSSION QUESTIONS

1. Whole language means different things to different people, which explains in part the confusion and controversy surrounding this particular approach to beginning literacy instruction. What are the key defining features of whole language?
2. Some reading specialists argue that beginning reading instruction should be modeled on first-language acquisition. Do you agree? Explain.
3. What is phonological recoding ability and why is it important in learning to read?
4. It is sometimes argued that English orthography contains so many irregularities that focusing too much attention on teaching children to take advantage of the mappings between subcomponents of written and spoken words will not only waste valuable time but possibly even confuse children and impede progress. Do you agree with this claim? Explain.
5. Should instruction in spelling-to-sound correspondences only arise incidentally in the context of reading connected text, or should such instruction be more explicit and systematic?
6. How does the metacognitive strategy teaching approach to beginning reading instruction differ from the skill-and-drill approach and the whole-language approach?
7. What are phonograms? What are some of the possible advantages of using phonograms in beginning reading instruction?

FURTHER READING

Adams, M. J. (1990). *Beginning to read: Thinking and learning about print.* Cambridge, MA: MIT Press.

Adams, M. J., & Bruck, M. (1993). Word recognition: The interface of educational policies and scientific research. *Reading and Writing, 5,* 113–139.

Gough, P. G., Ehri, L. C., & Treiman, R. (Eds.). (1992). *Reading acquisition.* Hillsdale, NJ: Erlbaum.

Juel, C. (1991). Beginning reading. In R. Barr, M. L. Kamil, P. B. Mosenthal, &
P. D. Pearson (Eds.), *Handbook of reading research* (Vol. 2; pp. 759–788). White
Plains, NY: Longman.

Stanovich, K. E. (1986). Matthew effects in reading: Some consequences of individual differences in the acquisition of literacy. *Reading Research Quarterly*,
21, 360–406.

Thompson, G. B., Tunmer, W. E., & Nicholson, T. (Eds.). (1993). *Reading acquisition processes*. Clevedon, UK: Multilingual Matters.

REFERENCES

Adams, M. J. (1990). *Beginning to read: Thinking and learning about print*. Cambridge,
MA: MIT Press.

Adams, M. J. (1991). Why not phonics *and* whole language? In W. Ellis (Ed.), *All
language and the creation of literacy* (pp. 40–53). Baltimore, MD: Orton Society.

Adams, M. J., Allington, R. L., Chaney, J. H., Goodman, Y. M., Kapinus, B. A.,
McGee, L. M., Richgels, D. J., Schwarts, S. J., Shannon, P., Smitten, B., &
Williams, J. P. (1991). Beginning to read: A critique by literacy profession-
als and a response by Marilyn Jager Adams. *Reading Teacher*, *44*, 370–389.

Adams, M. J., & Bruck, M. (1993). Word recognition: The interface of educational
policies and scientific research. *Reading and Writing*, *5*, 113–139.

Bergeron, B. (1990). What does the term whole language mean? Constructing a
definition from the literature. *Journal of Reading Behavior*, *22*, 301–329.

Bruck, M. (1992). Persistence of dyslexics' phonological awareness deficits. *Developmental Psychology*, *28*, 874–886.

Bryant, P. E., & Bradley, L. (1985). *Children's reading problems*. Oxford: Blackwell.

Byrne, B., Freebody, P., & Gates, A. (1992). Longitudinal data on the relations of
word-reading strategies to comprehension, reading time, and phonemic
awareness. *Reading Research Quarterly*, *27*, 141–151.

Calfee, R. C., & Drum, P. A. (1986). Research on teaching reading. In M. C.
Wittrock (Ed.), *Handbook of research on teaching* (pp. 804–849). New York:
Macmillan.

Chapman, J. W., & Tunmer, W. E. (1995). Development of young children's reading self-concepts: An examination of emerging subcomponents and their
relationship with reading achievement. *Journal of Educational Psychology*, *87*,
154–167.

Clay, M. (1985). *The early detection of reading difficulties*. Auckland, New Zealand:
Heinemann.

Clay, M. (1991). *Becoming literate: The construction of inner control*. Auckland, New
Zealand: Heinemann.

Croft, C. (1983). *Spell-write: An aid to writing, spelling and word study*. Wellington,
New Zealand: New Zealand Council for Educational Research.

Cunningham, A. E. (1990). Explicit versus implicit instruction in phonemic awareness. *Journal of Experimental Child Psychology*, *50*, 429–444.

Edelsky, C. (1990). Whose agenda is this anyway? A response to McKenna, Robinson & Miller. *Educational Researcher, 19,* 7–11.

Ehri, L. C. (1991). Development of the ability to read words. In R. Barr, M. L. Kamil, P. B. Mosenthal, & P. D. Pearson (Eds.), *Handbook of reading research* (Vol. 2; pp. 383–417). White Plains, NY: Longman.

Ehri, L. C. (1992). Reconceptualizing the development of sight word reading and its relationship to recoding. In P. Gough, L. Ehri, & R. Treiman (Eds.), *Reading acquisition* (pp. 107–143). Hillsdale, NJ: Erlbaum.

Ehri, L. C., & Robbins, C. (1992). Beginners need some decoding skill to read by analogy. *Reading Research Quarterly, 27,* 13–26.

Foorman, B. R., Francis, D. J., Novy, D. M., & Liberman, D. (1991). How letter-sound instruction mediates progress in first-grade reading and spelling. *Journal of Educational Psychology, 83,* 456–469.

Gaskins, I. W., Downer, M. A., Anderson, R., Cunningham, P. M., Gaskins, R. W., Schommer, M., & the Teachers of the Benchmark School. (1988). A metacognitive approach to phonics: Using what you know to decode what you don't know. *Remedial and Special Education, 9,* 36–41.

Gersten, R., & Dimino, J. (1993). Visions and revisions: A special education perspective on the whole language controversy. *Remedial and Special Education, 14,* 5–13.

Goodman, K. S. (1967). Reading: A psycholinguistic guessing game. *Journal of the Reading Specialist, 6,* 126–135.

Goodman, K. S. (1986). *What's whole in whole language: A parent–teacher guide.* Portsmouth, NH: Heinemann.

Goodman, K. S. (1989). Whole language research: Foundation and development. *Elementary School Journal, 90,* 207–221.

Goodman, Y. M. (1989). Roots of the whole-language movement. *Elementary School Journal, 90,* 113–127.

Goswami, U., & Bryant, P. (1990). *Phonological skills and learning to read.* Hove, UK: Erlbaum.

Gough, P. B. (1983). Context, form and interaction. In K. Rayner (Ed.), *Eye movements in reading: Perceptual and language processes* (pp. 203–211). San Diego, CA: Academic Press.

Gough, P. B. (1993). The beginning of decoding. *Reading and Writing, 5,* 181–192.

Gough, P. B., & Hillinger, M. L. (1980). Learning to read: An unnatural act. *Bulletin of the Orton Society, 30,* 179–196.

Gough, P. B., & Juel, C. (1991). The first stages of word recognition. In L. Rieben & C. Perfetti (Eds.), *Learning to read: Basic research and its implications* (pp. 47–56). Hillsdale, NJ: Erlbaum.

Gough, P. B., & Walsh, M. (1991). Chinese, Phoenicians, and the orthographic cipher of English. In S. Brady & D. Shankweiler (Eds.), *Phonological processes in literacy* (pp. 199–209). Hillsdale, NJ: Erlbaum.

Greaney, K., & Tunmer, W. E. (1996). Onset/rime sensitivity and orthographic analogies in normal and poor readers. *Applied Psycholinguistics, 17,* 15–40.

Iversen, S., & Tunmer, W. E. (1993). Phonological processing skills and the Reading Recovery program. *Journal of Educational Psychology, 85,* 112–126.

Juel, C. (1991). Beginning reading. In R. Barr, M. L. Kamil, P. B. Mosenthal, & P. D. Pearson (Eds.), *Handbook of reading research* (Vol. 2; pp. 759–788). White Plains, NY: Longman.

Liberman, I. Y., & Liberman, A. M. (1992). Whole language versus code emphasis: Underlying assumptions and their implications for reading instruction. In P. B. Gough, L. C. Ehri, & R. Treiman (Eds.), *Reading acquisition* (pp. 343–366). Hillsdale, NJ: Erlbaum.

Lundberg, I. (1994). Reading difficulties can be predicted and prevented: A Scandinavian perspective on phonological awareness and reading. In C. Hulme & M. Snowling (Eds.), *Reading development and dyslexia* (pp. 180–199). London: Whurr.

McKenna, M., Robinson, R., & Miller, J. (1990). Whole language: A research agenda for the nineties. *Educational Researcher, 19,* 12–13.

Nicholson, T. (1992). Historical and current perspectives on reading. In C. J. Gordon, G. D. Labercane, & W. R. McEachern (Eds.), *Elementary reading: Process and practice* (pp. 84–95). Needham, MA: Ginn.

Perfetti, C. A. (1991). The psychology, pedagogy, and politics of reading. *Psychological Science, 2,* 70–76.

Perfetti, C. A., Beck, I., Bell, L., & Hughes, C. (1987). Phonemic knowledge and learning to read are reciprocal: A longitudinal study of first grade children. *Merrill-Palmer Quarterly, 33,* 283–319.

Pinnell, G. S., De Ford, D., & Lyons, C. (1988). *Reading Recovery: Early intervention for at risk first graders.* Arlington, VA: Educational Research Service.

Read, C. (1986). *Children's creative spelling.* London: Routledge & Kegan Paul.

Rosenshine, B., & Stevens, R. (1984). Classroom instruction in reading. In P. D. Pearson, R. Barr, M. L. Kamil, & P. Mosenthal (Eds.), *Handbook of reading research* (pp. 745–799). New York: Longman.

Slavin, R. E., Madden, N. A., Karweit, N. L., Dolan, L. J., & Wasik, B. A. (1991). Research directions: Success for all: Ending reading failure from the beginning. *Language Arts, 68,* 404–409.

Smith, F. (1978). *Understanding reading.* New York: Holt, Rinehart & Winston.

Smith, J. W., & Elley, W. (1994). *Learning to read in New Zealand.* Auckland, New Zealand: Longman Paul.

Stahl, S. A., & Miller, P. (1989). Whole language and language experience approaches for beginning reading: A quantitative research synthesis. *Review of Educational Research, 59,* 87–116.

Stanovich, K. E. (1986). Matthew effects in reading: Some consequences of individual differences in the acquisition of literacy. *Reading Research Quarterly, 21,* 360–406.

Stanovich, K. E. (1990). A call for an end to the paradigm wars in reading research. *Journal of Reading Behavior, 22,* 221–231.

Stanovich, K. E. (1991). Commentary: Cognitive science meets beginning reading. *Psychological Science, 2,* 77–81.

Strickland, D., & Cullinan, B. (1990). Afterword. In M. J. Adams, *Beginning to read: Thinking and learning about print* (pp. 425–434). Cambridge, MA: MIT Press.

Thompson, G. B. (1993). Appendix: Reading instruction for the initial years in New Zealand schools. In G. B. Thompson, W. E. Tunmer, & T. Nicholson (Eds.), *Reading acquisition processes* (pp. 148–154). Clevedon, UK: Multilingual Matters.

Thompson, G. B., & Fletcher-Flinn, C. M. (1993). A theory of knowledge sources and procedures for reading acquisition. In G. B. Thompson, W. E. Tunmer, & T. Nicholson (Eds.), *Reading acquisition processes* (pp. 20–73). Clevedon, UK: Multilingual Matters.

Thompson, R. A. (1992). A critical perspective on whole language. *Reading Psychology, 13,* 131–155.

Treiman, R. (1992). The role of intrasyllabic units in learning to read and spell. In P. G. Gough, L. C. Ehri, & R. Treiman (Eds.), *Reading acquisition* (pp. 65–106). Hillsdale, NJ: Erlbaum.

Treiman, R. (1993). *Beginning to spell: A study of first grade children.* New York: Oxford University Press.

Tunmer, W. E., & Chapman, J. W. (1991). *An investigation of language-related and cognitive-motivational factors in beginning reading achievement.* Research proposal submitted to the Ministry of Education. Palmerston North, New Zealand: Massey University Educational Research and Development Centre.

Tunmer, W. E., & Chapman, J. W. (1993). To guess or not guess, that is the question: Metacognitive strategy training, phonological recoding skill, and beginning reading. *Reading Forum NZ, 8,* 3–14.

Tunmer, W. E., & Hoover, W. A. (1992). Cognitive and linguistic factors in learning to read. In P. G. Gough, L. C. Ehri, & R. Treiman (Eds.), *Reading acquisition* (pp. 175–214). Hillsdale, NJ: Erlbaum.

Tunmer, W. E., & Hoover, W. A. (1993). Components of variance models of language-related factors in reading disability: A conceptual overview. In M. Joshi & C. K. Leong (Eds.), *Reading disabilities: Diagnosis and component processes* (pp. 135–173). Dordrecht, The Netherlands: Kluwer.

Vellutino, F. R. (1991). Introduction to three studies on reading acquisition: Convergent findings on theoretical foundations of code-oriented versus whole-language approaches to reading acquisition. *Journal of Educational Psychology, 83,* 437–443.

Wise, B. W. (1992). Whole words and decoding for short-term learning: Comparisons on a "talking-computer" system. *Journal of Experimental Child Psychology, 54,* 147–167.

Wylie, R. E., & Durrell, D. D. (1970). Teaching vowels through phonograms. *Elementary English, 47,* 787–791.

Chapter 5

The Influence of Instructional Approaches
on Reading Procedures

VINCENT CONNELLY, RHONA S. JOHNSTON,
AND G. BRIAN THOMPSON

a) Is there more than one learning pathway to reading skill?

b) Do different instructional approaches lead children into different learning pathways?

c) What are the implications for our understanding of the development of reading skill?

For over a century, in many countries around the world there have been two opposed classes of approaches to teaching reading during the initial school years (Thompson, 1997). Analytic approaches include instruction about the sounds that correspond to the letters of print words, that is, explicit phonics instruction. In contrast, global approaches exclude such instruction and consider print words largely as tokens of meaning for the child's understanding of the text. Debate about the approaches continues to the present day (e.g., Adams, 1990), and a contemporary perspective on the various teaching strategies involved has been presented in the preceding chapter.

Which type of approach provides more rapid learning of reading skills? There has been much effort expended to answer this question (Bond & Dykstra, 1967; Chall, 1967; Dykstra, 1968b; Foorman, Francis, Novy, & Liberman, 1991). However, doubts remain about whether an adequate answer has been found (Dykstra, 1968a; Lohnes & Gray, 1972; Pflaum, Walberg, Karegianes, & Rasher, 1980; Rutherford, 1968; Sipay, 1968; Thompson, 1997). One problem is that many who ask this question presume that there is only one efficient universal learning pathway to reading skill.

There are theories of how children develop reading skill which propose that learning proceeds in a sequence of phases (e.g., Frith, 1985). (See Chapter 2 for further details and a comparison with other types of theories.) These developmental-phase theories are often interpreted as implying a single learning pathway that is followed through the successive phases. No consideration is given to the alternative possibility that different types of instruction may result in children following different learning pathways that lead to the same level of reading skill. It is the purpose of this chapter to consider whether different learning pathways result from reading instruction with and without explicit phonics. In explicit phonics instruction the child is taught sounds for letters and ways of using these in attempting to generate ("work out") the sound of print words. That is to say, the child is taught a procedure of phonological recoding, converting letters into corresponding sounds to identify words (see Chapter 2).

DOES PHONICS INSTRUCTION
INFLUENCE LEARNING PATHWAYS?

It may seem obvious that only children receiving explicit phonics instruction would be using phonological recoding. However, children are able to discover for themselves patterns of relations between letters and sounds within words and teach themselves to use phonological recoding (see Chapter 2; Thompson, Cottrell, & Fletcher-Flinn, 1996). It would be reasonable to suggest that any such self-teaching would be more extensive when the child has learned to read a larger vocabulary of words than when only a very small reading vocabulary is available. So the extent to which a child uses phonological recoding would be expected to change with the child's level of reading attainment. Hence, in order to obtain valid evidence, comparisons between children receiving and those not receiving phonics instruction would need to be made at the same level of reading attainment. In any case, this is the appropriate comparison if we wish to establish whether there are different learning pathways by which children may reach the same level of reading attainment.

Evidence from Types of Errors and Speed of Response

Only a very few research studies comparing teaching with and without explicit phonics have reported results that meet these requirements for matching levels of reading attainment. Elder (1971) collected data from a sample of 7-year-old children in Scotland who received beginning reading instruction with a strong phonics component and compared them with a sample from schools in Michigan where there was no such emphasis on phonics. The overall word-identification accuracy on oral reading passages was not significantly different. However, the children receiving the phonics instruction had a significantly higher percentage of nonword responses (e.g., "leb") among their errors. This result is consistent with the proposition that phonics instruction tends to increase the learner's time and attention spent on phonological recoding. A nonword error response would be the result of an attempt to obtain a word-identification response by phonological recoding where the attempt eventually failed.

This interpretation is also consistent with the finding by Elder that children who were taught phonics read paragraphs orally at a significantly slower rate (mean rate 87 words per minute) than the children without a phonics emphasis (mean rate 101 words per minute). This difference could be attributed to the phonics children taking more time attempting to obtain word-identification responses by phonological recoding procedures. Further evidence on speed of responding is provided in a study by Lesgold, Resnick, and Hammond (1985). Reaction times were measured for the oral reading of words, each one presented in isolation. Only reaction time data for correct responses were included. Comparisons were available between children receiving instruction with a phonics emphasis (including synthetic phonics, that is, "blending") and children in a "basal reader" program without a phonics emphasis. Both groups were from similar social environments in the United States. As the data were reported in subgroups by reading-attainment level, it was possible to compare children receiving the different types of reading instruction who were at approximately the same reading-accuracy level on the oral word-reading task. In first grade the children receiving instruction with the phonics emphasis showed much slower reaction times than those without. At subsequent grade levels there were no differences in reaction times between the children receiving the two types of instruction.

The time to execute a reading response obtained from phonological recoding procedures is generally greater than that for responses obtained by the principal alternative procedures of recall from orthographic memory of familiar print words (Thompson & Fletcher-Flinn, 1993). In the first year or so of reading instruction, an appreciable proportion of correct responses are likely to be obtained from phonological recoding procedures because there will be few familiar print words. Hence reading reaction times will be relatively slow. If learners exposed to phonics instruction obtain a larger proportion of their correct responses from phonological recoding procedures, then their reaction times will be even slower in comparison with learners not receiving such instruction. However, in subsequent years of instruction, whether including phonics or not, only a small proportion of correct responses are likely to be obtained from phonological recoding procedures. Average-progress learners will then have received enough experience of print words to obtain many of their correct responses by recall from orthographic memory of words (see Chapter 2). Hence differences in speed of responding between children taught phonics and those not would be expected to disappear in subsequent years.

Sowden and Stevenson (1994) compared the oral reading errors made to isolated words by two samples of 4- and 5-year-olds in England after 6 months of school instruction. One sample received explicit instruction in correspondences between letters and sounds. They also read from books that included texts devised to emphasize alliteration and rhyme comparisons between words. The other sample of children did not receive explicit phonics instruction and read from texts without selection of words for letter-sound patterns. Although total word-reading errors did not differ, the children receiving phonics instruction made more errors that were classified as resulting from phonological recoding.

Barr (1975) also reported errors in reading isolated words, but the data were collected from the same children over 8 months during the first year of school instruction. One sample of children was first taught phonics, including instruction on blending of sounds as well as letter-sound correspondences. The other sample had instruction first on responding to whole words, and phonics was introduced a little later. Both samples used reading texts. However, the texts for the children initially taught phonics were devised to provide words that exhibited the taught letter-sound correspondences. Although the two samples were matched at commencement on word-learning achievement, there was no information about these levels at the end of the study. Hence the two samples may have differed to some extent in reading-attainment level during the time the data were collected. A majority of the children receiving the initial phonics instruction made some nonword responses among their word-reading errors. Such nonword responses would result from attempts at phonological recoding where word-identification attempts had failed. Among the children receiving the initial whole-word instruction, nonword responses were rare.

Children in both samples tended to make some errors that were substitutions of other words that had appeared in their reading texts. However, such responses were less frequent among the errors of children receiving the initial phonics instruction. It was claimed that such responses are more likely to be produced by inaccurate memory for print words than by failed attempts at phonological recoding. Acceptance of this claim does not exclude the possibility that both samples of children could be storing orthographic memories of the words to the same extent, as they experienced the words in print. But the children with initial phonics instruction could have been making less use of their orthographic memory of words as they made more use of the alternative phonological recoding procedures.

Evidence from Tasks That Involve Orthographic Memory of Words

Recently a group of researchers have attempted a more direct examination of the alternative reading procedures that indicate different learning pathways. These researchers have used a variety of specially devised experimental tasks. Johnston, Thompson, Fletcher-Flinn, and Holligan (1995, Experiment 1) examined the extent to which children were able to use orthographic memories of print words. The children were administered a homophone word-meaning task. They were presented with items comprising a target word and four alternative words or phrases, for example,

won
___ a road
___ first in race
___ a number
___ leave it alone

The children were asked to choose which of the four alternatives was the best meaning for the target word. Among the three erroneous alternatives there was always one that was the meaning for the inappropriate homophone of the target word. In this example, *a number* was a meaning for the inappropriate homophone, "one." If the child had no orthographic memory of the letters of the target word, and had to rely exclusively on phonological recoding, which provides only the word sound, then there would be no way in which the child could distinguish between "one" and "won," as these words have the same sound. Hence, without orthographic word memory the child would be equally likely to respond *a number* as *first in race*.

Both phonics-taught 8- and 11-year-old children (in Scotland) and a matched sample of children without explicit phonics instruction (in New Zealand) were able to distinguish the meanings of a high proportion of these homophonic target words. This would not be possible without some orthographic memory of the words. (The two samples were matched on reading comprehension attainment level and aural vocabulary.)

Orthographic memory for words has also been examined using the pseudohomophone lexical decision task. The children had to decide whether each item was a real word (with correct spelling) or a made-up word. The following four items are examples:

stay
poast
help
loast

Only if the children had some orthographic memory for the real word, *post*, which corresponds to the pseudohomophone, *poast*, would they be able to discern that *poast* was a made-up word. If the children responded exclusively by phonological recoding procedures, without any orthographic memory of *post*, they would count *poast* as a real word because the sound resulting from the phonological recoding would be the same as that of the word "post." For these children, accuracy for lexical decisions on pseudo-homophones, such as *poast*, would not exceed the chance level.

Two research studies used this task with samples of 8-year-old children who had been taught phonics and compared them with matched samples without phonics (Johnston & Thompson, 1989, Experiment 1; Johnston et al., 1995, Experiment 1). The samples were matched on reading-attainment level and aural vocabulary. In both studies the children's accuracy in lexical decisions on pseudohomophones greatly exceeded chance level (and was not due merely to a bias to respond "made-up word," as indicated by a comparison with their responses to nonword control items, e.g., *loast*). The highest levels of accuracy on the pseudohomophones in this task would be expected to be achieved by children who responded using exclusively orthographic memory of words. Phonological recoding is inappropriate to lexical decisions about these items. It will tend to result in the child's accepting pseudohomophones as real words. In each of these two research studies, the children without phonics instruction were as accurate in their decisions on the pseudohomophones as they were on the nonword control items (which were as visually similar to real words as the corresponding pseudohomophones). In contrast, the children with phonics instruction were less accurate on pseudohomophones than control items. (Both the children with and without phonics were at the same level of accuracy on the control items.) This lower accuracy on pseudo-homophones among children with phonics instruction would be expected if the children continued to use phonological recoding even when it is inappropriate to the task.

Now it was shown that children without phonics instruction were able to use phonological recoding to some extent, indicating that some self-teaching of these procedures had taken place. The 8-year-old children in one of the studies (Johnston & Thompson, 1989, Experiment 2) were shown the pseudohomophone and nonword control items used in the lexical decision task, but they were obliged to attempt phonological recoding by being instructed to decide whether or not each item "sounds the same as a real word." Accuracy on this task was much higher among the children with phonics instruction than among those without. Nevertheless, the children without phonics instruction had some, more limited, capability at using phonological recoding procedures, as their accuracy was above chance level.

Preliminary Conclusions

Some preliminary conclusions can be drawn from these studies of error types, speed of response, and performance on experimental tasks. Children receiving explicit phonics instruction do not appear to use exclusively different learning pathways to reach the same level of reading attainment as children without phonics. Most children appear to have more than one learning pathway but differ in their capability at using one rather than the other. They also differ considerably in the extent to which they use their capabilities. Children taught phonics tend to be more capable at phonological recoding procedures and attempt to use these procedures more frequently, even when not appropriate to the task. Those children not taught phonics have also acquired some limited capability at phonological recoding, presumably through self-teaching. They tend not to attempt to use phonological recoding procedures so often. Both the children taught phonics, and those not, appear to acquire orthographic memory of words. Whether or not this has been acquired equally well is not clear, however, from the present evidence.

The studies reviewed have employed either the reading of test passages, isolated words, or a small number of specially devised experimental tasks. None of the studies have covered this range of multiple comparisons with the same sample of children. With a wider range of multiple comparisons, conclusions could be less tentative.

A STUDY: MULTIPLE COMPARISONS FOR BEGINNING READERS

The study we conducted and summarize here breaks new ground in having a very wide range of multiple comparisons for 5- and 6-year-old children with and without phonics teaching.

Method

One sample was taught with story texts and intensive early phonics instruction that included blending of sounds as well as correspondences between letters and sounds. The other sample received teaching without phonics, a "book experience" approach that emphasized the child's response to whole-story texts that were selected in a finely graded sequence for the individual child. No explicit phonics teaching was provided for this sample of children. The two teaching approaches are now described in further detail.

Teaching with Phonics. From the beginning of schooling, the children were taught the sounds of the letters and given instruction about the relationships between sequences of letters and their sounds in words. The children were shown, for example, that *cat* and *cub* start not only with the same sound but also with the same alphabetic letter. From about 3 months after starting school, they were taught to "sound and blend" simple sequences of letters (such as *c-u-p*) in order to pronounce unfamiliar words, using the taught letter-sound relationships. Soon more complex phonics relationships were taught, such as consonant blends (e.g., *track*) and vowel digraphs (e.g., m*ee*t). Some relationships were taught by verbalized rules (e.g., "Two Os make /oo/.") or descriptions (e.g., "magic e" for an *e* vowel marker as in *make*). This intensive training in letter-sound relationships was accompanied by the use of a reading series with story texts (Ginn & Co., 1988). The goal of the phonics instruction was to enable the children to build their knowledge of letter-sound relationships, using them effortlessly to identify unfamiliar words, so that they could rapidly become independent readers free to concentrate on the message of the text.

Teaching Without Phonics. From the outset "reading for meaning" was seen as paramount. This would be considered compromised if the children spent time looking at words in isolation and the letter-sound relationships within words. There was an emphasis, therefore, on the child's sampling the print as necessary to establish meaning and on the story line of the text. The child was taught to use the context of the story and to think ahead, drawing on his or her experience to predict the text. It was expected that only when meaning was lost would the child attend more closely to the print, perhaps rereading words or reading on. The child was taught to use the initial letter of a word as a final resort to help identify the word. The children were taught the names of the letters of the alphabet. The sounds of letters were not taught; neither did the instruction make use of prompted analogy cues (see Chapter 2). From commencement of schooling there was concurrent emphasis on the children expressing themselves in written language. In this, the teachers encouraged the children to invent spellings from the sounds of words. An important feature of the teaching of reading was the finely graded sequence used for the selection of each story text (usually a self-contained small book) for the individual child, according to the child's word accuracy of oral reading of texts, which was monitored systematically by the teacher. While the complete teaching approach can be regarded as compatible with "whole-language" approaches (see Chapter 4), this last feature is one not always present in implementations of "whole language." For further information on the teaching approach described here, see Thompson (1993).

Participants. The two samples of children were systematically selected and matched by age; time at school; aural vocabulary knowledge, based on the British Picture Vocabulary Scale (BPVS; Dunn & Dunn, 1982); short-term memory, based on the British Ability Scales (BAS) Recall of Digits Test (Elliott, Murray, & Pearson, 1979); and word-reading attainment, based on the BAS Word Reading Test (Elliott, Murray, & Pearson, 1979) (see Table 5.1). Eighty-two children participated in the study. There were 41 in the phonics-teaching sample who were drawn from two schools in Dundee, Scotland, and 41 in the nonphonics-teaching sample who were drawn from two schools in Wellington, New Zealand. The children were further classified as either year 1 or year 2 at school.

Results

The results showed that the phonics-taught children were, as expected, using phonological recoding procedures more than the children without phonics. They had a larger proportion of nonword responses among their reading errors. They read nonwords better. They were also better at spelling low-frequency words and nonwords. The children without phonics seemed to have less well developed procedures for dealing with unknown words. They made more refusal errors, whether the words were in context or not. They did, however, produce some nonword attempts at unknown words and could read some nonwords. Thus, they were developing phonological recoding procedures but more slowly than the phonics-taught children.

However, the phonics-taught children were much slower at reading text, which may be an indicator of greater dependence on phonological recoding procedures and less use of the more immediate recall of words from orthographic memory. They were also less accurate than the children without phonics in reading low-frequency words with irregular letter-

Table 5.1 Means and Standard Deviations of the Matched Variables for the
Children in Each Year Taught With and Without Phonics

Variables	Year-1 Children				Year-2 Children			
	Phonics		Nonphonics		Phonics		Nonphonics	
	M	SD	M	SD	M	SD	M	SD
	(n = 18)		*(n = 17)*		*(n = 23)*		*(n = 24)*	
Age (months)	67.3	2.5	68.0	1.9	76.8	2.5	77.3	1.9
Time at school (months)	6.8	0.3	7.0	1.8	14.7	0.2	14.9	2.6
BAS Word Reading age (months)	74.6	3.3	74.3	3.6	80.2	3.6	80.5	4.1
Aural vocabulary, BPVS standard score*	102.1	11.2	98.7	8.4	98.4	10.5	95.2	7.1
BAS Recall of Digits standard score*	108.1	13.7	110.2	13.7	117.7	20.7	118.0	13.2

Notes: M = Mean; SD = Standard Deviation; n = number of children. There were variations
from these values in the comparisons reported in the text for the Neale test in Year 2,
due to incomplete data. However, matching on the variables was maintained.
* Mean = 100, Standard Deviation = 15.

sound correspondences, again showing that they were more dependent on using phonological recoding procedures (which on their own will not produce accurate responses for irregular words). The slower reading of the phonics-taught children could partly be accounted for by their persistence with phonological recoding attempts on unknown and unfamiliar words. The phonics-taught children were a little more accurate in answering comprehension questions on the text they read than the children without phonics. Detailed results for each comparison are given in the following sections.

Types of Errors in Reading Isolated Words. The *total* oral word-reading errors on the BAS Word Reading Test were at the same level for both samples of children, as they had been matched on this measure. However, the types of error within these totals did differ between samples. Errors were categorized into three types: real-word responses, nonword responses (e.g., "leb"), and "refusals" (no spoken attempt). The mean percentages of these three error types produced by the phonics- and nonphonics-taught children are shown in Figure 5.1. The children without phonics made sig-

Figure 5.1 Mean Percentage of Types of Error on the BAS Word Reading Test for the Phonics- and the Nonphonics-Taught Children

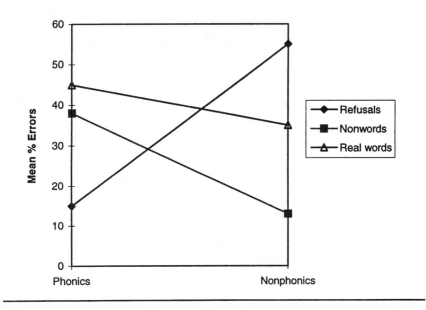

nificantly more refusal errors when responding to unknown words than the phonics-taught children, who in turn produced significantly more real word errors and more nonword responses. The production of nonword errors correlated significantly with accuracy of word reading for both the phonics and the nonphonics children, whereas refusal errors correlated negatively with word-reading accuracy in both samples of children.

The oral reading errors (not including refusals) on the BAS Word Reading Test were then further analyzed by examining letter differences between the stimulus word and the error, using categories based on Stuart and Coltheart (1988). The "first and last letters correct" error (e.g., "want" as a response to *wet*) was the most common "spoken attempt" error for both samples of children. The phonics-taught children produced significantly more of these as a proportion of the "spoken attempt" errors than the children without phonics instruction.

These error analyses make it clear that the two samples of children, even though they were matched for age, vocabulary, short-term memory, and word reading, differed in how they responded in reading the words.

The phonics-taught children made significantly more errors that matched first and last letters, gave more nonword responses, and made fewer refusals than the children without phonics instruction. However, the teaching approach without phonics heavily emphasized reading for meaning, and so it might be predicted that they would show fewer refusal errors when reading texts than isolated words and that they would have a better understanding of what they read than the children taught phonics.

Types of Word Errors in Reading Text. The year-2 children were also tested on the Neale Analysis of Reading Ability, Revised British edition (Neale, 1989). (See Connelly, Johnston, & Thompson 1996c for the full details of this data.) This test comprises a series of six short graded passages designed to provide separate scores each for accuracy, rate, and comprehension of children's oral reading of meaningful texts. As expected with groups matched on the BAS Word Reading Test, there was not a significant difference between the two samples of children in word-identification accuracy on the Neale test. The reading errors on the Neale test were also categorized as word, nonword, and refusal errors.

This analysis yielded a very similar pattern to that found in the isolated word reading. The phonics-taught children again produced significantly more real and nonword errors than the children without phonics, who again produced many more refusals. The percentages of refusal errors on the Neale test (which constituted 46% of the nonphonics sample's errors but only 11% of the phonics sample's errors) were very similar to those shown by the same children on the BAS Word Reading Test (49% of the nonphonics sample's errors and 6% of the phonics sample's errors). It can be concluded from this that if a child is not willing to attempt to decode when reading single words, then the influence of context will not alter that strategy.

Speed of Reading. It was found on the Neale test that the phonics-taught children were slow readers in terms of words read per minute. They were on average 10 months behind the age norms in rate of reading. The children without phonics instruction were faster readers, being 4 months ahead of the age norms. This large difference was likely due in part to the phonics-taught children stopping to sound out unfamiliar words. The children without phonics instruction did not do this. They tended to spend much less time on words on which they did not succeed. This was shown by their having a much larger proportion of refusal errors than the children taught phonics. As the phonics-taught children tended to spend more time on words on which they did not succeed, it may be considered that in this respect their reading was less efficient than that of the children without phonics. However, there are also other aspects of reading to consider, such as the children's comprehension of the text.

Connelly, Johnston, and Thompson (1996b) found in a related study on the same children (years 1 and 2) that the phonics-taught children showed a word-length effect in response time when reading isolated familiar words of 2 to 4 letters. The longer words had longer response times, a finding consistent with the children's use of phonological recoding procedures. The children without phonics, however, did not show any word-length effect and were significantly faster at reacting to all familiar words than the phonics-taught children. This speed difference persisted even when the words were presented in a distorted zig-zag format (e.g., $^h{_e}{^l}{_p}$). Therefore, children without phonics were not relying on word shape to allow them to read rapidly, so they were likely to be using stored information on at least some letters of the word, that is, orthographic storage of the word. This apparently enabled them to respond more rapidly to familiar words than the children with phonics instruction.

Reading Comprehension. The final measure on the Neale test was comprehension. It was expected that the nonphonics sample, having had the teaching emphasis on gaining meaning from text, would be more accurate in answering comprehension questions than the phonics sample. This was found not to be the case. The phonics-taught children were close to the age norms for comprehension, being only 1 month below the norms. The children without phonics instruction were 5 months below. However, it was noted that the average score for word accuracy on the Neale test was slightly, but not significantly, higher for the phonics-taught sample than the nonphonics sample. However, even when this was accounted for statistically (by an analysis of covariance), the phonics sample was still ahead of the nonphonics sample in average accuracy in answering the comprehension questions. Phonics teaching, combined with use of story texts, did not make the beginning readers poor comprehenders.

Irregular-Word Reading. The year-2 children from the two samples were asked to read isolated words with irregular letter-to-sound correspondences. Some of these irregular words were of high frequency (e.g., *said, water*) and others of lower frequency (e.g., *sword, broad*). There was no difference between the samples in accuracy of reading the high-frequency words (both samples scoring over 80% correct). However, the phonics sample (average 26%, standard deviation 18%) read significantly fewer of the low-frequency irregular words correctly than the nonphonics sample (average 43% correct, standard deviation 23%). The phonics-taught children may have been relying excessively on the letter-to-sound phonological recoding procedure, which in itself will not produce accurate responses for irregular words. The children without phonics instruction would be more sparing in their use of phonological recoding. Nevertheless, both samples had a high level of accuracy in reading high-frequency irregular words. This shows that the phonics-taught sample did not use phonological recoding procedures exclusively for familiar words.

Nonword Reading. The two samples from both years 1 and 2 were also tested on their ability to read regular nonwords, for example, *blum*, *druv* (Connelly, Johnston, & Thompson, 1996a). These were items that were totally unfamiliar to the children. It was expected that the phonics-taught children would be much better at this task, as they could use their greater phonological recoding capability to read the nonwords. This expectation was borne out. The phonics-taught children correctly read significantly more nonwords, on average 34% correct (standard deviation 19%) against an average 17% correct (standard deviation 15%) for the nonphonics children.

Spelling. From the commencement of schooling, the nonphonics sample spent much more time than the phonics-taught children expressing themselves in written language. In this the nonphonics children were encouraged to invent spellings of unfamiliar words. As this was not a feature of the teaching for the phonics sample, it might be expected that the nonphonics children would have an advantage in spelling unfamiliar words with regular sound-to-letter correspondences. The children from both years 1 and 2 were given monosyllabic words to spell. These words were in four categories: high-frequency regular words (e.g., "best," "green"), high-frequency irregular words (e.g., "come," "both"), low-frequency regular words (e.g., "luck," "beer"), and low-frequency irregular words (e.g., "wool," "lose"). It was found that in neither sample was there a significant difference in spelling accuracy between regular and irregular words. It was also found that the phonics-taught children spelled more low-frequency words correctly than the nonphonics children but that there was no difference between them in the spelling of high-frequency words. The year-2 children were given regular nonwords (e.g., "plam," "tain") to spell. The phonics-taught children correctly spelled significantly more nonwords than the children without phonics instruction. The children without phonics but with teaching that encouraged invented spelling clearly had no advantage in spelling unfamiliar items.

Phonological Awareness. Are the children without phonics instruction not as capable at phonological recoding because they failed to reach a sufficiently high level of phonological awareness? Work summarized by Goswami and Bryant (1990) can be interpreted to support this expectation. To test this, the children from both years 1 and 2 were administered two phonological awareness tasks, the Yopp-Singer Phoneme Segmentation Test (Yopp, 1988) and the Rosner Test of Auditory Analysis Skills (Rosner, 1975). The Yopp-Singer test is a measure of the ability to articulate the sounds (phonemes) in a spoken word separately and in the correct order (e.g., "Tell me all the sounds you can hear in the word dog"). On this task there was no statistically significant difference in performance between the phonics-taught children and the children without phonics instruction. The phonics-taught children scored an average of 15.9 items correct (standard deviation 4.5) out of 22 items and those without phonics, 14.3 items correct (standard deviation 4.8).

The Rosner (1975) test is more complex than the Yopp-Singer test and involves manipulating the sounds in words. The first few items involve picking out syllabic sounds in words (e.g., "Say sunshine. Now say it again but don't say shine."). In other items the child picks out a phoneme in a word (e.g., "Say meat. Now say it again but don't say the /m/ sound"), and in still others the child reassembles a word without particular phonemes (e.g., "Say stale. Now say it again but don't say /t/"). It was found in this task that there was also no significant difference between the phonics-taught and nonphonics samples. Phonics instruction would seem not to have made any difference on this more complex phonological awareness task.

On both phonological awareness tasks there was not a statistically significant difference between the two samples of children. Hence, contrary to expectation, the lower capability in phonological recoding of the children without phonics instruction cannot be explained as due to an insufficiently high level of phonological awareness. The results also indicate that the explicit phonics instruction did not significantly affect the children's level of phonological awareness. While this may also seem contrary to expectations, it is confirmed in other studies (Foorman et al., 1991; Thompson & Johnston, in press; Tunmer & Nesdale, 1985). All these agree in showing that phonics instruction resulted in greater phonological recoding capability but not in greater phonological awareness. Hence, phonological awareness skill in normal-progress beginning readers would appear to have its *source* in aspects of learning not closely related to phonological recoding capability. At the same time, specially devised instruction can improve the phonological awareness skill of beginning readers, particularly those whose skill is low. Moreover, such instruction for these children, along with teaching of letter-sound relationships, can yield gains in their phonological recoding capability (see Chapter 3).

Discussion

This study examined the influence of intensive early phonics instruction on the extent of use of different learning pathways by beginning readers, in comparison with a matched sample of children who had reached the same level of word-reading attainment but had received no explicit phonics instruction. The results show that teaching which includes explicit phonics instruction enhances children's phonological recoding procedures, that is, their use of letter-sound information when reading. Furthermore, we found that intensive phonics instruction (combined with instructional use of story texts) does not develop these word-identification skills at the cost of text comprehension. What is it about the different instructional approaches that may account for the findings? The phonics-taught children received direct instruction about the correspondences between letters and sounds, that is, the rules of English orthography; they were shown how to identify (regular) unfamiliar words using these rules; they were given the opportunity to practice this on isolated words and words in text. The children without phonics instruction received no direct tutoring on the rules of English orthography. The main emphasis in their "book-experience" approach was on actual reading of texts. Reading texts were selected by the teacher for individual children so that their word accuracy of oral reading of the unfamiliar text exceeded 90% for teacher-guided reading and 95% for the child's independent reading (Department of Education, 1985; Thompson, 1993). Time was taken up not in learning rules but in practicing reading of numerous story texts at difficulty levels adjusted to individual children. These differences between the teaching approaches suggest that instruction in reading can include two important factors: direct instruction of letter-sound correspondence rules and exposure to words of text (from which the children may discover the rules for themselves).

Both samples of children in this study possessed two different types of procedures for reading words. One procedure is word recall, which requires the building up of orthographic memories of words that are accessed without recourse to the letter-sound conversion of phonological recoding, the second type of procedure. Direct instruction of letter-sound correspondences can be expected to contribute more to the growth of phonological recoding procedures than word-recall procedures. Exposure to text would contribute to the build-up of a vocabulary of word memories for recall procedures (Juel, Griffith, & Gough, 1986). Word-recall procedures and phonological recoding procedures, however, both contribute to word identification (Coltheart, Curtis, Atkins, & Haller, 1993), and this may explain why both samples of children show the same level of overall skill at word identification. The teaching approaches we have examined influenced the child toward learning pathways that made greater use either of phonological recoding procedures or of word-recall procedures.

Explicit phonics instruction influenced the children to make very high use of phonological recoding procedures, as shown in the large proportion of nonword responses these children made to unknown words. They apparently spent much time persisting with phonological recoding procedures on unknown and unfamiliar words, thus contributing to their slow rate of reading. Their capability in phonological recoding procedures was shown in their relatively high level of (regular) nonword reading. The phonics-taught children were also exposed to print text, however, and did appear to build up recall of words from orthographic word storage, as shown by their ability to read high-frequency irregular words.

The nonphonics "book-experience" approach emphasizes "exposure to print," with words being read in many story texts. This experience is likely to build up the children's orthographic memory of the words they read. It can explain why these children were faster at reading familiar words than the phonics-taught children and were better at reading some irregular words. Without explicit phonics instruction they did not perform so well at tasks requiring phonological recoding procedures, such as the reading of regular nonwords. Therefore, they apparently depended on word-recall procedures much of the time. However, it is also evident that these children did have some phonological recoding capability, as they read some nonwords correctly and produced some nonword errors when reading words. There was some self-teaching of phonological recoding taking place.

CONCLUSIONS

Developmental theories of how children learn to read are often interpreted as implying that there is only one learning pathway to the same level of reading attainment. Such interpretation can give rise to educational recommendations based on a supposed single "right" way to learn to read. This can lead to adoption of teaching approaches that exclude from consideration the possibility that other approaches may work as well. The new research summarized here and that previously reviewed are consistent in showing that the type of instruction children receive from the commencement of schooling does influence the way they go about learning. Normal-progress children have more than one learning pathway. Their learning pathways include phonological recoding procedures and recall procedures that use orthographic memory of words. Although the presence or absence of explicit phonics instruction did not result in the children having exclusively different sets of learning pathways, it did result in their acquiring different capabilities in using one pathway rather than another and large differences in the extent to which they used the pathways.

REVIEW

There has been much research and debate about whether the inclusion of explicit phonics instruction in the teaching of reading results in more rapid learning progress. There has been very little research, however, on whether the phonics instruction influences children to follow different learning pathways to the same level of reading attainment as children without that instruction. The few published studies available were reviewed. The tentative conclusion from these studies was that, irrespective of exposure to explicit phonics instruction, normal-progress children had more than one learning pathway. They learned to use phonological recoding procedures, that is, the conversion of letters into corresponding sounds to identify words, and they also learned recall procedures using orthographic memory of words. Nevertheless, the evidence indicates that children taught phonics were more capable at phonological recoding procedures and used these more often than children without phonics.

Some new research was summarized that made a wide range of multiple comparisons not previously available. These comparisons examined the influences of the teaching approaches during the first 18 months of schooling. The children with phonics instruction had better-developed phonological recoding procedures. They were more capable at reading nonwords. They made much more use of phonological recoding, having more nonwords among their text-reading errors, and this apparently made them much slower at reading text than the children without phonics. However, this was not at the cost of their comprehension of the text. The children without phonics had nevertheless acquired some phonological recoding, apparently by self-teaching. On the other hand, they made more use of recall from orthographic memory of words. This was shown, for example, in their faster response to familiar words. The results of this new research were consistent with the more limited previous work in showing that normal-progress children acquire a similar set of learning pathways but that the type of instruction children receive influences their capabilities in using one pathway rather than another, as well as the extent to which they use the pathways. The evidence is against any developmental theory of reading which implies that most normal-progress children reach the same level of reading attainment in the same way.

STUDY AND DISCUSSION QUESTIONS

1. What are the two main learning pathways used by children as they learn to read?
2. (a) What kind of instruction would you expect to facilitate each of these two learning pathways?
   (b) Describe research evidence for your answer.
3. Does a faster reader always mean a better reader? If not, why not?
4. Would you expect the provision of explicit phonics instruction to increase the phonological awareness of children? Give a summary of research evidence and discuss.
5. What are the implications of the research summarized in this chapter for evaluating theories of the development of reading skill?

FURTHER READING

Adams, M. J. (1990). *Beginning to read: Thinking and learning about print.* Cambridge, MA: MIT Press.

Ehri, L. C. (1994). Development of the ability to read words: Update. In R. B. Ruddell, M. R. Ruddell, & H. Singer (Eds.), *Theoretical models and processes of reading* (4th ed.; pp. 323–358). Newark, DE: International Reading Association.

Ellis, A. W. (1993). *Reading, writing and dyslexia: A cognitive analysis* (2nd ed.). Hove, UK: Erlbaum.

Feitelson, D. (1988). *Facts and fads in beginning reading: A cross-language perspective.* Norwood, NJ: Ablex.

Gough, P. B., Ehri, L. C., & Treiman, R. (Eds.). (1992). *Reading acquisition.* Hillsdale, NJ: Erlbaum.

Johnston, R. S., & Thompson, G. B. (1989). Is dependence on phonological information in children's reading a product of instructional approach? *Journal of Experimental Child Psychology, 48,* 131–145.

REFERENCES

Adams, M. J. (1990). *Beginning to read: Thinking and learning about print.* Cambridge, MA: MIT Press.

Barr, R. (1975). The effect of instruction on pupil reading strategies. *Reading Research Quarterly, 10,* 555–582.

Bond, G.L., & Dykstra, R. (1967). The Cooperative Research Program in first-grade reading instruction. *Reading Research Quarterly, 2*(4), 5–142.

Chall, J. S. (1967). *Learning to read: The great debate.* New York: McGraw-Hill.

Coltheart, M., Curtis, B., Atkins, P., & Haller, M. (1993). Models of reading aloud: Dual-route and parallel-distributed processing approaches. *Psychological Review, 100*, 589–608.

Connelly, V., Johnston, R. S., & Thompson, G. B. (1996a). *Instructional method and approaches to reading development.* Manuscript prepared for publication.

Connelly, V., Johnston, R. S., & Thompson, G. B. (1996b). *Word distortion, reaction time and instructional approach.* Manuscript prepared for publication.

Connelly, V., Johnston, R. S., & Thompson, G. B. (1996c). *Word reading accuracy and text comprehension in beginning readers.* Manuscript prepared for publication.

Department of Education. (1985). *Reading in junior classes (with guidelines to the revised Ready to Read series).* Wellington, New Zealand: Government Printer.

Dunn, L. M., Dunn, L. M., & Whetton, C. (1982). *British Picture Vocabulary Scale.* Windsor, Berkshire, UK: NFER-Nelson.

Dykstra, R. (1968a). The effectiveness of code- and meaning-emphasis beginning reading programs. *Reading Teacher, 22,* 17–23.

Dykstra, R. (1968b). Summary of the second-grade phase of the Cooperative Research Program in primary reading instruction. *Reading Research Quarterly, 4*(1), 49–70.

Elder, R. D. (1971). Oral reading achievement of Scottish and American children. *Elementary School Journal, 71,* 216–230.

Elliott, C. C., Murray, D. J., & Pearson, L. S. (1979). *British Ability Scales.* Windsor, Berkshire, UK: NFER-Nelson.

Foorman, B. R., Francis, D. J., Novy, D. M., & Liberman, D. (1991). How letter-sound instruction mediates progress in first-grade reading and spelling. *Journal of Educational Psychology, 83,* 456–469.

Frith, U. (1985). Beneath the surface of developmental dyslexia. In K. E. Patterson, J. C. Marshall, & M. Coltheart (Eds.), *Surface dyslexia: Neuropsychological and cognitive studies of phonological reading* (pp. 301–330). London: Erlbaum.

Ginn & Co. (1988). *Reading 360.* Aylesbury, UK: Author.

Goswami, U., & Bryant, P. E. (1990). *Phonological skills and learning to read.* Hove, UK: Erlbaum.

Johnston, R. S., & Thompson, G. B. (1989). Is dependence on phonological information in children's reading a product of instructional approach? *Journal of Experimental Child Psychology, 48,* 131–145.

Johnston, R. S., Thompson, G. B., Fletcher-Flinn, C. M., & Holligan, C. (1995). The functions of phonology in the acquisition of reading: Lexical and sentence processing. *Memory & Cognition, 23,* 749–766.

Juel, C., Griffith, P. L., & Gough, P. B. (1986). Acquisition of literacy: A longitudinal study of children in first and second grade. *Journal of Educational Psychology, 78,* 243–255.

Lesgold, A., Resnick, L. B., & Hammond, K. (1985). Learning to read: A longitudinal study of word skill development in two curricula. In G. E. MacKinnon & T. G. Waller (Eds.), *Reading research: Advances in theory and practice* (Vol. 4; pp. 107–138). New York: Academic Press.

Lohnes, P. R., & Gray, M. M. (1972). Intellectual development and the cooperative reading studies. *Reading Research Quarterly, 8,* 52–61.

Neale, M. D. (1989). *The Neale Analysis of Reading Ability,* Revised British Edition. Windsor, Berkshire, UK: NFER-Nelson.

Pflaum, S. W., Walberg, H. J., Karegianes, M. L., & Rasher, S. P. (1980). Reading instruction: A quantitative analysis. *Educational Researcher, 9*(7), 12–18.

Rosner, J. (1975). *Helping children overcome learning difficulties.* New York: Walker.

Rutherford, W. (1968). Learning to read: A critique. *Elementary School Journal, 69,* 72–83.

Sipay, E. R. (1968). Interpreting the USOE cooperative reading studies. *Reading Teacher, 22,* 10–16, 35.

Sowden, P. T., & Stevenson, J. (1994). Beginning reading strategies in children experiencing contrasting teaching methods. *Reading and Writing, 6,* 109–123.

Stuart, M., & Coltheart, M. (1988). Does reading develop in a sequence of stages? *Cognition, 30,* 139–181.

Thompson, G. B. (1993). Reading instruction for the initial years in New Zealand schools. In G. B. Thompson, W. E. Tunmer, & T. Nicholson (Eds.), *Reading acquisition processes* (pp. 148–154). Clevedon, UK: Multilingual Matters.

Thompson, G. B. (1997). The teaching of reading. In V. Edwards, & D. Corson (Eds.), *Encyclopedia of language and education: Vol. 2, Literacy* (pp. 9–17). Dordrecht, The Netherlands: Kluwer.

Thompson, G. B., Cottrell, D. S., & Fletcher-Flinn, C. M. (1996). Sublexical orthographic-phonological relations early in the acquisition of reading: The Knowledge Sources account. *Journal of Experimental Child Psychology, 62,* 190–222.

Thompson, G. B., & Fletcher-Flinn, C. M. (1993). A theory of knowledge sources and procedures for reading acquisition. In G. B. Thompson, W. E. Tunmer, & T. Nicholson (Eds.), *Reading acquisition processes* (pp. 20–73). Clevedon, UK: Multilingual Matters.

Thompson, G. B., & Johnston, R. S. (in press). Are nonword and other phonological deficits indicative of a failed reading process? *Reading and Writing.*

Tunmer, W. E., & Nesdale, A. R. (1985). Phonemic segmentation skill and beginning reading. *Journal of Educational Psychology, 77,* 417–427.

Yopp, H. K. (1988). The validity and reliability of phonemic awareness tests. *Reading Research Quarterly, 23,* 159–177.

PART II

ACQUIRING READING COMPREHENSION

In Part I we examined the processes by which the child learns to identify print words. In this next part we consider the processes of learning to comprehend what is read. We have all experienced in our reading at some time or another the feeling of "losing the plot." Sometimes it is an unfamiliar word that is an obstacle. Sometimes the writing seems impenetrable and appears to lack structure. Why does this happen, and what can be done about it?

In Chapter 6 Tom Nicholson looks at two opposing models of how readers understand written text. Each model has its own explanation of reading comprehension. The "bottom-up" processing model offers a data-driven explanation, where the automaticity of word-decoding processes is considered the major influence on reading comprehension. The "top-down" processing model offers a context-driven explanation, which emphasizes the reader's use of comprehension strategies. Reading is seen as a transactional process where the meaning of the text is negotiated between reader and writer. A third view, the Simple View, is also considered. It accepts that reading comprehension involves more than decoding words but argues that decoding is also very important.

In Chapter 7 Tom Nicholson and Annette Tan look at the role of proficient word identification in acquiring reading comprehension. The principle of overlearning, which is practiced by athletes and other top performers, is also said to be relevant to reading. If children learn to identify words faster, so that they read words automatically, they will have more cognitive capacity to apply to comprehension processes. This chapter focuses on bottom-up processes.

Susan Dymock in Chapter 8 discusses children's learning about text structure to facilitate improvement in reading comprehension. Children often lack explicit knowledge of the structure of texts. This chapter reviews research on the structure of texts and describes teaching studies that show children how to "see" the structural design of texts. The chapter reviews comprehension strategies relating to the structures of narrative and of expository texts. Examples of how to teach these strategies are given. The ideas in this chapter focus on top-down processes.

The theme of Part II is that reading comprehension is multifaceted and requires both bottom-up and top-down processes.

Chapter 6

Reading Comprehension Processes

TOM NICHOLSON

a) What are the "bottom-up" and "top-down" process perspectives on reading comprehension?

b) What is the role of word-identification skill in reading comprehension?

c) What are the spin-off effects of early reading progress on reading comprehension?

d) Is it possible to teach reading comprehension?

What kind of a reader are you? Intensive or extensive? A stickler for detail, or like a windsurfer, skimming across the surface? The answer, naturally, is that we can read either way, depending on why we are reading. But how do you usually read, say, a magazine article, or the newspaper? As you would expect, opinions vary. Differences of opinion also reflect differences in theoretical views about how we process print. While the bottom-up perspective sees the reader as processing every word, and doing an intensive analysis, the top-down perspective sees the reader as sampling the text, using higher-level schemata, or knowledge structures, to construct the meaning. In this view, meaning is "negotiated."

THE BOTTOM-UP PERSPECTIVE

An excellent example of a bottom-up perspective is Gough's (1972) model of the skilled reader. At that time, very little was known about the specific workings of how we comprehend text. Thus, to assist in describing how the comprehension system worked, Gough used the metaphoric terms *Decoder, Librarian, Merlin,* and *TPWSGWTAU.*

The Decoder was responsible for analyzing the phonological structure of written input. The Decoder had a "code book" that enabled the reader to convert written language into an abstract phonological representation (called systematic phonemes). Words could then be looked up in the mental dictionary according to their phonological code (e.g., *city* is looked up as /sitee/). The Librarian was responsible for accessing the mental dictionary (i.e., our lexicon). Merlin then had to apply syntactic and semantic rules to work out the meanings of the strings of words that became available via the Decoder and Librarian. When Merlin had done its job of parsing the strings of words into sentences, it sent this information to long-term memory, which was called TPWSGWTAU (the place where sentences go when they are understood).

As Gough (1972) pointed out, the child's Librarian, compared with an adult's, had access to a mental lexicon that had fewer words. Also, information attached to words already in the lexicon was not as detailed or complete. Merlin was also still not fully developed, in that some complex grammatical structures still eluded the typical new entrant to school. The child's comprehension system was workable, though not up to the adult standard. In Gough's model, the main threat to reading comprehension for the child was the efficiency of the Decoder. If the Decoder was faulty, so that some of the written input was unable to be phonologically recoded, or was recoded too slowly, then the child would be unable to comprehend properly. There is evidence to support this idea. Incorrect information, in the form of reading errors, does interfere with comprehension (Nicholson, Pearson, & Dykstra, 1979). Also, slow and hesitant reading disrupts children's ability to make sense of text material (Perfetti, 1985). This is why the child must read reasonably quickly.

Unfortunately, if a word is too difficult, then the child has to guess what it might be. Otherwise, the flow of information will stop. Guessing helps to retain meaning, but it takes time and, as discussed in Chapter 4, it is more likely to be the strategy of a poor reader, or a beginner. In fact, even if the child is accurate, lack of fluency and speed will interfere with comprehension. To become a good reader, the child has to learn the letter-to-sound conversion rules of English and be able to apply these automatically (LaBerge & Samuels, 1974). This will ensure accurate information, at a reasonable speed, for the linguistic system to work on.

How does comprehension happen? As already indicated, the model argues that speed is necessary because of the way the mind is organized. Once the Decoder provides the phonemic form of a word, the Librarian looks it up and passes it on to short-term memory. Short-term memory has limited capacity and for the adult can only hold about seven chunks of information at a time (Miller, 1956). So, as words get deposited in short-term memory, it is important for Merlin to start working on them as soon as possible. This idea seems to be correct. Eye-movement research suggests that sentences are understood almost as soon as they are decoded. One theory, known as the "immediacy hypothesis" (Just & Carpenter, 1980), says that the eye does not move to the next word until the sentence's meaning up to that point is made clear. But other researchers say that "immediacy" is probably too much to expect, mainly because some word meanings, especially pronouns, are not clear until later in the sentence (Rayner, 1975; Rayner & Pollatsek, 1989).

Even so, sentence processing works quickly. It involves "snap decisions" (Matthei & Roeper, 1983), where we interpret phrases and clauses even before we get to the end of the sentence. This takes stress off short-term memory and makes the final processing of the sentence easier. The only problem is that the strategy can go wrong. For example, consider this sentence (Foss & Hakes, 1978, p. 130):

The horse raced past the barn fell.

The mistake that most of us make initially with the above sentence is to assume that *horse* is the subject of *raced*, when it is actually the subject of *fell*. In other words, the sentence is the same in structure as:

The horse, which was raced past the barn, fell.

Although these "garden-path" sentences trip up the language system, they do show that we unconsciously make snap judgments before the sentence is complete. In the "horse raced" example above, our tendency to make snap judgments caused an error. But this does not happen very often. The snap judgment strategy usually works very well. This strategy aims to take information out of short-term memory as soon as possible.

What this discussion is leading to is the idea that the reader must process words at speed. If information reaches the Librarian too slowly, it is lost from memory. Mental energy is diverted from comprehension when a child has to spend time working out a difficult word. This slows the system down and interferes with comprehension, which is why bottom-up theorists argue that the main threat to comprehension occurs when reading is slow, halting, and error-ridden, where there is a lack of "verbal efficiency" (Perfetti, 1984, 1985). When reading is fluent, however, the Librarian and Merlin can allocate all their cognitive capacity to comprehension.

The importance of speed and automaticity in reading comprehension may seem obvious. Skills in driving a car, in playing sports, and in many other activities all depend on lower-order skills becoming automatic and fast. The less mental energy put into these subskills, the more able we are to concentrate on higher-order skills, such as watching the flow of traffic or detecting gaps in the play of sporting opponents.

To ensure automaticity and speed of subskills, the usual advice is to practice, practice, practice. In the area of reading comprehension, this suggests that training children to read words faster would enable more mental energy to be put into higher-order processes, which would improve comprehension. Training studies, however, have produced inconclusive results. Fleisher, Jenkins, and Pany (1979) taught fourth- and fifth-grade poor readers (9- and 10-year-olds) to read words more quickly. They did this by showing key words on flashcards. After training, the pupils read a passage containing the key words. Tests of comprehension, however, showed no improvement in comprehension. Similar inconclusive results were obtained by Samuels, Dahl, and Archwamety (1974), using similar training procedures. However, Tan and Nicholson (see Chapter 7) have replicated the study of Fleisher and colleagues (1979) and obtained different results. The children in their study were 8-, 9-, and 10-year-olds. They were all poor readers.

Tan and Nicholson used flashcards, but the training was more extensive. The children in their study were trained not just on one set of words, but on several. Also, they used a variety of question types when assessing comprehension, including literal questions, where the answer was "right there" in the text, and inferential questions, where clues to the correct answer were in the text but the children had to do some thinking as well ("think and search"). These questions were designed to quiz pupils on what was in the text, without focusing too much on prior knowledge. Prior-knowledge questions can often be answered without reading the text at all (Nicholson, 1982; Nicholson & Imlach, 1981; Pearson & Johnson, 1978; Pearson & Nicholson, 1976; Raphael & Wonnacott, 1985). As a result of the flashcard training, Tan and Nicholson obtained significant gains in reading comprehension. These results support the concept of fast decoding as an important factor in reading comprehension. Is automaticity sufficient to ensure comprehension? The answer is no. The ability to pronounce words quickly and accurately is important, but the Librarian and Merlin must be able to extract their meaning.

THE "SIMPLE VIEW"

In recent work, Gough has explained more clearly the importance of both decoding skill (the Decoder) and linguistic comprehension skills (the Librarian and Merlin). The updated view states that reading has two components: decoding and linguistic comprehension. The updated view predicts that poor readers are either poor in decoding, poor in linguistic ability, or poor in both. It is called the Simple View of reading and reading disability (Gough & Tunmer, 1986).

The Simple View has been tested by following the reading progress of 129 children from first through fourth grade in a large, lower-middle-class school in Austin, Texas (Juel, 1988, 1994). The study found support for the model, though the evidence was correlational. That is, we can't be sure that the variables in the model actually *do* cause children to learn to read and write. In the end, we have to be guided by the weight of evidence. Fortunately, the evidence seems to be pointing in the same direction (Juel, 1991; Vellutino, 1991).

The Simple View can explain "word calling" (see also Stanovich, 1986). The popular image of this is a "parrot reader" who does not read for meaning. The child can pronounce words fluently and accurately but not understand what is read. The explanation of word calling is that a child has learned to decode yet has poor linguistic comprehension. An extreme case is a pupil who is learning to speak English as a second language. It is unusual for native speakers of English to have poor linguistic comprehension (i.e., be unable to understand even if a book is read aloud to them) but it may happen if the child lacks access to books, or does not like reading, or lags behind in language and cognitive development. For example, if a pupil did not get much exposure to print outside school, through reading of books or through being read to, then there would be less opportunity to learn new words and ideas, which are important for linguistic comprehension. Some children live in print-rich environments, where reading at home is likely to occur. Others, however, live in home surroundings where books are not available and visits to the library do not occur. So they do not do as much reading. This could have a negative effect on linguistic comprehension ability, even if the child has reasonable decoding skills.

There is not much research on children who seem to be adequate decoders but poor comprehenders. However, a recent study of 16 word callers (good decoders, poor comprehenders) found that they just didn't read as much as a matched control group of 16 good readers (good decoders, good comprehenders). This may explain why it turned out that, even when passages were read aloud to them, the so-called word callers did not comprehend as well as the good readers (Dymock, 1993). The important result of the study was that these 11- and 12-year-old word callers had poor linguistic comprehension. Their poor reading comprehension had nothing to do with word calling. If word calling was the problem, then they should have achieved higher comprehension scores when all they had to do was listen to passages read aloud to them. But their comprehension of the read-aloud passages was just as poor as when they read the passages themselves. If the Simple View is correct, then the best way to help these poor readers would be to increase their linguistic knowledge. One way to achieve this would be through easy reading, on their own, and/or by reading *to* them (Juel, 1991).

Another finding of the Dymock (1993) study was that these word callers didn't like reading, which may have caused them to lag behind in linguistic knowledge. When asked whether they would rather watch television or read, 73% of good readers said they would prefer to read but only 27% of poor readers said this. When asked whether they would rather play with their friends or read, both groups preferred to play with their friends. But each group gave different reasons. The good readers implied that they enjoyed the company of their friends yet still liked reading (Dymock, 1991, p. 84):

> "I think it is necessary to have some outdoor activities."
> "Most of the time I don't have many [friends], so I don't want to miss out on the opportunity."
> "I don't see my friends very often and I can read at night instead."
> "Reading will always be there but friends have to be there when you are."
> "I haven't got any brothers or sisters, and I get lonely."

In contrast, poor readers implied (or stated outright) that they just did not like reading (Dymock, 1991, p. 84):

> "You can play sport or make things, which is better than reading."
> "It's [sport is] more interesting and exciting."
> "I don't like reading."

Such findings are in line with the Simple View. Children may appear to be word callers, but the reason they are behind their classmates may be poor listening comprehension. They may not necessarily need help with decoding (though we should check that these skills are truly "automatic"). Instead, they may need to improve their vocabulary and general knowledge. As Juel, Griffith, and Gough (1986) put it:

> Thus, we believe that given perfection in decoding, the quality of reading will depend entirely on the quality of the reader's comprehension; if a child's listening comprehension of a text is poor, then his reading comprehension will be poor, no matter how good his decoding. (p. 244)

THE TOP-DOWN PERSPECTIVE

Top-down theorists have a different way of explaining word calling. The word caller is seen as a child who has been taught inappropriate reading strategies. For example, Goodman (1973) has described the word caller as someone who has been taught to say words but not to think about their meanings: "Remedial reading classes are filled with youngsters in late elementary and secondary schools who can sound out words but get little meaning from their reading" (p. 491). In Goodman's top-down model, good readers "sample" the text. Prior knowledge is crucial for reducing the amount of text information processed. By using syntactic and semantic information (i.e., context) it is possible to avoid reading every word in the text. Top-down theorists such as Goodman rely on the use of higher-level processes to help explain how this happens. As Goodman (1985) put it:

> Inference and prediction make it possible to leap toward meaning without fully completing the optical, perceptual and syntactic cycles. Yet the reader, once sense is achieved, has the sense of having seen every graphic feature, identified every pattern and word, assigned every syntactic pattern. (p. 835)

It ought to be noted that this model of the reading process is now considered wrong by many researchers (e.g., Stanovich, 1986, 1992). What distinguishes good readers is not their ability to read better in context but their ability to read words even in isolation. Poor readers do not read words well in isolation. They rely on context to help them read (Nicholson, 1991). Good readers read words well in isolation because they use their knowledge of letter-sound rules, a skill that poor readers lack. For good readers, eye-movement data show fairly complete processing of the words on the page (Rayner & Pollatsek, 1989). Very few words are skipped, and if they are, they tend to be words like *the*. In all, it seems that the good reader processes almost all the print, does it very quickly, and tries to make decisions about meaning at the same time (Matthei & Roeper, 1983).

To end on a positive note, the top-down emphasis on predicting from context may be important for other reasons. "Guessing" helps good readers to figure out letter-sound rules (Tunmer, 1990). They are able to use context clues as tools for learning how to decode. An emphasis on reading for meaning is also important for motivating children to read more often and to want to read. Top-down theorists have always argued that children learn to read by reading, and extensive reading seems an important way for children to refine their decoding skills and add new words and ideas to the language system. Let's now talk about this process in a bit more detail.

MATTHEW EFFECTS IN READING

There is quite a lot of evidence to suggest that the spin-off effects of learning to read extend beyond word recognition, to reading and listening comprehension, and to spelling and writing. In short, problems in the early stages of learning to read, where children get stuck at the decoding stage, unable to use letter-sound rules fluently, can have escalating negative effects, so that poor decoders get further and further behind. These effects reflect the Matthew principle (Stanovich, 1986). This principle is based on a statement from the Gospel according to Matthew (25:29): "To everyone who has will be given more, and they will have more than enough; but from those who have not, even what they have will be taken away." Applied to reading, the Matthew principle suggests that children who get off to a bad start in learning to read will get further and further behind in all aspects of literacy, including comprehension. As a result, there are rich-get-richer effects and poor-get-poorer effects.

Causes of Matthew Effects

The source of these Matthew effects can be traced to problems with phonemic awareness skills at school entry (see the discussion in Chapter 1). There is evidence that children who are deficient in phonemic awareness skills are likely to lag behind in learning to decode and may never catch up. Stanovich (1986) has argued that initial differences in phonological awareness are a major causal factor in producing later differences in reading achievement. The long-term effects of initial differences in phonemic awareness were traced in a longitudinal study of 54 children, whose progress was followed from first through to fourth grade (Juel, 1988):

> In my research, the children who became poor readers entered first grade with little or no phonemic awareness. Although their phonemic awareness steadily increased in first grade, they left this grade with a little less phonemic awareness than that which the children who became average or good readers possessed upon entering first grade (p. 444).

Reciprocal Causation Effects

Children who enter school with phonemic awareness are better equipped to learn the spelling-to-sound system. This enables them to start reading for themselves. Then the process of reading provides children with "positive learning trials" (Stanovich, 1986, p. 376). A positive learning trial occurs when the child successfully reads a word. Each time a child reads a word, there is an opportunity to store it in memory and to reinforce the child's emerging knowledge of letter-sound rules. As they learn more and more letter-sound rules, this helps to refine their phonemic awareness even further. The child's word-recognition skill is improved, and his or her phonemic awareness is improved as well. In the later stages of reading development, the effects of phonemic awareness are less important and give way to another two-way payoff of reading and linguistic comprehension. These two-way payoffs are called "reciprocal relationships" (Stanovich, 1986, p. 378), where one skill helps to improve the other, and vice versa.

Rich-Get-Richer Effects

The snowball effect of learning to read is increased by *active* "organism environment correlations" (Stanovich, 1986, p. 381). These correlations refer to things that the child has control over, that produce rich-get-richer effects. Children who learn to read easily and quickly can "shape" a positive environment, for example, by asking for books as a present. They can "select" a positive environment, for example, by choosing friends who like to read. They can "evoke" a positive environment, for example, by showing a strong interest in books, which then will encourage their parents to read to them and buy books for them. Parents are more likely to buy books for their children if their children show interest.

Differences between good and poor readers are also related to things that the child has no control over. These are passive organism–environment correlations. If a child is lucky, and is a winner in the biological lottery of life, he or she will be born with natural ability. If a child is lucky, he or she will grow up in a home environment that is educationally and financially advantaged, will attend schools where most of his or her classmates are above-average achievers. These social and educational advantages are sometimes called "cultural capital" (Bourdieu, 1974). They are positive Matthew effects.

The positive effects of attending a school in which most children are above-average have been documented in several studies. An Australian study of 500 children in the first two years of school found that the higher the average ability level of the classroom, and the school, the better the child's progress in acquiring phonemic awareness (Share, Jorm, Maclean, & Matthews, 1984).

Poor-Get-Poorer Effects

In contrast, an unlucky child will be born less able, will grow up in a home where there is poverty and where his or her parents lack education themselves. The child will probably attend a school where most children are below-average readers. These are passive organism–environment correlations that are outside the child's control and produce negative Matthew effects.

These negative Matthew effects were found in Juel's (1988) longitudinal study of 54 children:

> In my research, a vicious cycle seemed evident. Children who did not develop good word recognition skill in first grade began to dislike reading and read considerably less than good readers, both in and out of school. They thus lost the avenue to develop vocabulary, concepts, ideas, and so on that is fostered by wide reading. (p. 445)

The interesting thing about the Juel study was that the 54 children were all from a low-income area. Low socioeconomic status is associated with negative, passive organism–environment correlations. Nevertheless, there were children in Juel's sample who became good readers. The 30 children who became good readers started school with much higher levels of phonemic awareness than the 24 who became poor readers. The average pretest score on a phonemic awareness test for those who became good readers was 21.7; the average pretest score for those who became poor readers was 4.2. In fact, the modal score (most frequent score) was zero for those who later became poor readers. Also, those children who started with good phonemic awareness skills were well ahead in terms of decoding ability by the end of first grade. Their average posttest score on a word-recognition test was 26.4, while the poor readers averaged 8.3. Their average reading comprehension posttest score was at the 2.4 grade level, whereas poor readers were still at kindergarten level.

On a pure test of decoding (e.g., using made-up words such as *tiv* and *exyoded*), where children could not rely on memory for words already seen in their reading, the difference between good and poor readers was very clear. For good readers, the average number of words correct on a posttest of pseudowords (e.g., *tiv, blor, sanwix*) was 24.9, whereas the average for the poor readers was only 8.3, even though all these children had gone through a mandatory phonics program. Also, 9 of the poor readers could still not read any words on the pseudoword test, even after a year in school. Juel's (1988) findings have two implications. One is that children from low-income areas *can* succeed if they start school with high levels of phonemic awareness. The other implication is that the phonic method is not *the* answer to the problem of learning to decode, especially when children start school with low levels of phonemic awareness. It may be that no method will work unless certain prerequisites, like phonemic awareness, have been attained.

Another point to consider is that all these children started school with similar levels of listening comprehension. Their scores were below average, but similar to one another. Yet, after 2 years in school, children who had become poor readers made no further progress in listening, while good readers continued to make gains. Here are their grade-average scores, in listening comprehension, keeping in mind that they were all tested at the *end* of each school year. Poor readers: grade 1 = 1.4, grade 2 = 2.5, grade 3 = 2.5, grade 4 = 2.6. Good readers: grade 1 = 1.5, grade 2 = 3.2, grade 3 = 4.9, grade 4 = 5.2. To summarize, children who became poor readers started behind average in grade 1 and never caught up. In contrast, children who became good readers were well ahead in decoding even at the end of grade 1, and by the end of grade 3 they were well ahead in listening as well. These data illustrate the way in which reading failure impacts not only on decoding skill but also on comprehension in general.

There is evidence, from data collected in the 1960s, that at the end of the first year of school those in the top 25% in terms of reading skill will have read four times as many words as those in the bottom 25% (Clay, 1967). The estimated ratio in Clay's study was 20,000 versus 5,000 words. These data, though old, are in line with data from more recent work described above, where Juel (1988) found that first-grade good readers were exposed to twice as many words in their classroom readers as poor readers (18,681 words, as against 9,975 words). Also by fourth grade, good readers had read roughly 178,000 words in their school readers, while poor readers had read 80,000 words, less than half as many (Juel, 1991).

This is in line with another study, based on observations of children's reading in 24 classrooms (Allington, 1980). The findings were that poor readers in first and second grade read fewer than half the number of words that good readers did during their daily reading time (average number of words = 237 versus 539). As mentioned earlier, these differences, even from the first days of school, create Matthew effects that serve to create widening gaps between good readers and poor. The effects also extend to writing, since the extra reading done by good readers will give them a deeper knowledge base to draw on for ideas to write about (Juel, 1994).

The Matthew principle has policy implications. It points to the importance of ensuring that all children get off to as good a start as possible in learning to read and spell. But is this the end? Not really. Even good readers will come across material that is difficult, or complex in content. How do they tackle such material? This brings us to the topic of metacomprehension.

METACOMPREHENSION

From about age 5 through to adolescence, children become aware of how their language system works. Although adults usually know when a word rhymes, or when a sentence is grammatically correct, preschoolers find this difficult. Yet by the time they start school, most children show signs of being able to do these things. At this age, there is a change in children's ways of thinking, involving the development of cognitive control, sometimes called *metacognition*.

Metacognition is an umbrella term that includes other areas of thinking as well, such as metamemory, metalearning, and meta-attention (see Tunmer & Bowey, 1984). The *meta* means "knowledge about." Metacognition refers to knowledge of how the mind works. It involves the ability to reflect on and control one's own thought processes. The part of metacognition that is of interest to us is metacomprehension. This is the part that applies to reading comprehension. There are several aspects to this (Baker & Brown, 1984; Wagoner, 1983). One has to do with the ability to reflect on your own cognitive processes, so that you have a sense of when you don't understand something. This is called *knowing about comprehension*. It means being aware of when something is not making sense to you, for example, if a message is incomplete or contains inconsistencies.

A second aspect of metacomprehension refers to the ability to regulate your own thinking while reading. This is called *knowing how to comprehend*. It refers to the kinds of problem-solving strategies that the reader uses during the comprehension process. These are fix-up strategies that the reader puts into action when there is an awareness of comprehension failure. For example, the reader may look back, reread, summarize, look for inconsistencies, think about what is missing from the text, and so on. These strategies are not possible when listening, but they are possible when reading. Poor readers do not do this. Studies of fourth-grade poor readers suggest they do not have the fix-up strategies of good readers. As Paris and Oka (1989) put it, "Poor readers in fourth grade do not detect errors in text, study main ideas, or organize text information as well as their classmates who read well" (p. 34).

In the 1980s a number of training studies were carried out to improve children's skills in these areas (Baker & Brown, 1984; Palincsar & Brown, 1984; Paris, Wasik, & Turner, 1991; Pearson & Fielding, 1991). The aim was to see if training of cognitive monitoring skills would lead to improvements in reading comprehension. This is called *strategic reading* (Paris et al., 1991). In one study third- and fifth-graders were taught to predict what would happen, to look for main ideas, to skim a passage for meaning, to look back and check what happened, or to read forward to understand a difficult word (Paris, Cross, & Lipson, 1984). In another study sixth- and seventh-graders were taught to coach each other, by posing questions, asking for clarification, making predictions, and summarizing while reading (Palincsar & Brown, 1984). In yet another study sixth-graders were taught question-answering strategies, distinguishing between literal (Right There), inferential (Think and Search), and general knowledge (On your Own) questions (Raphael, 1982; Raphael & Wonnacott, 1985). These question-answering strategies are illustrated in Table 6.1. Positive effects on reading were obtained when these strategies were used.

However, a criticism of these studies (Carver, 1987) is that the training did not improve global comprehension, as measured on standardized tests. Instead, the effect was local. For example, children had a better understanding of a specific story, or did a better job of answering questions about a particular story. But that was all. A local effect is what we would expect when we ask children to spend more *time* on text material. The more time we spend on something, and the more we *practice* it, the better we usually get. The effect is not due to comprehension monitoring. It may instead be due to the extra effort put into the task. We haven't skills that will transfer to all reading. We have just asked students to do some extra study of specific texts. We have spent time explaining the text to them, but we haven't improved their overall comprehension ability. All we have done is given them some *prior knowledge* for just one topic. These are the kinds of arguments that have been put forward as a criticism of direct instruction in metacomprehension training (Carver, 1987). Is it fair for teachers to assign reading material that requires extra coaching, or a set of fix-up strategies, just so that students can comprehend such material? Carver concluded that the teaching of comprehension skills should

Table 6.1 Answering Strategies for Three Kinds of Questions (Based on Raphael, 1982)

The Answer Is Right There
 The answer is in the story and easy to find. The words used to make the question and the words that make the answer are right there in the same sentence.

Think and Search for the Answer
 The answer is in the story, but a little harder to find. You would never find the words in the question and the words in the answer all in the same sentence, but you would have to think and search for the answer.

Answer On My Own
 The answer won't be told by words in the story. You must find the answer in your head. Think: "I have to answer this question on my own. The story won't be much help."

be queried if taught to unskilled readers. Such skills were "study skills in disguise" (p. 125). They were the kinds of skills that come into operation when normal comprehension processes break down (i.e., when text is too difficult).

Carver's alternative to teaching such comprehension skills was to argue that reading materials should be written well enough so that pupils can learn new things on their own, without having to use "study skills." Reading material was considered well written by Carver if it was not too difficult for students to read. Carver was concerned that teachers were being encouraged by metacomprehension researchers to provide reading material to children that was too difficult for them. Carver suggested that giving frustration-level material to children was "poor teaching" (p. 124). He suggested that pupils should not be confronted with really difficult material until they could read at the eighth-grade level (13-year level). This was the level at which newspapers were written for the general population and was the point at which reading ability met with pupils' natural ability to understand spoken language. After that, teaching study skills would make much more sense, since the content of the reading material would be beyond students' general knowledge.

Carver's criticisms are important, but even he concedes that there are times when metacomprehension instruction is useful. In high school, pupils may need these extra study skills to cope with their textbooks. Local effects will help them to pass their exams! Carver's argument against teaching comprehension applies more to younger children, who should be able to "read to learn" without having to expect all sorts of difficulties along the way. His alternative suggestion is that children be assigned material that is appropriate for them. In this way, through further reading, they will be able to build up a richer lexicon and more sophisticated general knowledge.

There is evidence to support this. A recent study (Cunningham & Stanovich, 1991) of 34 fourth-grade, 33 fifth-grade, and 67 sixth-grade children found that knowledge of book titles, which indirectly measured out-of-school reading, was significantly correlated with decoding, spelling, knowledge of word meanings, and general knowledge. Dymock (1995) adapted the Cunningham and Stanovich (1991) Title Recognition Test (TRT) and tested it on 38 8-year-olds, 40 9-year-olds, and 40 10-year-olds. She found significant correlations between children's TRT scores (e.g., recognizing titles like *James and the Giant Peach*) and reading comprehension. Children who do lots of reading improve in reading comprehension. Stanovich (1993) argues that they will be smarter as well. Still, we must be cautious. Correlation is not causation. The only real test of this idea would be to let children do more reading and see what happens. This has been done in "book floods" and "sustained silent reading" programs. But research on these efforts is equivocal (Pearson & Fielding, 1991). Why should this be so? A possible reason is that simply asking children to read is no guarantee that they will do so. Who knows what actual reading goes on in a sustained silent reading lesson? (You can lead a horse to water, but . . .) Another possible reason is that poor decoding skills may undermine the positive effects of reading books. Poor readers, during free reading time, tend to select books that are too difficult for them (Anderson, Higgins, & Wurster, 1985). Children will improve their comprehension only if they can decode the material with ease. Otherwise, their mental energy is tied up with decoding difficulties instead of the content of the story.

Letting children read does not solve the Matthew effects dilemma. Good readers will cover more text per minute of silent reading and will engage with a higher level of text than will poor readers. So they learn more words and acquire more ideas. For example, Nicholson and Whyte (1992) tested 56 children aged 8 to 10 years on their ability to work out new words from listening to a William Steig story book, *Farmer Palmer's Wagon Ride*. Poor readers did not learn the meanings of new words when the story was read aloud to them, though they were able to work out the meanings of *some* words when the written sentences in which the words occurred were re-read to them. In contrast, average and good readers learned far more new words. Thus, even if we let children "learn to read by reading," the gap between good and poor readers will not disappear. It will increase.

Despite these rich-get-richer and poor-get-poorer effects, it is still important to teach metacognitive strategies, so that children will monitor their comprehension. If they sense that they are losing track of the story, they can stop and try some repair techniques (e.g., rereading, checking the meanings of key words). If these repair strategies fail, they will at least know they have wandered into a "too hard" area. At that point, it may be time to try another book.

What if the book that is too hard is a required text that pupils have to deal with? Dealing with hard text content is a feature of the middle grades of schooling, as pupils "read to learn." Harbaugh (1988) illustrates the difficulties faced by many pupils with the following case study:

> Meghan was doing fine in third grade. She had no trouble grasping third grade reading materials. But suddenly, in fourth grade, her rate of progress took a serious dive. Her teacher couldn't get her to move ahead. Meghan became increasingly frustrated. Her parents were worried. Meghan was suffering from what educators know as the infamous "fourth grade slump," the phenomenon that often occurs during the tricky transition students must make from learning to read to reading to learn. (p. 26)

This quotation highlights the increased reading demands of the middle grades, but these difficulties extend well into secondary school (Nicholson, 1984, 1988).

TEACHING ABOUT TEXT STRUCTURE

In addition to strategic reading strategies, which have already been discussed, children can be taught structural strategies for learning new words and remembering texts (see Figure 6.1). First, let us consider how these apply to *vocabulary*. Calfee (1984) and Calfee and Patrick (1995) suggest several structural techniques, including webs, weaves, and hierarchies. The web is like a spider's web. It helps the child to remember more about new words, since they are deliberately linked with other words and ideas through group discussion and brainstorming. For example, you can take a general concept such as "birds" and build a lot of information around it in web form, with subheadings such as "kinds of birds," "what they eat," "where they nest," "common features," and so forth. Lots of new words thus get included in the web and are clarified by the web. More complex structures, a step up from the web, include weaves, continuums, and the hierarchies. A weave is like a tapestry. Ideas are more strongly connected, in matrix fashion. A matrix pattern is a useful framework for making comparisons and contrasts, as in a comparison of New Zealand and the United States in terms of geographic size, population, ethnicity, famous persons, favorite foods, sports, and so on. A continuum structure is a time line that shows events in history, but in chronological order (e.g., kings and queens of England, presidents of the United States). A hierarchy structure, for example, can show how different things such as spiders, insects, and whales are all animals.

Structural strategies also apply to *texts*. Calfee and Patrick (1995) separate narrative text from expository and teach children to visualize them differently. Diagrams are used to show different structural patterns. Their definition of narrative is that it is a story. Narratives have a plot and characters. One way to show the plot is to use a *time line*. This can be drawn on a large sheet of paper to show high and low points of the story over time. Events in many narratives build slowly toward a high point, or climax. Children chart the key events, in order, and think about their relative importance in the flow of the story. During discussion, children can be asked to justify their decisions about high and low points in the action. They can also refer back to the text for support when making decisions about the order of key events (see Figure 6.1).

Another technique with narratives is to break the plot into a few chunks, and then list the supporting details that go with each chunk. The

Figure 6.1 Structural Diagrams for Teaching Vocabulary and Text Comprehension (based on Calfee & Patrick, 1995)

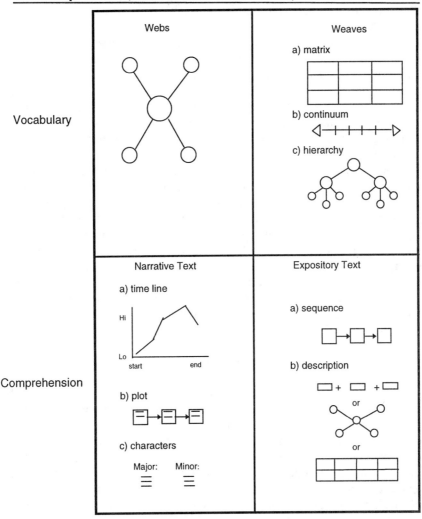

chunks can be very simple, such as beginning, middle, and end. Children discuss why certain chunks should be categorized as beginning, middle, and end. A final narrative technique is to break the characters into major and minor, group the various characters under each heading, and describe them. Children discuss the reasons for their decisions about major/minor characters and refer to the text for evidence. This adds text verification to the way they see the characters and builds a group consensus as to the structure of the story.

Expository text can be defined as *not* a story. This separates it from narrative text. There are different kinds of expository text. A sequence text (like a continuum) shows something happening over time, such as the life cycle of the monarch butterfly. There is a cause-effect structure in this life-cycle pattern. The events follow a set order. They can't be scrambled. Again, in discussion, children should talk about why the sequence is the way it is, and they can check the text to verify their ideas. A description text, on the other hand, can have a list structure in which there is no set order. It may be a list of things to take when you go fishing, or a list of animals found in Australia, or a list of products made in Japan. It doesn't matter what goes first in the list. Children discuss whether or not the text fits a list structure. Could it be sequence? Why not? And so on. Other kinds of description text include the topical net structure (like a web) and the matrix structure (like a weave). Chapter 8 gives a description of text-structure research. The chapter explains in detail the structural approach to texts and research related to it, and it gives specific examples of how pupils can apply metacognitive structural strategies. The use of structural strategies will work better if children are already fluent decoders of words, since they will not get stuck on pronunciation of difficult words. It is a metacognitive approach that is proactive. It encourages children to look for specific patterns in text. It can also be useful for poor readers, though the teacher would have to read the text aloud to them first.

REVIEW

Children can already comprehend language when they get to school. The native speaker of English comes to the reading task with an impressive comprehension system, including a Librarian and a Merlin. The Librarian has access to the meanings of words stored in the child's lexicon, while Merlin consists of a complex set of syntactic and semantic rules to apply to sentences in order to derive their meanings. According to the bottom-up perspective on comprehension, all the child needs is to be able to decode printed language, and comprehension will follow. This is because the child already has a comprehension system that is designed to process spoken language. Once the child knows how to recode the written form into a more abstract, phonological form, then the author's written message can be fed directly into the regular linguistic comprehension system.

In the bottom-up model, reading comprehension problems will be due to bottlenecks caused by poor decoding skill. When this happens, the Librarian and Merlin receive information that contains errors. Poor decoding skill will produce slow, erratic information flow. This will interfere with comprehension, because top-down processes will be diverted from comprehension to help the child guess what the words on the page mean. The bottom-up model requires automaticity of word identification to ensure comprehension.

The Simple View extends the bottom-up model to show that reading comprehension depends not just on decoding but also on linguistic comprehension. A child who is a good reader must be a good decoder and have good linguistic comprehension. If the child is deficient in one of these areas, or in both, then the child will not read well.

The literature on Matthew effects suggests that the child who learns to read easily gets to read more and, in the process, learns more new words and ideas. The positive spin-off effects of learning to read have been termed rich-get-richer effects. For the good reader, learning to decode leads to more reading, which improves decoding skills even more, and comprehension as well.

Finally, by making use of metacomprehension strategies, children can enhance and deepen their vocabulary knowledge and understanding of text. Complex ideas will be better understood and remembered more easily, which is what effective comprehension is all about.

STUDY AND DISCUSSION QUESTIONS

1. What are the key points that distinguish a bottom-up perspective on reading comprehension from a top-down perspective?
2. Some teachers find that their pupils are adequate decoders but can't understand what they decode. How does the *Simple View* explain this phenomenon?
3. How does the concept of automaticity apply to reading comprehension? What evidence is there to support training of automaticity?
4. The top-down perspective has links with metacomprehension training, especially strategic reading. What are the goals of strategic reading? What are the limitations?
5. Good readers are better than poor readers in many ways. They are better at predicting what will happen in a story, they are better at summarizing what happens, they are better at finding main ideas, and so on. But are these the skills that make good readers good, or are these skills the *result* of other factors? How does the literature on Matthew effects explain the superior comprehension skills of good readers?
6. Researchers have found that pupils often have trouble remembering what they read. How can group discussion, along with simple organizational frameworks, be used to teach better comprehension of text?

7. Imagine that your school principal wants you to increase the reading comprehension levels of all pupils in the school, but especially those who are presently below-average. What suggestions would you make, given previous research on automaticity, reading practice, strategic reading, and structural frameworks?

FURTHER READING

Calfee, R. C., & Patrick, C. L. (1995). *Teach your children well: Bringing K–12 education into the 21st century.* Stanford, CA: Stanford Alumni Association.

Juel, C. (1994). *Learning to read in one elementary school.* New York: Springer-Verlag.

Nicholson, T. (1997). *Solving reading problems* (rev ed.). Wellington, New Zealand: New Zealand Council for Educational Research.

REFERENCES

Allington, R. L. (1980). Poor readers don't get to read much in reading groups. *Language Arts, 57,* 872–876.

Anderson, G., Higgins, D., & Wurster, S. R. (1985). Differences in the free-reading books selected by high, average, and low achievers. *Reading Teacher, 39,* 326–330.

Baker, L., & Brown, A. L. (1984). Metacognitive skills and reading. In P. D. Pearson, R. Barr, M. L. Kamil, & P. Monsenthal (Eds.), *Handbook of reading research* (pp. 353–394). New York: Longman.

Bourdieu, P. (1974). The school as a conservative force. In J. Eggleston (Ed.), *Contemporary research in the sociology of education* (pp. 32–46). London: Methuen.

Calfee, R. C. (1984). *The book: Components of reading instruction.* Unpublished manuscript, Stanford University, Stanford, CA.

Calfee, R. C., & Patrick, C. L. (1995). *Teach our children well: Bringing K–12 education into the 21st century.* Stanford, CA: Stanford Alumni Association.

Carver, R. P. (1987). Should reading comprehension skills be taught? In J. E. Readance & R. S. Baldwin (Eds.), *Research in literacy: Merging perspectives* (pp. 115–126). Rochester, NY: National Reading Conference.

Clay, M. M. (1967). The reading behaviour of five year old children: A research report. *New Zealand Journal of Educational Studies, 2,* 11–31.

Cunningham, A. E., & Stanovich, K. E. (1991). Tracking the unique effects of print exposure in children: Associations with vocabulary, general knowledge, and spelling. *Journal of Educational Psychology, 83,* 264–274.

Dymock, S. J. (1991). *Poor comprehension amongst good decoders: Is the problem due to "word calling" or language comprehension?* Unpublished master's thesis, University of Waikato, Hamilton, New Zealand.

Dymock, S. J. (1993). Reading but not understanding. *Journal of Reading, 37,* 2–8.

Dymock, S. J. (1995). Measuring print exposure in New Zealand classrooms. *Best of Set: Assessment* (No. 2., Item 6). Wellington, New Zealand: New Zealand Council for Educational Research.

Fleisher, L. S., Jenkins, J. R., & Pany, D. (1979). Effects on poor readers' comprehension of training in rapid decoding. *Reading Research Quarterly, 15,* 30–48.

Foss, D., & Hakes, D. (1978). *Psycholinguistics: An introduction to the psychology of language.* Englewood Cliffs, NJ: Prentice-Hall.

Goodman, K. S. (1973). The 13th easy way to make learning to read difficult: A reaction to Gleitman and Rozin. *Reading Research Quarterly, 8,* 484–493.

Goodman, K. S. (1985). Unity in reading. In H. Singer & R. B. Ruddell (Eds.), *Theoretical models and processes of reading* (pp. 813–840). Newark, DE: International Reading Association.

Gough, P. B. (1972). One second of reading. *Visible Language, 6,* 291–320.

Gough, P. B., & Tunmer, W. E. (1986). Decoding, reading, and reading disability. *Remedial and Special Education, 7,* 6–10.

Harbaugh, M. (1988, October). Climbing out of the fourth grade slump. *Instructor,* pp. 26–27.

Juel, C. (1988). Learning to read and write: A longitudinal study of 54 children from first through fourth grades. *Journal of Educational Psychology, 80,* 437–447.

Juel, C. (1991). Beginning reading. In R. Barr, M. L. Kamil, P. B. Mosenthal, & P. D. Pearson (Eds.), *Handbook of reading research* (Vol. 2; pp. 759–788). White Plains, NY: Longman.

Juel, C. (1994). *Learning to read in one elementary school.* New York: Springer-Verlag.

Juel, C., Griffith, P. L., & Gough, P. B. (1986). Acquisition of literacy: A longitudinal study of children in first and second grade. *Journal of Educational Psychology, 78,* 243–255.

Just, M. A., & Carpenter, P. A. (1980). A theory of reading: From eye fixations to comprehension. *Psychological Review, 87,* 329–354.

LaBerge, D., & Samuels, S. J. (1974). Toward a theory of automatic information processing in reading. *Cognitive Psychology, 6,* 293–323.

Matthei, E., & Roeper, T. (1983). *Understanding and producing speech.* Bungay, Suffolk, England: Fontana.

Miller, C. A. (1956). The magical number seven, plus or minus two: Some limits on our capacity for processing information. *Psychological Review, 63,* 81–97.

Nicholson, T. (1982). *An anatomy of reading.* Sydney: Martin Educational.

Nicholson, T. (1984). Experts and novices: A study of reading in the high school classroom. *Reading Research Quarterly, 19,* 436–458.

Nicholson, T. (1988). *Reading and learning in the junior secondary school.* Wellington, New Zealand: Department of Education.

Nicholson, T. (1991). Do children read words better in context or in lists? A classic study revisited. *Journal of Educational Psychology, 83,* 444–450.

Nicholson, T., & Imlach, R. (1981). Where do their answers come from? A study of the inferences which children make when answering questions about narrative stories. *Journal of Reading Behavior, 13,* 111–129.

Nicholson, T., Pearson, P. D., & Dykstra, R. (1979). Effects of embedded anomalies and oral reading errors on children's understanding of stories. *Journal of Reading Behavior, 11,* 339–354.

Nicholson, T., & Whyte, B. (1992). Matthew effects in learning new words while reading. In C. K. Kinzer & D. J. Leu (Eds.), *Literacy research, theory and practice: Views from many perspectives* (pp. 499–503). Chicago: National Reading Conference.

Palincsar, A. S., & Brown, A. L. (1984). Reciprocal teaching of comprehension-fostering and comprehension-monitoring activities. *Cognition and Instruction, 1,* 117–175.

Paris, S. G., Cross, D. R., & Lipson, M. Y. (1984). Informed strategies for learning: A program to improve children's reading awareness and comprehension. *Journal of Educational Psychology, 76,* 1239–1252.

Paris, S. G., & Oka, E. R. (1989). Strategies for comprehending text and coping with reading difficulties. *Learning Disability Quarterly, 12,* 32–42.

Paris, S. G., Wasik, B. A., & Turner, J. C. (1991). The development of strategic readers. In R. Barr, M. L. Kamil, P. B. Mosenthal, & P. D. Pearson (Eds.), *Handbook of reading research* (Vol. 2; pp. 609–640). White Plains, NY: Longman.

Pearson, P. D., & Fielding, L. (1991). Comprehension instruction. In R. Barr, M. L. Kamil, P. B. Mosenthal, & P. D. Pearson (Eds.), *Handbook of reading research* (Vol. 2; pp. 815–860). White Plains, NY: Longman.

Pearson, P. D., & Johnson, D. D. (1978). *Teaching reading comprehension.* New York: Holt, Rinehart & Winston.

Pearson, P. D., & Nicholson, T. (1976, December). *Scripts, texts and questions.* Paper presented at the annual meeting of the National Reading Conference, Atlanta, GA.

Perfetti, C. A. (1984). Reading acquisition and beyond: Decoding includes cognition. *American Journal of Education, 93,* 40–60.

Perfetti, C. A. (1985). *Reading ability.* New York: Oxford University Press.

Raphael, T. E. (1982). Question-answering strategies for children. *Reading Teacher, 36,* 186–191.

Raphael, T. E., & Wonnacott, C. A. (1985). Heightening fourth grade students' sensitivity to sources of information for answering comprehension questions. *Reading Research Quarterly, 20,* 282–296.

Rayner, K. (1975). The perceptual span and peripheral cues in reading. *Cognitive Psychology, 7,* 65–81.

Rayner, K., & Pollatsek, A. (1989). *The psychology of reading.* Englewood Cliffs, NJ: Prentice-Hall.

Samuels, S. J., Dahl, P., & Archwamety, T. (1974). Effect of hypothesis/test training on reading skill. *Journal of Educational Psychology, 66,* 835–844.

Share, D. L., Jorm, A. F., Maclean, R., & Matthews, R. (1984). Sources of individual differences in reading acquisition. *Journal of Educational Psychology, 76,* 1309–1324.

Stanovich, K. E. (1986). Matthew effects in reading: Some consequences of individual differences in the acquisition of literacy. *Reading Research Quarterly, 21,* 360–407.

Stanovich, K. E. (1992). Speculations on the causes and consequences of individual differences in early reading acquisition. In P. B. Gough, L. C. Ehri, & R. Treiman (Eds.), *Reading acquisition* (pp. 307–342). Hillsdale, NJ: Erlbaum.

Stanovich, K. E. (1993). Does reading make you smarter? In H. Reese (Ed.), *Advances in child development* (Vol. 24; pp. 133–180). London: Academic Press.

Tunmer, W. E. (1990). The role of language prediction skills in beginning reading. *New Zealand Journal of Educational Studies, 25,* 95–114.

Tunmer, W. E., & Bowey, J. A. (1984). Metalinguistic awareness and reading acquisition. In W. E. Tunmer, C. Pratt, & M. L. Herriman (Eds.), *Metalinguistic awareness in children: Theory, research and implications* (pp. 144–168). Berlin: Springer-Verlag.

Vellutino, F. R. (1991). Introduction to three studies on reading acquisition: Convergent findings on theoretical foundations of code-oriented versus whole-language approaches to reading instruction. *Journal of Educational Psychology, 83,* 437–443.

Wagoner, S. A. (1983). Comprehension monitoring: What it is and what we know about it. *Reading Research Quarterly, 18,* 328–346.

Chapter 7

Proficient Word Identification for Comprehension

TOM NICHOLSON AND ANNETTE TAN

a) How important is word identification in improving reading comprehension?

b) What is the role of automaticity in learning and reading?

c) Will gains in proficiency of word identification improve reading comprehension?

Reading is a multicomponent skill that involves several cognitive processes, including word identification, retrieval of word meanings from memory, grammatical and semantic analysis of sentences, and interpretation of paragraphs and texts. Most of these linguistic processes are already in place for the native speaker. They require little or no mental effort in that they are part of an inbuilt ability to understand speech (Pinker, 1994). One component that is not automatic, taking several years to acquire, is the ability to read words quickly. Word identification is the hard part of learning to read. It needs to be learned for the reader to understand the meaning of the text.

WORD IDENTIFICATION AND READING ABILITY

The relationship between word-identification skill and reading comprehension is well explained by the "Simple View" of reading and reading disabilities (Gough & Tunmer, 1986; see Chapter 6). The Simple View proposes that reading comprehension depends on both word-identification skill and linguistic comprehension. Identifying words without understanding them is not reading. Understanding words (as in listening to a story) yet not being able to identify them in print is also not reading. There is now considerable evidence to suggest that word-identification skill is very important in the beginning stages of reading, when children are faced with text that is well within their linguistic comprehension but they are unable to access the meaning because they have trouble identifying written words. But once word-identification skills are well developed, reading comprehension is more influenced by children's linguistic comprehension ability. This is because children have to cope with text that is more difficult to understand as they move through the school grades (Calfee & Patrick, 1995; Juel, 1994; Juel, Griffith, & Gough, 1986).

Linguistic comprehension can take more or less cognitive effort, depending on the difficulty of the ideas being expressed. Understanding what is read is not something that can be done without effort. But researchers have found that word-identification skills, when well developed, can involve very little cognitive effort. Word-identification skills can become automatic, thus making the task of reading comprehension not too different from that of listening comprehension. Reading the words can become so effortless that reading a written text is almost like listening to a spoken message. In this chapter we will consider how it is that word identification can become automatic and how automaticity can in turn facilitate reading comprehension.

THE IMPORTANCE OF AUTOMATICITY

What is it that concert pianists, sculptors, tennis stars, champion swimmers, and research mathematicians have in common? The answer is automaticity, the ability to do something in an effortless way. Bloom (1986) studied the careers of outstanding performers. He found that top performers took at least a dozen years to reach the top, though some of them started very early in life. These top performers spent many hours practicing to the point where they overlearned certain skills. Tennis players practiced certain shots every day; pianists practiced specific pieces of music for up to 6 months before they felt ready to play them. They had overlearned these skills to the point where they were automatic, that is, they could be performed without having to think about them.

Automaticity and Learning

Overlearning can apply to everyday skills as well as specialist skills. Bloom (1986) gives the example of walking. Anyone who has watched 2-year-olds walking knows that they have definitely not yet overlearned this skill. They still put mental effort into walking. They look where they are walking, learn to adjust their pace, and so on. But walking, for the adult, requires no conscious attention—except, as Samuels (1976) pointed out, when the ground is icy and attention must be used to avoid falling. In addition, while walking, the mind can be thinking about something else other than the process of walking. This is another aspect of automaticity. The mastery of one skill to the point of effortlessness enables you to do something else at the same time.

Automaticity in Reading

The impact of automaticity on reading can be demonstrated in what is called the Stroop task (for a review, see Jensen & Rohwer [1966]). In this task, words that name colors (e.g., red, green, blue) were printed in different colors. The task was either to read the words or else ignore the words and name the colors that they were written in. The person who introduced this test into American psychology, John Ridley Stroop, found that subjects were slower to name the color of a printed word (e.g., a word written in a red color) if the printed word was also the name of a different color (e.g., if the printed word was *blue*, but it was written in the color red).

The reason for the Stroop effect is that the word-reading identification process has become automated for the skilled reader, to the point where it resists external control and interferes with the color naming (Bloom, 1986). For example, imagine you are one of Stroop's subjects. You are shown a written word on a screen. The word is *black*, but it is printed in green letters. Your task is to name the color of the letters as quickly as possible. You see the green-colored letters of the word and desperately try to say "green." But it's too late. Your automatic reading processes have already identified the word *black*. You thus have two possible responses in your mind competing against one another, "green" and "black." The involuntary, automatic reading of the printed word *black* is the competing response. You then have to sort out which response is correct. You have to suppress "black" and permit "green." This takes a little bit of time and effort, which is why Stroop found that subjects were slower to name colors when the written word spelled the name of a color different from the color of the letters it was printed in. These results provide support for the principle of automaticity in reading. They suggest that the skilled reader has internalized the skills of word identification to the point where they can be operationalized without mental effort and without conscious control. In short, word identification has become automatized.

Similar Stroop-type findings are reported in Underwood and Batt (1996). Researchers have also used a different task. An example is a picture of an object alongside which is printed a word that names a semantic associate (e.g., a picture of bread, with the word *butter* written below the picture). Researchers have found that even children in their first year of school are slower to name pictures if they are accompanied by a highly associated word. This suggests that for many young readers, the automatization of word-reading identification skills appears very quickly.

When we first start to practice a skill, it is obvious that we have limited capacity in what we can do. When we first start swimming, for example, it is hard to do everything at once. We use our arms but forget to use our feet, we can't keep to a straight line, and so on. We can do one or two aspects of the task, but that is all. Samuels (1976) calls this the *cocktail party problem*, since it is similar to the experience of being at a function where there may be several interesting conversations going on. You can only listen to one at a time, so you give the appearance of listening to one conversation while you tune into another.

The cocktail party metaphor can be applied to the problems of poor readers in that their attention is constantly switching between word identification and comprehension. Similarly, unskilled swimmers or tennis players give most of their attention to particular subskills, whereas skilled sportspersons have overlearned certain skills to the point where they do not have to allocate attention to these subskills. When you have achieved automaticity of subskills, you can't easily stop them from operating. Someone who is skilled in reading, for example, can find it very difficult not to read signs in the street or on the bus. Our eyes just start reading.

Automaticity Theory

Stanovich (1990) notes that the concept of automaticity was discussed early in this century by Huey (1908/1968). After that, according to Stanovich (1990), there was "darkness." This was the period when cognitive theory lost popularity and was replaced by behaviorist theory. By the 1970s, however, cognitive theory was once again acceptable, and this coincides with new work on automaticity and reading.

The first paper to be published on automaticity theory and reading was by University of Minnesota researchers, LaBerge and Samuels (1974). They proposed that specific word-identification processes become automated over time: first letters, then spelling patterns, then words. A fluent reader identifies words in text automatically. This leaves attention free for comprehension. Beginning readers, in contrast, lack automaticity. They must devote attention to the task of identifying words. In a follow-up paper on automaticity, Samuels (1979) proposed three stages in the development of word-identification skills. First, there is the nonaccurate stage, where the child has trouble identifying words. Second, there is the accuracy stage. Reading is accurate, but slow, halting, expressionless, and effortful. Word identification still requires mental effort. Third, there is the automatic stage. The child reads with expression and with ease. Attention can then be fully applied to the task of comprehension.

Similar findings to those of LaBerge and Samuels were reached independently by University of Pittsburgh researchers, Perfetti and Hogaboam (1975). They published data showing that good and poor comprehenders differed in the speed of decoding single words. They compared children in third and fifth grade who were either good or poor comprehenders. The children were presented with words on a screen and had to read them aloud as quickly as possible. Good comprehenders were faster at reading words than were poor comprehenders, especially low-frequency, unfamiliar words. Perfetti and Hogaboam (1975) concluded that poor comprehenders lacked automatic word-identification skills. They proposed a "shared limited capacity hypothesis" (p. 468) to explain why word reading speed was important. Automaticity of word identification meant that there were fewer demands on higher-order linguistic skills (i.e., grammatical and semantic processes), which are important for comprehension. The mind can only process a limited amount of information at any one time, so mental work required for word identification would put pressure on limited memory capacity available at any one time for comprehension.

Perfetti and Lesgold (1977) used the term *bottleneck* to describe the problem of shared limited capacity. What would a comprehension bottleneck be like? Imagine a traffic jam. When a multilane highway reduces to just one lane, there are a lot of cars wanting to move into the one lane. If you could reduce the number of cars, the traffic would flow more smoothly. Likewise in reading, if word-identification processes were automatic, then the meaning of the text would be processed more quickly and efficiently. Fewer cognitive resources would share the same mental space. In terms of the bottleneck metaphor, there would be fewer cars wanting to share the road. Since automaticity of word identification requires little memory capacity, the traffic flow of words would move more easily.

In recent writing, Perfetti has used the term *verbal efficiency* (Perfetti, 1985) to explain differences between good and poor readers. Verbal efficiency refers to the efficiency with which the reader is able to recognize letters, identify words, and also retrieve word meanings from memory. Good readers are better than poor readers in all these aspects of verbal efficiency. Thus verbal efficiency theory predicts that context-free word identification is the hallmark of reading ability.

Automaticity and Speed Reading

Automaticity (or verbal efficiency) refers to the ability to identify words and recall their meanings without effort. Comprehending phrases and sentences, however, may require a great deal of time and effort, depending on the difficulty of the text. Carver (1990) has shown that readers increase their comprehension if given more time to read. The time we take to read depends on text difficulty. Some texts will take longer to read and understand than others. Verbal efficiency applies just to the part of reading that involves word identification. If this part of the process is attention-free, then the reader is able to allocate full cognitive resources to comprehension. We should not confuse verbal efficiency with speed reading. Skilled readers recognize words quickly, yet the time it takes them to read a text can vary considerably, depending on the difficulty of the text.

What Is It That Becomes Automatic?

In the LaBerge and Samuels (1974) model, automaticity occurs at the letter level, the spelling-pattern level, and the word level. The skilled reader might identify words by analyzing them as whole units (e.g., *the*) or by a phonological recoding process whereby the spoken form of the word is realized by using letter-sound rules. These rules are internalized and operate automatically. For example, the skilled reader does not think about the sound made by *ch*. The *ch* correspondence has been overlearned to the point where *ch* is recoded into sound automatically. Johnson and Pearson (1984) and Juel (1991) note that skilled readers can easily identify made-up words that follow regular spelling patterns (e.g., *glick, poon, sanwixable*). This ability to read made-up words is related to reading progress. In a 4-year longitudinal study, Juel (1988) found that all the poor readers in her study were much worse than the good readers in terms of reading made-up words. Felton and Wood (1992) also found that the ability to read made-up words is more closely related to reading ability than is IQ. The development of word-identification skills is discussed in Chapter 2.

Automaticity or Modularity?

Automaticity theory is based on the idea of limited capacity and attentional processes. But it may be that these concepts are not really central to what happens when automaticity is achieved. Stanovich (1990) reviews research that has moved away from the automaticity perspective to one of modularity, where word identification is viewed as an independent, autonomous processing system. This processing system consumes some mental resources, but for the skilled reader the system is so good that mental resources are used as efficiently as possible. Thus, rather than thinking about fast word identification in terms of more or less processing resources, the modular approach suggests that it is better to think of the quality of the processing instead. Even if fast identification takes some resources, this may not matter. What does matter is whether the identification process is done in the most efficient way possible. Perfetti's (1985) idea of verbal efficiency comes closer to the idea of quality processing and fits in with much of the 1980s research on context effects in word identification. A great deal of research across a range of research paradigms, such as oral reading error studies, eye-movement studies, timed text reading, and text disruptions, now suggests that good readers are able to read words without the use of context clues, linguistic guessing, background knowledge, and so on.

The quality of the good reader's word-identification skills is such that these skills consume a minimum of mental resources. Stanovich (1986) cites many studies showing that skilled readers do not make more use of context than unskilled readers. Contrary to the finding of 1960s research on this topic, unskilled readers are in fact more reliant on context than are skilled readers (Nicholson, 1991; Nicholson, Bailey, & McArthur, 1991; Nicholson & Hill, 1985; Nicholson, Lillas, & Rzoska, 1988; Stanovich, 1986). The word-identification abilities of skilled readers are so good that they do not need to invoke other cognitive processes. Poor readers, however, are more reliant on context because their word-identification skills are not as efficient. Even when given material that is within their reading ability and that they can read with accuracy, research has shown that poor readers rely on contextual clues to achieve this accuracy (for a summary, see Nicholson [1993]). Thus their word-identification skills are not context-free in the way that the skills of good readers are. By having to rely on context to read words accurately, poor readers have less opportunity to concentrate on comprehension.

Many words are not predictable in text. Gough (1983) has calculated that only one in ten content words is predictable from context alone. The ability to read words in a context-free way is therefore a huge advantage for the good reader over the poor reader. The good reader has very high-quality word-identification processes, which are modular in the sense that they operate independently of higher-level processes.

The modular approach to the notion of automaticity (Stanovich, 1990), that is, the idea that word recognition is a functionally autonomous system, not open to higher-order effects such as context, may be a more appealing approach in the long run because it fits well with recent reading research on context effects in reading. Much research now indicates that reliance on high-level processes (e.g., prediction, guessing) for word identification is more descriptive of poor and novice readers than skilled readers (Nicholson, 1991). Use of context to compensate for poor word-identification skills may help the poor or novice reader to read some words accurately or else guess a substitute word that has the same meaning. But such guesswork diverts cognitive energies from the task of comprehension, thus limiting the quality of comprehension that can be achieved.

Samuels (1994), in a revisit of the classic LaBerge and Samuels (1974) paper, acknowledges Stanovich's criticisms of automaticity theory but suggests that the concept of limited attentional resources is still very descriptive of what distinguishes a skilled reader from an unskilled one. It is tempting to say "yes" to this, but there is a small problem in that Samuels still allows for the possibility that context can facilitate word identification. He gives the example of text material that is very familiar to a child (e.g., a text on soccer), arguing that such text could facilitate word identification. A child with inefficient word-identification skills who knows nothing about soccer will have more difficulty with a word like *penalty* than will another child with similar poor word-identification skills but a familiarity with soccer. Samuels (1994) comments that: "When judging the degree of automaticity in readers' decoding skills based on their comprehension and recall of text, familiarity with the subject matter must therefore be taken into account" (p. 831). But such a role for context is not consistent with modularity theory. Yes, a poor reader may be helped by familiar context, as in a text on soccer, but use of context to facilitate word identification is not characteristic of good readers. It seems, then, that there is a difference between automaticity theory and modularity theory.

DOES TRAINING CHILDREN TO READ WORDS FASTER IMPROVE COMPREHENSION?—A REPLICATION STUDY

A simple test of the importance of word identification in reading comprehension would be to train beginning readers or poor readers to read words more rapidly, to see if this results in better reading comprehension. This has been done in several studies, but with inconclusive results.

Fleisher, Jenkins, and Pany (1979) had no success when they tested the "bottleneck hypothesis." These researchers used flashcards to teach poor readers to read words faster. In one experiment, they taught 11 fourth- and 11 fifth-grade poor readers to read single words that were each printed on a single-word flashcard (e.g., *spider*). In a second experiment they taught 27 fourth- and 6 fifth-grade poor readers with phrase flashcards, so as to give more context help (e.g., the word *spider* was presented as a phrase, as in *spider in the shower*). The aim was to teach children all the words from a passage that they had not seen before. Then, once they could identify all the words, they would read the unseen passage aloud. Their comprehension of the passage would also be assessed, to see if the flashcard training had helped comprehension. The researchers taught the children to read all the words from one of two passages. One passage had 74 different words, while the other passage had 75 different words. The two sets of words were printed on flashcards for teaching. The two passages were necessary, in order to control for the effects of the flashcard training. Each child was taught all the words from one or the other of the two passages, depending on which set of flashcard words the researchers randomly selected. The untrained words were from the control passage. After the flashcard teaching, each child read the trained-words passage, answered comprehension questions, and completed a cloze test of the passage (fill-in-the-blanks). They also read the control passage, answered comprehension questions, and completed a cloze test of the passage. In both experiments, using either one-word flashcards or phrase flashcards, the results showed that the flashcard teaching had worked in terms of speed and accuracy of word reading. Children read the flashcard-trained words (from one passage) faster than the untrained words (from the other passage), and with fewer errors. But there was no improvement in reading comprehension for the trained-words passage over the untrained-words control passage. This was a blow to the bottleneck hypothesis, which would have predicted a comprehension advantage for children who had been taught to read words faster.

The results of Fleisher and colleagues (1979) have been questioned by Blanchard and McNinch (1980) and Holt-Ochsner and Manis (1992). Yet similar inconclusive results have been reported by other researchers who have used single-word flashcard training (Perfetti, 1985; Samuels, Dahl, & Archwamety, 1974; Van den Bosch, Van Bon, & Schreuder, 1995; Yuill & Oakhill, 1988).

The failure of these training studies has caused some textbook writers to reach despondent conclusions about whether training children to read words faster can improve their comprehension. Rayner and Pollatsek (1989) state that "merely training a child to say words quickly will not necessarily result in improved comprehension" (p. 391). A similar conclusion was reached by Just and Carpenter (1987), who noted that "efficient word recognition is not sufficient for good reading. A number of training studies that improved the word recognition speed of poor readers did not find commensurate increases in their reading level" (pp. 458–459). However, we have replicated the study of Fleisher and colleagues (1979) and found support for the bottleneck hypothesis. The first replication used a very small sample of three Asian adults learning English as a second language (Tan, Moore, Dixon, & Nicholson, 1994). In a second replication, with a larger and younger sample, we again found support for the bottleneck hypothesis. We think this latter study was important, so we will describe it in some detail (Tan & Nicholson, 1997).

Method

Participants and the Research Design. We selected 42 poor readers whose ages ranged from 7 to 10 years. Our screening tests showed that these children scored poorly in word identification and in reading comprehension. We matched the children in triplets, according to age levels. Each child in each triplet had approximately the same reading ability level. This procedure gave us a total of 14 sets of triplets. Each child in each triplet was given a different training procedure. Training sessions lasted 20 minutes. Each child was trained individually. Each session focused on words from a single story. There were five sessions for each child, covering five different stories.

Materials. Since there was a range of reading ability within each training group, we used 25 different stories, some from the *New Zealand School Journal* and others from three different commercial programs: Literacy 2000, Literacy Links, and Jelly Bean Books. The stories were of different lengths, according to the reading difficulty level of each story. Children were given stories that were no more than 1 year above their own reading age. The shortest stories were 200 to 300 words; the longest were 350 to 450 words. Although we used many stories, the matched triplets in each of the three training conditions all received the same stories. There were no cases where children in one training condition read stories different from those of their matched partners in the other training conditions.

Word Lists. The lists of training words varied in number. The rule was to select about 8% of words of the story. The words chosen were those likely to present identification difficulties. Lists varied in number, so that a 200-word story would have a list of 15 training words, while a 300-word story would have a list of 25 words.

Assessment Measures. Comprehension of the stories was assessed with comprehension questions (8 factual and 4 inferential). The factual questions were explicit, in that answers to these questions were explicitly stated in the stories. The inferential questions were implicit, in that answers to these questions were implied in the text and required inferences on the part of the child, which meant combining information from the stories with the child's prior knowledge (Pearson & Johnson, 1978; Nicholson, 1982; Raphael & Wonnacott, 1985). These types of questions, and how they can be distinguished from each other, are discussed in Chapter 6.

The comprehension questions were open-ended in that children gave their own answers. The questions were also designed so that children could not guess the answers from general knowledge. We asked the questions orally and recorded each child's answers. In addition, after answering the questions, children were asked to retell the story in their own words. Another point about the questions is that they were not deliberately tagged to the training words. The preparation of the questions was done independently of the training words, though sometimes the answers to the questions did include training words.

Training Procedures. The training was different for each of the three matched groups. The first training condition received flashcard training with single words. The meanings of the flashcard words were explained. If the child did not know what a word meant, he or she was shown the word in a two-word phrase on the back of the card and the meaning was explained. Once it was clear that the meaning of the trained words were understood, all further training involved just the single-word flashcards. The flashcards were presented one at a time, and the child had to say the word as quickly as possible. The presentation of the flashcards continued until the time ran out (20 minutes) or until the child could say the word on each card in less than 1 second. The aim was to achieve a speed of about 90 words per minute. For example, 15 flashcard words read in 10 seconds is equivalent to 90 words per minute. At the end of the training session, the child was given a list of the trained words in scrambled order. The child had to read the list as fast as possible. Reading errors were recorded. A stopwatch was used to record times. Not all children achieved the 90-words-per-minute criterion, but they read the words as fast as was possible for them, given the 20 minutes of training allowed.

After the word list, each child was given the story from which the trained words had come and was asked to read it aloud. We recorded the time it took to read the story and the number of reading errors that were made. Then the child answered our 12 comprehension questions and retold the story in his or her own words. We recorded all responses to the questions as well as the retellings.

In the phrase condition, children were trained in the same way except that the flashcards were long strips of paper that had phrases and sometimes sentences on them containing the target words. We thought that the extra phrase and sentence contexts might enable the children to learn to read the target words more efficiently. For example, the target word *lemonade* was taught as part of a long phrase on the flashcard, *A cool lemonade drink*. The word *raspberry* was taught in a sentence, *I like raspberry jam on bread*. At the end of the 20-minute training session, each child was given a word list containing the key words. Then the child read the story aloud, answered comprehension questions, and retold the story.

In the control condition, the children did not see the trained words. There were no flashcards. But each word was orally explained and discussed with the child during the 20-minute session. For example, the child was asked. "What does the word *lemonade* mean to you? Can you say it in a sentence? If you can't, I'll say it in a sentence and you tell me what it means in my sentence." This was done for each word on the list. At the end of the session, the child was shown (for the first time) the written words on a list. The child read the words aloud, then read the story aloud, answered comprehension questions, and retold the story. The children in the control condition therefore discussed the same words, for the same amount of time, and with the same help with meaning as occurred for children in the other conditions. The only difference was that they did not see the words and did not receive the flashcard training.

At the end of each of the five training sessions, children were given a questionnaire that had a Likert Attitude Scale format. There were questions such as "Did you like the lesson?" and "Would you like to come to another lesson?" Alongside each question there were five pictures of a dog, with the dog's expression ranging from very happy to very sad. The children would circle the picture of the dog that matched their feelings. They would then take the questionnaire back to class to show their teachers. This was done in order to check that the children were not becoming bored with the flashcard training.

Analysis of Data. The marking of the comprehension questions was done in a strict way (i.e., the answer had to be exactly right in terms of the story) and in a lenient way (i.e., the answer could be reasonably close). For example, in one story called *When the Moon Was Blue*, where there were a lot of imaginary events, children were asked the question, "What was the hat made of?" A strictly correct answer was "orange peel" (which was mentioned in the story) but a leniently correct answer would be "banana skin," which was plausible, since a banana is also a fruit. The retelling of the story was scored in terms of idea units. The child could get up to 4 points for mentioning each main idea in the story. The child could get up to 4 more points for mentioning details from the story (e.g., 1 point for one detail; 4 points for six details).

Results

How effective, then, was the flashcard training? The training did not show any effect for speed of reading of the stories. This result seemed odd at first, since we had trained target words from the stories. But it is understandable if we take into account that only 8% of the words were trained.

The effects of the training would have been canceled out by the large number of untrained words in each story. When it came to speed of reading the words in lists, the effects of the training were more obvious. The children who were trained with single-word flashcards and with phrase flashcards were significantly faster than children in the control condition.

What was the effect of the training on accuracy? We found that the children who had received the flashcard training were significantly more accurate than the control children in word-reading accuracy for both the lists and the stories. This was a concern, however, in that possible effects of the training on reading comprehension might be due not so much to speed of reading as to accuracy of reading. We do know that inaccuracy interferes with comprehension (Nicholson, Pearson, & Dykstra, 1979), so it could be argued that the trained children, if they turned out to be better at comprehension, were only better because they made fewer reading errors than the control children.

To deal with this concern, we went back and counted up all the words that the children had read correctly in the lists. We then checked, for each child, to see whether they read correctly in the stories the words that they had read correctly in the lists. Each child in each of the conditions was checked. Since each child had read five stories, we checked all five stories for each child. We then calculated the percentage of words read correctly on the lists that were also read correctly in the stories (e.g., if the child read 10 words correctly on a list, but only read 6 of those words correctly in a story, then he or she got a score of 60%). What we found was that the children who had received flashcard training got higher percentage scores than the control children (single word = 94%, phrase = 95%, control = 83%). This showed that the control children were less accurate in the story than were the flashcard children, even for words that they had read correctly on the lists. This may seem odd, but it is in line with anecdotal reports from teachers that poor readers are erratic. They can read a word correctly on one page but misread it on another (Gough & Hillinger, 1980). This is because they have inefficient word-identification processes. In contrast, the trained children had learned the flashcard words to such an extent that they were able to read the trained words in the story with more accuracy than did the control children. Thus, it seemed that the flashcard training had effects that went beyond accuracy. Even if all three conditions had achieved the same levels of accuracy on the word lists, the control condition would still have been less accurate in the stories because they had not experienced the benefits of overlearning that had come with the flashcard training. This automaticity training was a factor contributing to any possible differences in comprehension among the three conditions.

And there were differences. We found statistically significant differences favoring the flashcard-trained children in terms of correct answers to our comprehension questions, for both the strict and lenient ways of scoring. We also found significant differences favoring the flashcard-trained children on story recall. These were consistent differences, across all five stories. Was there any difference between the single-word training and the phrase training with flashcards? We found only one difference between the single-word condition and the phrase condition. This occurred for inferential comprehension questions (strict scoring only). Apart from this difference, the results for the two kinds of flashcard training were the same. Visual summaries of the comprehension results are shown in Figures 7.1 and 7.2.

Implications of the Study

We have explained our study in quite a bit of detail because we think it makes an important contribution to the automaticity literature. Our results supported the bottleneck hypothesis. Previous literature had shown a relationship between reading words faster and reading comprehension, but the fact that two things are related does not prove that they are causally related. Only training studies can provide that link between cause and effect. Our study was able to establish that link. We found that training poor readers to read faster improved their comprehension of stories. Our findings, however, were different from those of previous researchers, especially Fleisher and colleagues (1979). In their study, like ours, the trained poor readers were both quicker and more accurate than the untrained poor readers, yet in their study the trained children were no better in comprehension than the control children.

Why did we find training effects when Fleisher and colleagues did not? It may be that the children in our study responded better to the training. Our children were from a school that adhered to a very strong whole-language philosophy. When we proposed using flashcards to the school, they were very concerned that the flashcard training, especially the single-word flashcards, would undermine what they were trying to achieve, which was that their children read in context and read for meaning. In the whole-language approach, children do not receive explicit phonics instruction. Instead, attention to letter and word detail is minimized. Children make use of context and picture clues so as to reduce the need to analyze words on a letter-by-letter basis. The poor readers in our study may therefore have differed from children in previous studies, which had been carried out in the United States and England. In these other studies, children may have received regular school instruction in which they were exposed to phonics instruction and word drills. As a result, the flashcard

Figure 7.1 Accuracy Scores on Reading Comprehension Questions for
Passages of Successive Sessions in the Two Training Groups and the
Control Group

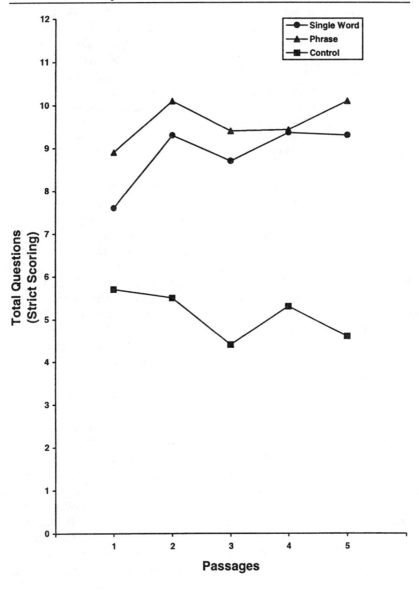

Figure 7.2 Accuracy Scores for Recall of the Passages of Successive Sessions by the Two Training Groups and the Control Group

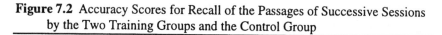

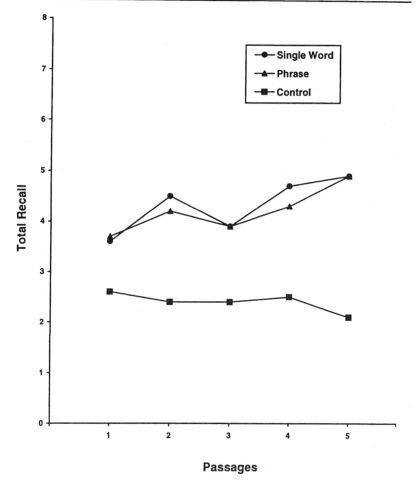

training may have seemed less interesting. The positive results of our "puppy-dog" attitude questionnaire suggest that the children in our study may have been more positive toward flashcard training because it was new and different from their regular instruction. This new flashcard instruction, which focused on context-free word identification, when added to their previous experiences of reading for meaning, may have made the effects of our training more pronounced for the children in our study than it was for children in other studies.

Another possible difference between our study and previous studies was that the difficulty levels of the stories were only a year above the children's reading ages, whereas in the study of Fleisher and colleagues, for example, the material was 3 years above the reading ages of their poor readers. This may have given our children an advantage in that the stories were easier to comprehend.

Another explanation is that in our study we ensured that the meanings of the trained words were well understood by all the children. That way, we knew that they would understand the words that they recognized. Even the control children were given an explanation of the meanings of the words. As a result, the trained children, when they read the stories, were reading for meaning. They were not "radic readers" who were saying the words without necessarily comprehending what they meant. In previous studies, children may have been able to read words faster but may not have understood all their meanings. This may have offset the advantages gained by the flashcard training. Our combination of reading words faster and understanding what the words meant may have accounted for the trained children's improved comprehension compared with the control children. The combination was important. All children in the study, including the control children, were helped with the meanings of the target words. But the children who received the instruction in word meaning *and* the flashcard training achieved higher comprehension than did the control children, who only received instruction in word meanings.

CONCLUSIONS

Our findings were in line with the concept of overlearning that was described in Bloom's (1986) report on top performers in sports and music. The overlearning we provided enabled the poor readers in our study to read and comprehend more effectively the specific stories we gave them. The training did not turn the children into good readers. But it did illustrate the added value that comes from being able to read words quickly.

What else is needed to turn poor readers into good readers? Flashcard training may help, but there are problems with an overreliance on flashcards. McCullough (1955) has reported that children remember flashcards by using extraneous clues. Harris (1970) gives some examples: "The card with the dirty thumb mark on it is *baby*. I always know it by that else I'd swear it was *lady*. *Saw* is the one with the corner cut off" (p. 317). Gough (1993) has reported a study of kindergarten children which found that this reliance on extraneous cues did indeed happen.

Flashcards will not be useful if children lack word-identification skills. But if beginning or poor readers are initially given instruction in phonemic awareness and letter-sound rules, so that they have a foundation of word-identification skills (Castle, Riach, & Nicholson, 1994; Nicholson, 1997a), then flashcards may provide supplementary opportunities for children to practice and overlearn their emerging word-identification skills. Flashcards can also be valuable in firming up children's ability to recognize quickly those words that are irregular in spelling but highly frequent in stories (e.g., words such as *after, because, come, one, put, there, would*). Other teaching procedures, such as repeated reading (Rashotte & Torgesen, 1985; Samuels, 1979), can also give opportunities to increase fluency and speed (though see Gibbs & Nicholson [1998] for an unsuccessful use of the repeated reading method with beginning readers). As poor readers get faster at reading words, this will encourage them to read more, and this in turn will give them the practice they need to read words quickly. The instructional ideal is to get poor readers to the point where they do not need flashcard training and can improve their word-identification skills simply by reading (Stanovich, 1986).

Another practical approach is the use of new computer technology, which can give more interesting word practice than is provided by flashcards. A number of researchers have reported improvements in children's word-identification abilities by making use of computer technology (e.g., Rashotte & Torgesen, 1985; Van der Leij & Van Daal, 1989).

If computer technology is unavailable, there may still be merit in using flashcards to improve speed of word identification. Try using a "first dictionary card" (Butterflies, 1993), or something similar, which has lists of high-frequency words arranged in alphabetical order. A dictionary card is like a mega-flashcard. You can train the poor reader to identify the high-frequency words on the card without having to use separate flashcards for each word. Spending 10 minutes each day on this word training can be useful without becoming dull. Old basal grade readers are often a good source of stories that use a lot of high-frequency words. These stories give poor readers the opportunity to internalize in memory frequently occurring words through the process of reading them again and again in context. If you are unable to get this type of material, try writing stories yourself, using as many words as possible from the dictionary card (or let the good readers in your classroom write some stories for you).

It is often virtually impossible to find interesting stories that poor readers can read fluently. Yet by using flashcards as a kind of scaffolding technique, poor readers are able to read stories that they could not cope with otherwise. A short session of flashcard training (say, 20 minutes), with 15 to 20 difficult words from the story, can set up the poor reader for a positive reading experience. The flashcard training can be even more enjoyable if children are given the flashcards so that they can train themselves. As the self-training proceeds, they put the easy cards to one side, and then revise the harder cards until they are easily identified. Be sure to make yourself available to help children with words they do not recognize. Another technique, during the training session, is to ask the child to guess what the story will be about, just from the flashcards. Children are usually unable to guess the story; however, it is a good way of discussing the words while they are being trained. And children can come up with some very funny predictions of what the story will be about. After the training, they read the story and answer some comprehension questions for you. It is surprising how this simple technique can make a difficult-to-decode story more accessible to the poor reader (Nicholson, in press).

Flashcard and repeated reading activities may be a useful addition to regular reading instruction. They are an extra and should not be a major part of the reading instruction given. If children can read stories on their own, then there is no need for flashcard practice at all, since story reading is practice in itself. If flashcards are used, be aware that children may be relying on inefficient strategies for reading flashcards. If this is happening, then don't use flashcards. Research has shown clearly that the major aim of instruction is to enable children to understand the alphabetic principle, so that they can recognize words accurately and quickly (Nicholson, 1997b; Stanovich, 1986). They should not rely on trivial details for word identification (e.g., the "tail" on the word *dog*) or rely excessively on context clues.

Many children, even after several years of schooling, are unable to read grade-level material with adequate fluency (Pinnell et al., 1995). The research discussed in this chapter is of relevance to this problem. We have presented evidence which suggests that children who are not reading fluently enough to maximize their comprehension may benefit from further instruction in the skills of word identification.

REVIEW

Reading is a multicomponent skill. One important component of reading skill is the ability to read words quickly. Researchers who have compared skilled and unskilled readers have found significantly faster word-identification rates among skilled readers compared with unskilled readers. One theory about this difference is called automaticity theory. It argues that skilled readers have automatized their word-reading skills to the point where these skills require very little in the way of cognitive resources, which leaves them able to apply almost all their cognitive resources to the task of comprehension. A similar concept, verbal efficiency theory, proposes that word-identification skills are highly efficient for the skilled reader. Skilled readers are able to read words in a context-free way, whereas unskilled readers are forced to rely on context clues to compensate for their inefficient word-identification skills. A third theory, modularity theory, proposes that the word-identification skills of the good reader are so efficient that they are a modular system, impenetrable to the influence of other factors, such as context clues. Modular word-identification systems do not require contextual processes and do not use them. All these theories have a common theme, which is that the good reader spends very little mental effort on the task of word identification. This component of reading skill has been overlearned to the point that it is like walking. The reader is able to use word-identification processes without detracting from the cognitive resources needed for comprehension. In this chapter, we have presented a detailed description of a study we carried out which found that practice in reading words quickly, with the use of flashcards, enabled poor readers to improve their comprehension of stories. Our results suggest that such teaching of word-identification skills may have a positive effect on reading comprehension, especially for beginning and poor readers.

STUDY AND DISCUSSION QUESTIONS

1. What evidence is there that being able to read words quickly gives skilled readers an advantage in reading comprehension?
2. What is meant by the term *automaticity*?
3. Can you give an example of the role of automaticity in the success of Olympic athletes?
4. How does automaticity apply to reading?
5. Can you explain the following theoretical terms?
   (a) Automaticity theory
   (b) The "bottleneck hypothesis"
   (c) Verbal efficiency theory
   (d) Modularity theory
6. What is the evidence to show there is a cause-effect relationship between reading words faster and reading comprehension?
7. Is there a role for using flashcards (or something similar) as a supplement to the regular reading program?

FURTHER READING

Bloom, B. S. (1986). Automaticity. *Educational Leadership, 43*, 70–77.
Gough, P. B. (1993). The beginning of decoding. *Reading and Writing, 5*, 181–192.
Nicholson, T. (1994). *At the cutting edge*. Wellington, New Zealand: New Zealand Council for Educational Research.

Nicholson, T. (1997). *Solving reading problems across the curriculum.* Wellington, New Zealand: New Zealand Council for Educational Research.

Perfetti, C. A. (1977). Language comprehension and fast decoding: Some psycholinguistic prerequisites for skilled reading comprehension. In J. T. Guthrie (Ed.), *Cognition, curriculum and comprehension* (pp. 20–41). Newark, DE: International Reading Association.

Samuels, S. J. (1994). Toward a theory of automatic information processing in reading, revisited. In R. B. Ruddell, M. R. Ruddell, & H. Singer (Eds.), *Theoretical models and processes of reading* (pp. 816–837). Newark, DE: International Reading Association.

Tan, A., & Nicholson, T. (1997). Flashcards revisited: Training poor readers to read words faster improves their comprehension of text. *Journal of Educational Psychology, 89,* 276–288.

REFERENCES

Blanchard, J. S., & McNinch, G. H. (1980). Testing the decoding sufficiency hypothesis: A response to Fleisher, Jenkins and Pany. *Reading Research Quarterly, 15,* 559–564.

Bloom, B. S. (1986). Automaticity. *Educational Leadership, 43,* 70–77.

Butterflies. (1993). *First dictionary card.* Auckland, New Zealand: Author.

Calfee, R. C., & Patrick, C. L. (1995). *Teach our children well.* Stanford, CA: Stanford Alumni Press.

Carver, R. P. (1990). *Reading rate: A review of research and theory.* San Diego, CA: Academic Press.

Castle, J. M., Riach, J., & Nicholson, T. (1994). Getting off to a better start in reading and spelling: The effects of phonemic awareness instruction within a whole language program. *Journal of Educational Psychology, 86,* 350–359.

Felton, R. H., & Wood, F. B. (1992). A reading level match study of nonword reading skills in poor readers with varying IQ. *Journal of Learning Disabilities, 25,* 318–326.

Fleisher, L. S., Jenkins, J. R., & Pany, D. (1979). Effects on poor readers' comprehension of training in rapid decoding. *Reading Research Quarterly, 15,* 30–48.

Gibbs, C. J., & Nicholson, T. (1998). *When you've heard it all before and still can't read.* Unpublished manuscript, Massey University, New Zealand.

Gough, P. B. (1983). Context, form, and interaction. In K. Rayner (Ed.), *Eye movements in reading* (pp. 203–211). New York: Academic Press.

Gough, P. B. (1993). The beginning of decoding. *Reading and Writing, 5,* 181–192.

Gough, P. B., & Hillinger, M. L. (1980). Learning to read: An unnatural act. *Bulletin of the Orton Society, 30,* 179–196.

Gough, P. B., & Tunmer, W. E. (1986). Decoding, reading and reading disability. *Remedial and Special Education, 7,* 6–10.

Harris, A. J. (1970). *How to increase reading ability.* New York: McKay.

Holt-Ochsner, L. K., & Manis, F. R. (1992). Automaticity training for dyslexics: An experimental study. *Annals of Dyslexia, 42,* 222–241.

Huey, E. B. (1968). *The psychology and pedagogy of reading.* Cambridge, MA: MIT Press. (Original work published 1908)

Jensen, A. R., & Rohwer, W. D. (1966). The Stroop word-color test: A review. *Acta Psychologica, 60,* 157–171.

Johnson, D. D., & Pearson, P. D. (1984). *Teaching reading vocabulary* (2nd ed.). Orlando, FL: Holt, Rinehart & Winston.

Juel, C. (1988). Learning to read and write: A longitudinal study of 54 children from first through fourth grades. *Journal of Educational Psychology, 80,* 437–447.

Juel, C. (1991). Beginning reading. In R. Barr, M. L. Kamil, P. B. Mosenthal, & P. D. Pearson (Eds.), *Handbook of reading research* (Vol. 2; pp. 759–788). White Plains, NY: Longman.

Juel, C. (1994). *Learning to read and write in one elementary school.* New York: Springer-Verlag.

Juel, C., Griffith, P. L., & Gough, P. B. (1986). Acquisition of literacy: A longitudinal study of children in first and second grade. *Journal of Educational Psychology, 78,* 243–255.

Just, M. A., & Carpenter, P. A. (1987). *The psychology of reading and language comprehension.* Newton, MA: Allyn & Bacon.

LaBerge, D., & Samuels, S. J. (1974). Toward a theory of automatic information processing in reading. *Cognitive Psychology, 6,* 293–323.

McCullough, C. (1955). Flash cards—The opiate of the reading program? *Elementary English, 32,* 379–381.

Nicholson, T. (1982). *An anatomy of reading.* Sydney: Horwitz-Grahame.

Nicholson, T. (1991). Do children read words better in context or in lists? A classic study revisited. *Journal of Educational Psychology, 83,* 444–450.

Nicholson, T. (1993). The case against context. In G. B. Thompson, W. E. Tunmer, & T. Nicholson (Eds.), *Reading acquisition processes* (pp. 91–104). Clevedon, UK: Multilingual Matters.

Nicholson, T. (1994). *At the cutting edge.* Wellington, New Zealand: New Zealand Council for Educational Research.

Nicholson, T. (1997a). Closing the gap on reading failure: Social background, phonemic awareness and learning to read. In B. A. Blachman (Ed.), *Foundations of reading acquisition and dyslexia: Implications for early intervention* (pp. 381–407). Mahwah, NJ: Erlbaum.

Nicholson, T. (1997b). *Solving reading problems across the curriculum.* Wellington, New Zealand: New Zealand Council for Educational Research.

Nicholson, T. (in press). The flashcard strikes back. *The Reading Teacher.*

Nicholson, T., Bailey, J., & McArthur, J. (1991). Context cues in reading: The gap between research and popular opinion. *Journal of Reading, Writing and Learning Disabilities, 7,* 33–41.

Nicholson, T., & Hill, D. (1985). Good readers don't guess—Taking another look at the issue of whether children read words better in context or isolation. *Reading Psychology, 6,* 181–198.

Nicholson, T., Lillas, C., & Rzoska, M. A. (1988). Have we been misled by miscues? *The Reading Teacher, 42,* 6–10.

Nicholson, T., Pearson, P. D., & Dykstra, R. (1979). Effects of embedded anomalies and oral reading errors on children's understanding of stories. *Journal of Reading Behavior, 11,* 339–354.

Pearson, P. D., & Johnson, D. D. (1978). *Teaching reading comprehension.* New York: Holt, Rinehart & Winston.

Perfetti, C. A. (1985). *Reading ability.* New York: Oxford University Press.

Perfetti, C. A., & Hogaboam, T. (1975). The relationship between single word decoding and reading comprehension skill. *Journal of Educational Psychology, 67,* 461–469.

Perfetti, C. A., & Lesgold, A. M. (1977). Coding and comprehension in skilled reading and implications for reading instruction. In L. B. Resnick & P. A. Weaver (Eds.), *Theory and practice of early reading* (Vol. 1.; pp. 57–84). Hillsdale, NJ: Erlbaum.

Pinker, S. (1994). *The language instinct.* New York: Morrow.

Pinnell, G. S., Pikulski, J. J., Wixson, K. K., Campbell, J. R., Gough, P. B., & Beatty, A. S. (1995). *Listening to children read aloud: Data from NAEP's integrated reading performance record (IRPR) at grade 4.* Washington, DC: National Center for Education Statistics.

Raphael, T. E., & Wonnacott, C. A. (1985). Heightening fourth-grade students' sensitivity to sources of information for answering comprehension questions. *Reading Research Quarterly, 20,* 282–296.

Rashotte, C. A., & Torgesen, J. K. (1985). Repeated reading and reading fluency in learning disabled children. *Reading Research Quarterly, 20,* 180–188.

Rayner, K., & Pollatsek, A. (1989). *The psychology of reading.* Englewood Cliffs, NJ: Prentice-Hall.

Samuels, S. J. (1976). Automatic decoding and reading comprehension. *Language Arts, 53,* 323–325.

Samuels, S. J. (1979). The method of repeated readings. *The Reading Teacher, 32,* 403–408.

Samuels, S. J. (1994). Toward a theory of automatic information processing in reading, revisited. In R. B. Ruddell, M. R. Ruddell, & H. Singer (Eds.), *Theoretical models and processes of reading* (pp. 816–837). Newark, DE: International Reading Association.

Samuels, S. J., Dahl, P., & Archwamety, T. (1974). Effect of hypothesis/test training on reading skill. *Journal of Educational Psychology, 66,* 835–844.

Stanovich, K. E. (1986). Matthew effects in reading: Some consequences of individual differences in the acquisition of literacy. *Reading Research Quarterly, 21,* 360–406.

Stanovich, K. E. (1990). Concepts in developmental theories of reading skill: Cognitive resources, automaticity, and modularity. *Developmental Review, 10,* 72–100.

Tan, A., Moore, D. W., Dixon, R. S., & Nicholson, T. (1994). Effects of training in rapid decoding on the reading comprehension of adult ESL learners. *Journal of Behavioral Education, 4,* 177–189.

Tan, A., & Nicholson, T. (1997). Flashcards revisited: Training poor readers to read words faster improves their comprehension of text. *Journal of Educational Psychology, 89,* 276–288.

Underwood, G., & Batt, V. (1996). *Reading and understanding*. London: Blackwell.

Van den Bosch, K., Van Bon, W. H., & Schreuder, R. (1995). Poor readers' decoding skills: Effects of training with limited exposure duration. *Reading Research Quarterly, 30*, 110–125.

Van der Leij, A., & Van Daal, V. H. (1989). Repeated reading and severe reading disability. In H. Mandl, E. DeCorte, N. Bennett, & H. F. Friedrich (Eds.), *Learning and instruction* (pp. 235–251). Oxford: Pergamon.

Yuill, N., & Oakhill, J. (1988). Effects of inference awareness training on poor reading comprehension. *Applied Cognitive Psychology, 2*, 33–45.

Chapter 8

Learning About Text Structure

SUSAN J. DYMOCK

a) What is text structure?

b) What does research have to say about children's understanding of text structure?

c) Can children's awareness of text structure enhance their reading comprehension?

d) How can children be taught about text structure?

By the time most pupils have entered high school, they have encountered a multitude of different texts. The ability to comprehend such texts depends on many variables, including decoding ability, language comprehension, background knowledge, and knowledge of text structures. While the above variables all play a part in comprehension, it is the structure of text that this chapter will focus on. Good writers structure their ideas in patterns in order to compose well-organized discourse. Good readers know these structures and are able to use them to comprehend more effectively.

According to Meyer and Rice (1984), text structure refers to the way in which "the ideas of a text are interrelated to convey a message to the reader" (p. 319). Text structure relates to the order of sentences, paragraphs, and the passage as a whole, whether it be a short article, a novel, or a chapter in a science textbook. How the text is structured plays an important role in comprehension (Meyer, Brandt, & Bluth, 1980; Taylor, 1980).

Text is usually defined as a "coherent written message" (Calfee & Drum, 1986, p. 835). *Cohere* means "to stick together," so textual coherence is an important characteristic for comprehension. The extent to which a text is coherent depends on its structure. As Calfee (1984) puts it, "structure is the key to comprehension—to comprehend a passage is to create a mental structure" (p. 82).

To comprehend better, the reader should be able to recognize the particular structure of the passage being read. With this knowledge, the reader can construct a more detailed and memorable representation of the text. Some readers intuitively acquire text-structure knowledge through continual exposure to different text structures. However, many readers are not so lucky. It is up to the classroom teacher to inform not-so-lucky students about different text structures and how to look for these structures as they read.

As Calfee (1984) explains, "Learning to use a microscope can be a frustrating experience. In order to see what you are looking for, you have to know what is there" (p. 87). If pupils know what to look for when peering through the microscope (e.g., knowing about the structure of cells through the use of diagrams), they will have a better chance of recognizing what they are looking at. Likewise, pupils can read a multitude of different text types and not comprehend them very well because they are unaware of their various structures. However, if they have an understanding of different text types, they will know what to look for in order to create a better mental representation of the meaning of the text.

Not all texts are well structured (see Armbruster, 1984). By assisting students to understand text structures, teachers can indirectly help them to recognize poorly written material, or what Armbruster (1984) has labeled "inconsiderate text." The reader needs to develop strategies for mentally reorganizing a poorly constructed text into a coherent structure.

Research on the structural characteristics of text (Meyer, 1975) suggests that there are three levels at which text can be analyzed. The first level is the microproposition level (sometimes referred to as the microstructure). At this lowest level of text structure, the focus is on interrelationships among sentences, how sentences cohere, and how sentences are organized within a text. Each new item of information, whether it is a part of a sentence or whole sentence, refers to what has preceded it. At this level, the structure is a highly detailed representation of the text.

The second level is the macroproposition level (sometimes referred to as macrostructure). Here the concern is with main ideas, represented by larger portions of text, such as paragraphs. Macropropositions represent the global meaning, or "gist," of the text (see Meyer & Rice, 1984). At the macropropositional level, the concern is with the essential points of a passage.

The third, or top-level structure (sometimes referred to as a schematic superstructure), refers to the overall organizing principles of the text. Macropropositions are found within the top-level structure. Top-level structures are like an architect's drawings and are the designs into which text content will fit. These designs will differ according to the content material (e.g., research reports, narratives, descriptive texts, argument texts). For example, a writer may use a sequence-design in writing an expository text about the life cycle of the monarch butterfly. This sequence-design is a top-level superstructure that the writer follows in writing the text. The text will start with the laying of an egg on a milkweed leaf, then the hatching of the caterpillar, and so on. A very interesting feature of top-level designs is that they may not be transparent to the novice reader, just as an architect's drawings of a house may not be transparent to nonexperts when they view the completed house.

The concern of this chapter is with this top level of text structure. We will be looking at different structural designs for texts in order to see how macrostructure information fits into these designs.

NARRATIVE TEXT

Narratives are stories. Stories are often written to entertain and excite. A story usually has a beginning, middle, and end. Narratives can easily be identified because they usually contain a setting, characters, plot, and theme. However, even though most children upon entering school have a general understanding of how stories are built, they lack a detailed, analytic understanding of the structure of narrative text (Calfee, 1984).

Modern research on the structure of simple narrative text and memory for such text began with work on story grammars. Rumelhart (1975) provided one of the first story grammars that could be applied to a wide range of story types as a model for story comprehension. Story grammars comprise rules that are used to produce a structure for any story. The rules outline relationships among the components of the text. It is this organization (or macrostructure) that creates a well-formed story rather than a sequence of unrelated sentences.

Thorndyke (1977), like Rumelhart, used a set of story-grammar rules for generating simple narratives. These rules describe the top-level structure of a story. Thorndyke (1977) stated that narratives have their own internal structure, which consists of four main components. The components include setting, theme, plot, and resolution. Each component can be expanded to give a total of 10 categories of rules. A story can thus be rewritten using the set of rules shown in Figure 8.1 (based on Thorndyke, 1977, p. 79).

These rewrite rules form a hierarchical structure, or "tree." At the top of the hierarchy is the setting, overall theme, plot, and resolution (Rule 1). Subplots are located lower down in the hierarchy. As you read a story, you attempt to fill in the slots, beginning with setting, theme, plot, and resolution and working down the hierarchy. The slots contain macro- and microstructure information. Memory for the story will depend on where

Figure 8.1 Example of Story-Grammar Rules (Based on Thorndyke, 1977)

1. STORY → SETTING + THEME + PLOT + RESOLUTION
2. SETTING → CHARACTERS + LOCATION + TIME
3. THEME → (EVENT)* + GOAL
4. PLOT → EPISODE*
5. EPISODE → SUBGOAL + ATTEMPT* + OUTCOME
6. ATTEMPT → EVENT* or EPISODE
7. OUTCOME → EVENT* or STATE
8. RESOLUTION → FINAL EVENT or STATE
9. SUBGOAL/GOAL → DESIRED STATE
10. CHARACTERS/LOCATION/TIME → STATE

Note: Each arrow means the item on the left consists of the structural elements on the right. The symbol "+" shows the combination of elements in sequential order. The asterisk (*) means the element may be repeated. The parentheses around "event" mean this element is optional.

each sentence is located in the hierarchy. The higher the sentence is in the hierarchy, the more likely it will be recalled. Thorndyke found that stories with complex hierarchies were not recalled as well as stories with clear, easily defined hierarchies.

While much research has focused on the structure of narrative text, the structure of expository text has also drawn considerable attention.

EXPOSITORY TEXT

Expository text is designed to interpret, explain, or appraise. Magazine articles, encyclopedias, and science textbooks are examples of expository texts. A dictionary definition of expository text is "a setting forth of meaning" (American Heritage, 1969), where the author's purpose is to inform rather than entertain. Calfee, Henry, and Funderburg (1988) state: "The passage is expository if it describes an event, person, or thing, presents a logical time sequence for a factual event, or gives a logical set of directions or steps, and makes an argument or attempts to persuade" (p. 132).

Meyer (1975) and others (e.g., Frederiksen, 1975; Kintsch, 1974) suggest that expository texts, like stories, also have structure. The most common structural patterns include cause-effect, compare-contrast, time-order relations (chronology), simple listing, and problem-solution.

A cause-effect text structure is common in science, social studies, and English textbooks. Here, one or more ideas or events are causal, while others are effects or results. For example, a history text may cover the causes and effects of revolutions (e.g., the Russian Revolution of 1917).

A compare-contrast structure shows similarities and differences between two or more things. This structure is often found in English, health, and science textbooks. For example, in science comparisons can be made between black bears, brown bears, and polar bears in terms of size, color, habitats, and so on.

A time-order structure is common in history books, where a chronological description of events is given (e.g., events leading up to the war in Bosnia). This organizational pattern is structured in a sequence over a passage of time. Or it could refer to a sequence to follow in working out a mathematics problem; or in science, a sequence for dissecting a frog.

A simple listing structure is not affected by time, as in a time-order structure, and can be found in mathematics, health, science, and social studies textbooks. Simple listing is like a shopping list. For example, in mathematics textbooks, the various attributes of logarithms may be listed. Or in science, the attributes of penguins may be listed (e.g., black and white, eat fish, can't fly, etc.).

Finally, a problem-solution organizational structure is similar to a cause-effect structure, where two factors are related. However, in this text structure a problem is stated and then a solution to that problem is given. While this structure is found in several types of textbooks, it is common in science and health textbooks. For example, a serious problem related to inadequate diet in school-age children is poor concentration, lethargy, and lack of motivation. A possible solution is for schools to provide breakfast and lunch.

These five structures are top-level structures. As discussed earlier, top-level structures are like architectural designs for a text. Using these designs, writers convey their ideas in a way that is coherent and thus make texts more easily understood.

CHILDREN'S UNDERSTANDING OF NARRATIVE TEXT

Research suggests that comprehension and recall of narrative text will be reduced if authors do not structure their stories to well-known patterns. Thorndyke (1977) found that recall of narrative text was poor if the theme or goal was moved to the end of the story, if the theme was removed altogether, or if sentences were randomly ordered.

Kintsch, Mandel, and Kozminsky (1977) had university students read well-structured stories and stories with little structure in which the paragraphs had been scrambled. Students were divided into two groups: one group read both types of stories with no time restriction; the other group had time restrictions imposed. Subjects then summarized the passages they read. Subjects in the no-time-limit condition took longer to read scrambled text, but there was no difference in writing time or quality of summaries between the well-structured stories and the scrambled stories. When a time limit was imposed, students produced better summaries of well-structured stories than of scrambled stories. This research suggests that stories are easier to understand if they follow a particular pattern and that if they don't, comprehension and recall will be diminished.

Mandler and Johnson (1977) compared children's and adults' ability to recall story details. Six-year-olds, 10-year-olds, and adults listened to and recalled two stories. Results showed that adults recalled more than 10-year-olds, and 10-year-olds recalled more than 6-year-olds. The researchers found that the children in their study were sensitive to the structure of narrative text but that children and adults differed in what parts of the story they recalled. For example, children recalled setting, beginning, and outcome but, unlike adults, failed to recall how the outcome was achieved.

The results of these studies support the story-grammar construct, suggesting that text comprehension involves readers matching their knowledge of story-grammar structure to the passage they are reading. If the text is well structured, in terms of story grammar, comprehension is better than if the text is poorly structured. These results also suggest that while children are sensitive to the structure of narrative text, their understanding or memory capacity may not be sufficient to recall all components of the story grammar (e.g., how characters reacted, what they did, how the story ended).

CHILDREN'S UNDERSTANDING OF EXPOSITORY TEXT

As pupils approach the end of elementary school, most of the school text material they encounter is expository. Content-area reading is at times technical, the topic is unfamiliar, vocabulary is new, and text structure takes on a new form. It is not surprising, then, that pupils encounter, at about age 10, what Chall (1983) calls "the fourth-grade slump" in reading comprehension.

Chall (1983) states that during the initial stages of reading, text material is narrative in structure and familiar to the young reader; therefore comprehension is good. As children progress through school, they encounter increasingly complex text material that is expository in structure. It is this more complex expository text structure that causes problems for the older elementary school reader as well as the high school reader. Chall (1983) notes, "Some are able to read the stories in their 'readers,' but not their content textbooks which contain a more extensive vocabulary and concept load and require more background knowledge" (p. 68). Texts at the 9- to 10-year-old level, as Chall (1983) points out, "begin to contain more unfamiliar 'bookish,' abstract words and a higher proportion of long and complex sentences" (p. 21). Such text material also contains many viewpoints, theories, and sets of facts, and if the reader lacks adequate tools for dealing with the increasing complexity of text, then comprehension will be poor. One important tool could be knowledge of text structure.

McGee (1982) asked good and poor 11-year-old students and good 9-year-old students to read and recall two expository passages. She found that good 11-year-old students were more aware of expository text structure and used this knowledge to recall text details. While poor 11-year-old students showed some awareness of text structure, good 9-year-old students did not. She concluded that good older readers had more awareness of text structure then poor or younger readers.

Taylor and Samuels (1983) divided average or better 10- and 11-year-old readers into two groups based on their awareness of expository text structure. Pupils were identified as aware of text structure if their written recalls followed the text structure of the passage. The two groups were then compared on their ability to recall normal and scrambled passages. Results showed that pupils who were aware of text structure were able to recall normal (or well-structured) passages significantly better than scrambled passages. This result suggests that good readers made use of text structure to organize the ideas in the text and were later able to recall this structure to assist in comprehension. However, for pupils who were unaware of text structure, recall of passage details was no better for normal passages than for scrambled passages. This result suggests that the unaware students were not using text-structure awareness to assist with comprehension. Results also showed that there was no significant difference between the two groups for recall on three of the four scrambled passages. This suggests that the aware pupils were able to use text structure to help recall rather than rely on superior memory.

These results of McGee (1982) and Taylor and Samuels (1983) have implications for teaching. Many students are not familiar with the structure of expository text. Training in how to recognize and use these structures should improve comprehension and recall. As Englert and Hiebert (1984) put it, "knowledge of discourse types underlies effective expository comprehension" (p. 65).

As mentioned earlier, knowledge about how narrative and expository text is structured will not guarantee comprehension, but having a clear understanding of how the text is structured may help the reader to build a coherent model of the text. Teaching children how to identify these structures, therefore, may improve their overall comprehension of text material. In this next section, we will discuss practical ideas on how to teach text structure.

TEACHING ABOUT TEXT STRUCTURE

Teaching students about text structure involves teaching them to think metacognitively. Metacognition (Tunmer & Bowey, 1984) refers to the ability to think about your own cognitive processes. There are various kinds of metacognition (see Chapter 6). Metamemory is knowing how well, or how badly, your memory works; metalearning is knowing what strategies help you to learn better; and metalanguage is knowing about the structure of your language. One metalanguage skill involves pragmatic awareness, which is knowing about discourse structure, whether it is coherent or not and appropriate to the purpose.

Calfee (1981) states that metacognitive strategies enable pupils to remember better by helping them to organize information more efficiently. Humans are capable of remembering a great deal. However, they find it difficult to think about many different things at any one time. Because of the human mind's limited capacity, information that is to be stored in long-term memory must be well organized. And this is where metacognitive strategies, such as knowledge of text structure, are useful.

Teaching About Narrative Text

Pupils can be taught that well-formed stories follow a pattern. Young readers easily understand that stories include characters, setting, and plot. The *characters* in a story can be divided into major and minor characters. Pupils can be taught to analyze individual characters, focusing on their appearance and personality and how their individual traits influence the story as a whole. Different characters in the story can also be compared and contrasted.

The *setting* establishes where and when the story takes place. For example, is the story set in Poland during World War II, in a modern industrialized city, or in a remote village in South America? Awareness of settings can help the reader get a feel for the situation. The *plot* (or story plan) includes a sequence of episodes that occur over a period of time, involving the characters in resolving an overall problem. Each episode is a sub-plot that includes its own problem, response action, and outcome. Some simple stories have as few as three episodes, while others have far more. To understand the story plan, readers, like scientists using the microscope, need to have some awareness of what to look for. Calfee (1984) suggests that readers can learn to divide up the episodes of narrative text.

To illustrate the concept of episode analysis, Figure 8.2 shows how a simple story was broken into chunks or episodes by a 10-year-old pupil. The story, *A Lost Shoe and a Broken Window* (Crayford, 1992), has three episodes; an extract from the story is provided in the chapter Appendix. To understand how stories are put together, young readers must be able to analyze episodes. Each episode consists of a *problem*. Characters *respond* to the problem and then do something about the problem (*action*). Finally, the episode ends (*outcome*). Usually as the story develops, episodes become exciting, leading to a high point and final conclusion. *A Lost Shoe and a Broken Window*, however, breaks somewhat from this pattern. It begins on a high note, with a shoe flying through a window.

Figure 8.2 Example of an Episode Analysis from *A Lost Shoe and a Broken Window* (Crayford, 1992)

Episode 1:

Problem: The shoe smashes through the window.
Response: Then they [children] are silent.
Action: They [children] clean up the mess.
Outcome: Gran comes home and the house is clean.

Episode 2:

Problem: She [Gran] realized that the window was smashed.
Response: The kids feel scared.
Action: They run away.
Outcome: Gran had got over being angry.

Episode 3:

Problem: She [Gran] can't find her shoe.
Response: The children feel scared because they know where the shoe was [it was lost].
Action: She [Gran] searched the whole place.
Outcome: Never found the shoe.

Resolution/Conclusion:

[Years later]. The son told Gran what happened to her shoe.

Teaching About Expository Text

Calfee and Curley (1984) analyzed prose structures found in textbooks at the high school level. They found cause-effect, compare-contrast, time-order, and listing to be the most common structures. These rhetorical patterns can be divided into two categories, sequential and descriptive (Calfee, 1984; Calfee & Patrick, 1995). Sequential structures present a series of events that progress over time. Descriptive structures focus on the attributes of something. Figure 8.3 shows three sequence and three descriptive structures. In my experience, the most common expository text structures found in elementary school texts are linear string, topical net, and matrix (after Calfee, 1984). Calfee and Patrick (1995) also refer to linear string as string, topical net as web, and matrix as weave. I will now briefly describe these three text patterns and provide examples from my research.

Sequence Structures. A string or linear string pattern is a common sequential structure. The string is set out in a first-to-last pattern (e.g., events leading up to the Industrial Revolution). Another example is the sequence involved in making bread. The string structure as shown in Figure 8.4 is based on the *School Journal* article "Joab Bakes Bread" (Westra,

Figure 8.3 Six Expository Text Structures (Copyright 1995 by R. C. Calfee and C. L. Patrick, p. 88. Reprinted with permission.)

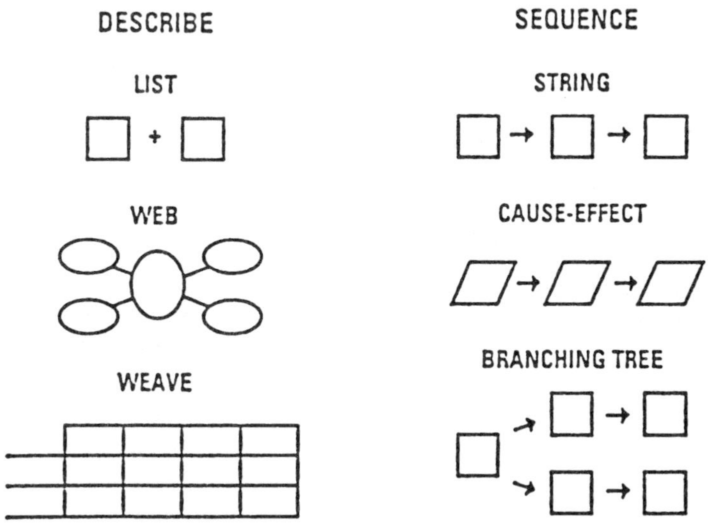

Figure 8.4 A Sequential Structure (Linear String) Based on "Joab Bakes Bread" (Westra, 1988)

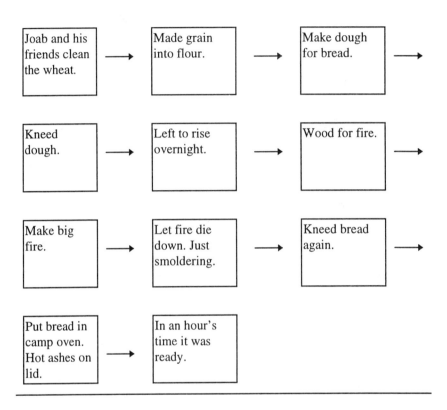

1988). The example was produced by an 8-year-old pupil. An extract from the article is shown in the Appendix to this chapter.

Descriptive Structures. The web or topical net structure is sometimes compared with a spider web. Various aspects of the central topic are discussed in the text. Each aspect is linked to the central topic, like the parts of a spider web. A web pattern is shown in Figure 8.5. It was produced by a 9-year-old and is based on a short article titled "The Brown Rat" (Clements, 1972). An extract from the article can be found in the Appendix. Note that the text talks about features and habits of brown rats: appearance, where they live, food, and so on. The web separates out these various points, so that the structure of the text becomes clear.

Figure 8.5 A Descriptive Structure (Topical Net or Web) Based on "The Brown Rat" (Clements, 1972)

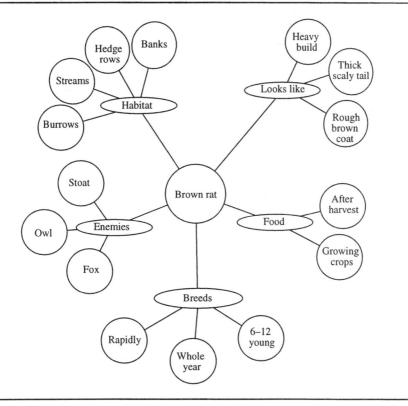

The weave or matrix structure compares and contrasts two or more topics. In the weave shown in Table 8.1, the characteristics of brown bears, black bears, and polar bears are compared and contrasted. An extract from the text, *Bears* (Wexo, 1991), can be found in the Appendix. This pattern is quite common in science books. This weave was produced in a small-group situation, with myself helping the pupils to figure out the text structure. Note that the text is more sophisticated than the web structure. It focuses on more than one topic and shows how bears differ on several dimensions: weight, length, where they are found, types of homes, features, and so forth.

As this section demonstrates, expository texts follow different text structures. So it is not surprising that many children, as they progress

Table 8.1 A Descriptive Text Pattern (Matrix or Weave) Based on *Bears* (Wexo, 1991)

	Weight	Length	Habitat	Den	Features
Black Bears	136 kg	Up to 1.7 m	Forest Canada/USA	Cave or hole from fallen tree	Large ears. Climbs trees. Not all are black. Long straight noses.
Brown Bears	Up to 726 kg	Up to 3.35 m	Open meadow Europe/Asia North America	Dig a hole for themselves	Small ears. Large hump of muscle/fat over shoulder. Many sizes.
Polar Bears	1,002 kg	Over 3.35 m	Snow/ice Polar region	Hollow out a snowbank	Best hunters. Thick layer of fat. Good eyesight. Swim 97 km without a rest. Front feet are webbed.

through school and begin to encounter more expository text, have difficulty with comprehension. The young high school reader may become exasperated if the text is poorly structured.

SUMMARY

Pupils who have awareness of text structure may have fewer problems with text comprehension. There are several things teachers can do to help pupils "see" the structure of text. First, teachers can ensure that texts presented to pupils are well structured and of a high quality. Second, teachers can show children how to identify the macrostructures of both narrative and expository texts, and provide many opportunities for analyzing text.

PUTTING TEXT STRUCTURE INTO PERSPECTIVE

I recently carried out a study that compared teaching about text structure with two alternative ways of teaching, namely sustained silent reading and guided reading (Dymock, 1998, in press). I reasoned that by teaching pupils about text structure, I would be able to give them explicit knowledge of what top-level text structures were like, so that they would be able to read text material with more control. They would be able to see more clearly the architectural design of text material, and this would help them remember the context of material more effectively.

I had three groups of pupils (30 in each group, aged 8, 9, and 10 years). The text-structure group was taught about the top-level structures of narrative and expository texts. The sustained silent reading group engaged in supervised reading of stories, which included computer checks of their comprehension of text. The guided reading group engaged in prereading and postreading discussions of text material, where the focus was not on top-level structures but on predicting what the text material would be about and bringing their own experiences to the discussion.

The teaching part of the study took 17 weeks for each group, based on twice-weekly sessions of 30 minutes each. Each of the three instructional groups consisted of four subgroups. I taught each subgroup separately. At the end of the study, the three different teaching methods were compared, using pupils' standardized test performance scores on both pre- and posttests.

Although my study was inconclusive, in that text-structure instruction did not prove to be clearly superior to sustained silent reading or guided reading, text-structure instruction still has value. The study showed that text-structure instruction held its own against other teaching methods. It has a place in the teaching program. Text-structure instruction may be of special value when analyzing content material that needs to be carefully read and remembered. It may also be a useful approach for teaching pupils about the different ways in which writers use top-level structures to present their ideas.

REVIEW

Reading comprehension depends on many variables, including background knowledge, decoding ability, language comprehension, and awareness of text structure. While not underestimating the importance of the above variables on comprehension, this chapter has focused on the influence of text structure. Text structure refers to the way in which ideas in the text are organized, that is, to the pattern the author has used to organize information.

Research on this topic has focused on the two major structures of discourse: narrative and exposition. Narratives are stories. They include characters, setting, plot, and theme. Expository text is designed to interpret, explain, or appraise. The structural characteristics of expository text are more complex than narrative text. There are many different expository structures (Grimes, 1975), though this chapter has focused on just some of these textual patterns.

Most children have only a basic understanding of the structure of narrative and little understanding of the structure of exposition. Some children, through continual exposure to different text structures, are intuitively able to develop a good understanding of expository as well as narrative structures and to use this knowledge to assist with comprehension. However, many children lack such understanding.

Children who are taught to identify the structures of expository and narrative text will be able to use this metacognitive knowledge to improve their comprehension of text material. To illustrate such strategies, we have discussed several text structure patterns, as suggested by Calfee and Patrick (1995), which are designed to improve pupils' ability to understand texts. Current research suggests that children can learn and use metacognitive strategies to enhance their ability to comprehend written language.

Finally, my own research suggests that text-structure instruction is not the only approach of value, but it warrants a place in the instructional portfolio of every teacher.

STUDY AND DISCUSSION QUESTIONS

1. Text comprehension depends on many variables, including decoding ability, language comprehension, background knowledge, and knowledge of text structure. How is text structure related to reading comprehension?
2. Narrative text follows a basic structure. While there are variations of this pattern ranging from a preschool book with a simple plot to a lengthy adult novel with a complex plot, the overall structure can be the same. Can you apply narrative text structure to a children's book? (Try one of Bill Peet's books, such as *Farewell to Shady Glade* [1967].)
3. This chapter has outlined the most common expository text structures found in some school texts (i.e., string, topical net [or web], matrix [or weave]). Find an example of each organizational pattern, and apply an appropriate structure to each text.
4. How is research on children's understanding of text structure of relevance to the classroom teacher?
5. Metacognitive strategies may help the reader to remember better. How can the content of a lesson be structured so that the reader is able to

understand and organize information more effectively? (Try the topic
of "Birds of the world," and use diagrams to show the structure.)

FURTHER READING

Barton, J., & Calfee, R. C. (1989). Theory becomes practice: One program. In
    D. Lapp, J. Flood, & N. Farnan (Eds.), *Content area reading and learning:
    Instructional strategies* (pp. 366–378). Englewood Cliffs, NJ: Prentice-Hall.
Calfee, R. C., & Drum, P. A. (1986). Research on teaching reading. In M. Wittrock
    (Ed.), *Handbook of research on teaching* (pp. 804–849). New York: Macmillan.
Calfee, R. C., & Patrick, C. L. (1995). *Teach our children well: Bringing K–12 educa-
    tion into the 21st century*. Stanford, CA: Stanford Alumni.
Chambliss, M. J. (1993). Assessing instructional materials: How comprehensible
    are they? In C. J. Gordon, G. D. Labercane, & W. R. McEachern (Eds.), *Ele-
    mentary reading: Process and practice* (2nd ed.; pp. 319–340). Needham Heights,
    MA: Ginn.
Dymock, S. J. (1993). Reading but not understanding. *Journal of Reading, 37*, 2–8.
Tunmer, W. E., & Bowey, J. A. (1984). Metalinguistic awareness and reading
    acquisition. In W. E. Tunmer, C. Pratt, & M. L. Herriman (Eds.), *Metalinguistic
    awareness in children: Theory research and implications* (pp. 144–168). Berlin:
    Springer-Verlag.

REFERENCES

American Heritage. (1969). *The American Heritage dictionary of the English language*.
    New York: Author.
Armbruster, B. B. (1984). The problem of "inconsiderate text." In G. Duffy,
    L. Roehler, & J. Mason (Eds.), *Comprehension instruction* (pp. 202–220). New
    York: Longman.
Calfee, R. C. (1981). Cognitive psychology and educational practice. *Review of
    Research in Education, 9*, 3–72.
Calfee, R. C. (1984*). The book: Components of reading instruction*. Unpublished manu-
    script, Stanford University, Stanford, CA.
Calfee, R. C., & Curley, R. (1984). Structure of prose in the content areas. In
    J. Flood (Ed.), *Understanding reading comprehension* (pp. 161–180). Newark,
    DE: International Reading Association.
Calfee, R. C., & Drum, P.A. (1986). Research on teaching reading. In M. Wittrock
    (Ed.), *Handbook of research on teaching* (pp. 804–849). New York: Macmillan.
Calfee, R. C., Henry, M., & Funderburg, J. (1988). A model for school change. In
    S. J. Samuels, & P. D. Pearson (Eds.), *Changing school reading programs*
    (pp. 121–141). Newark, DE: International Reading Association.
Calfee, R. C., & Patrick, C. L. (1995). *Teach our children well: Bringing K–12 educa-
    tion into the 21st century*. Stanford, CA: Stanford Alumni.

Chall, J. S. (1983). *Stages of reading development.* New York: McGraw-Hill.

Clements, H. (1972). *Rodents.* London: Frederick Muller.

Crayford, K. (1992). A lost shoe and a broken window. *School Journal,* Part 2, No. 4, 2–8. [Wellington, New Zealand: Learning Media, Ministry of Education.]

Dymock, S. J. (1998). *The effects of text structure training, reading practice, and guided silent reading on reading comprehension.* Doctoral thesis, University of Auckland, New Zealand.

Dymock, S. J. (in press). A comparison study of the effects of text structure training, reading practice, and guided reading on reading comprehension. In T. Shanahan (Ed.), *Yearbook of the National Reading Conference* (Vol. 47). Rochester, NY: National Reading Conference.

Englert, C. S., & Hiebert, E. H. (1984). Children's developing awareness of text structures in expository materials. *Journal of Educational Psychology, 76,* 65–74.

Frederiksen, C. H. (1975). Acquisition of semantic information from discourse: Effects of repeated exposures. *Journal of Verbal Learning and Verbal Behavior, 14,* 158–169.

Grimes, J. E. (1975). *The thread of discourse.* The Hague: Mouton.

Kintsch, W. (1974). *The representation of meaning in memory.* Hillsdale, NJ: Erlbaum.

Kintsch, W., Mandel, T., & Kozminsky, E. (1977). Summarizing scrambled stories. *Memory and Cognition, 5,* 547–552.

Mandler, J. M., & Johnson, N. S. (1977). Remembrance of things parsed: Story structure and recall. *Cognitive Psychology, 9,* 111–151.

McGee, L. M. (1982). Awareness of text structure: Effects on children's recall of expository text. *Reading Research Quarterly, 17,* 581–590.

Meyer, B. J. F. (1975). *The organization of prose and its effects on memory.* Amsterdam: North-Holland Publishing.

Meyer, B. J. F., Brandt, D. M., & Bluth, G. J. (1980). Use of top-level structure in text: Key for reading comprehension of ninth grade students. *Reading Research Quarterly, 16,* 72–103.

Meyer, B. J. F., & Rice, G. E. (1984). The structure of text. In P. D. Pearson (Ed.), *Handbook of reading research* (pp. 319–351). New York: Longman.

Peet, B. (1967). *Farewell to Shady Glade.* London: Deutsch.

Rumelhart, D. E. (1975). Notes on a schema for stories. In D. G. Bobrow & A. M. Collins (Eds.), *Representation and understanding: Studies in cognitive science* (pp. 211–236). New York: Academic Press.

Taylor, B. M. (1980). Children's memory for expository text after reading. *Reading Research Quarterly, 15,* 399–411.

Taylor, B. M., & Samuels, S. J. (1983). Children's use of text structure in the recall of expository material. *American Educational Research Journal, 4,* 517–528.

Thorndyke, P. W. (1977). Cognitive structures in comprehension and memory of narrative discourse. *Cognitive Psychology, 9,* 77–110.

Tunmer, W. E., & Bowey, J. A. (1984). Metalinguistic awareness and reading acquisition. In W. E. Tunmer, C. Pratt, & M. L. Herriman (Eds.), *Metalinguistic awareness in children: Theory, research, and implications* (pp. 144–168). Berlin: Springer-Verlag.

Westra, A. (1988). Joab bakes bread. *School Journal*, Part 2, No. 2, 9–14. [Wellington, New Zealand: School Publications Branch, Department of Education.]
Wexo, J. B. (1991). Bears. *Zoobooks*, 9, 1–18.

APPENDIX

An Extract from *A Lost Shoe and a Broken Window* (Crayford, 1992, pp. 2–3):

One day, Gran was out at work and my father and all his brothers and sisters were home, larking about. One of the children invented a new game. They each put on a shoe that was too big for them, and then kicked hard. The winner was the one who could make their shoe fly highest and farthest. They got noisier and noisier, with shoes flying about all over the place and everyone arguing and laughing and shouting as they tried to decide who'd won.

The game came to a sudden end when my father put on one of Gran's best shoes and sent it crashing through the window.

After the crash there was an awful silence.

The girls went down into the street to look for the shoe, while the boys wondered what to do about the broken window.

Very carefully, they removed all the bits of glass from the window frame. This made it look neater, but the light that streamed through the place where the glass had been was much brighter than the light coming in through the other windows. So they decided to clean all the other windows.

(Copyright 1992 by K. Crayford. Reprinted with permission.)

An Extract from "Joab Bakes Bread" (Westra, 1988, pp. 10–11):

The children help with many of the jobs. When I was there, Joab made bread, from beginning to end for the first time. It was quite exciting, and his friends came to watch and help.

First Joab and his friends cleaned the wheat, by standing on a little hill-side and dropping them slowly through the air. The wind blew away any dust and husks left in the grain. They did this over and over again.

Then they made the grain into flour by grinding it in a hand-mill. This was hard work, and they all took turns at turning the mill.

The next step was to make dough for the bread, using the fresh flour. Joab's mother helped him to mix in all the right things. Then she showed him how to knead the dough. It was such a big lump of dough that this was hard work, too.

When the dough was ready, it was left to rise overnight.

(Copyright 1988, by Ans Westra. Reprinted with permission.)

An Extract from "The Brown Rat" (Clements, 1972, p. 15):

[The brown rat] can be recognised by its heavy build and rough, brown coat. It has a thick, scaly tail, shorter than that of the black rat, but longer than that of a water vole. Its ears are more prominent than those of the water vole, and its snout is more pointed. It swims well, and will colonise the banks of streams, especially if there is a good supply of food. It lives for most of its life in a series of tunnels, which it burrows out itself. Above ground it likes the shelter of hedgerows or coarse vegetation. In summer it moves to the fields to feed on growing crops, and after the harvest it moves back to farm buildings and warehouses, where it finds plenty of food.
(Copyright 1972, by Frederick Muller Ltd.)

An Extract from *Bears* (Wexo, 1991, pp. 5–6):

Black bears are small bears compared to their cousins, the brown and polar bears. They usually weigh no more than 136 kilograms, and are less than 1.7 metres. They have long, straight noses and the largest ears of any bears.

Trees are a black bear's best friends. Whenever they are in danger, black bears climb trees. They have rather short claws that are ideal for scrambling up a tree. It is not surprising that black bears stay as close to trees as they can. They rarely leave the forest.

The dens of different kinds of bears are different. Most black bears use a cave or a hole that has been opened by a falling tree. Brown bears nearly always dig a hole for themselves. Polar bears usually hollow out a snowbank, and the warmth of their breath often creates a vent in the roof to let in fresh air.
(Copyright 1991 by Wildlife Education, Ltd./Zoobooks. Reprinted with permission.)

PART III

LEARNING
LITERATURE APPRECIATION

Part II was about the child understanding the ideas of the passage being read. Now in Part III our interest widens to consider the diversity of books and the various ways the child reader may use them. In Chapter 9 Joan Gibbons considers the features of books that constitute "children's literature." This literature ranges from books that are read to preschool children to complex literary art that is appreciated by the very able adolescent reader. Selections of books from within this range have an important role in school reading instruction, irrespective of whether this instruction has an emphasis on explicit teaching of letter-sound correspondences. But children's literature provides more than instruction in reading. It is also to be enjoyed for its own sake and for recreation. In Chapter 10 Deborah Widdowson, Dennis Moore, and Robyn Dixon look at teachers' modeling of the child's engagement in silent reading for recreation.

While reading skills are a means of gaining knowledge and a means of recreation, yet other dimensions can be added as young people gain experience of literature. In Chapter 11 Chanda Pinsent considers how young people can reflect on their reading experience in order to make an evaluation of a book as a work of literary art. The chapter also examines evidence about the ages at which children are able to be guided toward making literary evaluations.

Chapter 9

Literature for Children

JOAN GIBBONS

a) What is children's literature?

b) What are the features of children's literature?

c) What is the role of children's literature in teaching children to read?

d) Which books will extend children's reading capabilities?

It is through the reading of literature that children learn one of the essential components of the reading task: how to read a book. This task takes reading beyond the identification of words and comprehension of sentences to the understanding and appreciation of informative and creative works. The process of learning to read is not complete until this is accomplished. In childhood, learning to read is a continuing task. It has been noted (e.g., by Watson, 1992, p. 7) that children may have made progress toward this aspect of reading before they can read a single word. When worthwhile books are enjoyed daily from early childhood onward, children begin to appreciate the pleasures of literature and to respond to stories with understanding.

Learning to appreciate literature and to discern different qualities in literature are skills that are learned alongside other tasks, such as word identification and comprehension of information. This is best achieved by listening to, reading, and discussing stories. Just as phonological awareness can be increased by reading alphabet books and books that rhyme, and the early stages of reading are facilitated by books with regular patterns of sound and repetition of words and phrases, so too do reading and discussing in depth a variety of texts help children learn to cope with more complex texts. There is evidence that reading to children in their early years contributes to their success in learning to read (Clark, 1976; Durkin, 1966; Gibbons, 1981; Teale, 1978, 1981). Teachers and children's literature theorists have examined the benefits of reading to children and of children's discussing the literature they read, both among themselves and with adults (Huck, Hepler, & Hickman, 1987). Being read to enables children to learn what kind of activity reading is. It creates expectations from books and lays down patterns that children can use as guides when they are later involved in reading independently.

Those teachers who have used children's literature (often referred to as "real books" in Britain and "trade books" in the United States) in the classroom for direct or guided instruction as well as for independent reading have found that children gain from it a more enthusiastic attitude toward reading as well as a better understanding of texts (Nicoll & Roberts, 1993).

CHARACTERISTICS OF CHILDREN'S LITERATURE

Children's literature is written and read because children require a special range of literature of their own. Children's literature is characteristically simple and straightforward, repetitious, fast-paced, focused on action, dialogue-based, optimistic, didactic, about childhood; it expresses a child's point of view and a viewpoint of innocence; it tends toward fantasy or pastoral idyll. (In discussions of literature, *pastoral* has come to mean embodying old-fashioned values, such as those of home and family.) Townsend (1971) wrote that "the only practical definition of a children's book" (p. 10) was that it appeared on a publisher's children's list, but in a less cynical mood he referred to the "wild blood" of children's literature: "Its ancestry lies in the long ago ages of storytelling which preceded the novel" (p. 12). The tendency toward fantasy, pastoral idyll, and innocence identified in Townsend's account is also discussed by Nodelman (1992). Not all of these characteristics are present in all children's books, and many books for adults share some of these characteristics. For instance, Dick Francis's *Decider* (1993), like many popular novels, is simple and straightforward, focuses on action, is partly about childhood, is optimistic, has elements of pastoral idyll, and exhibits a tendency toward the didactic. Popular light fiction appears to have much in common with children's fiction. Children's literature is often thought to be "less rational" than adult fiction, but those who so characterize it are disregarding the majority of adult fiction and looking only at a particular kind of literature (Rudd, 1992). It can be argued from the basis of such novels as *A Wizard of Earthsea* (Le Guin, 1971), *The Mouse and His Child* (Hoban, 1969), and *Drift* (Mayne, 1985) that some of the best literature for children is not particularly simple or straightforward but shares more with "quality" literature for adults than it does with light fiction.

The need to pinpoint what is essential to children's literature has led some literary theorists to argue that it can be identified by one particular characteristic. Wall (1991), for instance, argues persuasively that the presence of a narrator's voice that speaks "to the child" is the only reliable indicator of a book for children. She says that both William Mayne and Enid Blyton "write to the child reader," taking only their needs and interests into consideration, whereas J. M. Barrie (1911/1988) in *Peter Pan* writes with frequent asides to the adult.

It is only relatively recently that literary critics and academics have shown much interest in children's literature. To some extent these critics have stirred the debate about essential differences between children's and adult literature. Even now, most books about children's literature are written by child educators, who tend to see the advantages of reading literature in terms of improvements in reading ability and the development of the child through the ideas generated (e.g., Cullinan, 1981; Huck et al., 1987; Norton, 1987).

Any literature that is read with appreciation by children can be thought of as children's literature. What is thought suitable for children varies over time and from place to place. However, there is more agreement about quality among significant critics than one might expect. The biggest disagreement tends to be not among established critics but between them and people who think that popularity is the most important criterion for a good children's book. Popularity is not irrelevant, and it can be the key to getting reluctant children to read regularly, but it is not necessarily an indicator of quality. However, quality and popularity can be found in combination, as they are, for instance, in *How Tom Beat Captain Najork and His Hired Sportsmen* (Hoban, 1974) and *Whispers in the Graveyard* (Breslin, 1994). Reading instruction for competent readers should gradually include the reading of more complex and more subtle texts.

Simplicity

Simplicity is a common feature of children's literature. Features such as repetition, rhythm, and regular patterns of sound make the reading of first books easier. Joy Cowley's (1983) *Greedy Cat* repeats sounds, words, and phrases in a satisfying manner:

Along came greedy cat.
He looked in the shopping bag.
Gobble, gobble, gobble,
And that was the end of that. (p. 3)

Dr Seuss set out to show what could be done within the restrictions of a very simple vocabulary with his Beginner Books. *The Cat in the Hat* (Seuss, 1958) tells a complex story with simple, mostly one-syllable, words, and much repetition, with lines such as "All that cold, cold, wet day" (p. 1).

A simple vocabulary is used in other books that children can learn to read very quickly, such as *Bears in the Night* (Berenstain & Berenstain, 1971). Here lines are characteristically short but action-ridden; for example, "Down the tree." Successful low vocabulary picture books such as this help make children's early independent reading experiences enjoyable.

A similar facility with simple language is shown in *Titch* (Hutchins, 1972), where the sizes of the children and their possessions are contrasted, but Titch's tiny seed grows into a huge plant. Another brilliant example of the art of brevity appears in *Dog In, Cat Out* (Rubinstein & James, 1991), where the entire text consists of various arrangements of the words in the title.

What makes these particular books welcome as literature is the sophisticated way in which the simple language is arranged, raising them above the level of many easy readers. Contrast is evident amidst the repetition. The quality of the interaction of the text with the illustrations also contributes to the notability of certain picture books.

Repetition

Repetition of words and phrases is common in stories for young children. It makes the stories easier to read and also has universal appeal. The refrain ending "Millions and billions and trillions of cats" is oft-repeated in the classic picture book *Millions of Cats* (Gag, 1929). The vocabulary is not simple, but the repetition makes it easy to remember and read. Likewise with another old favorite, Burton's (1942) *Mike Mulligan and His Steam Shovel*. Much repetition is involved in this story, and language patterns are formed both orally and visually:

> It was Mike Mulligan and Mary Anne and some others who dug the great canals for the big boats to sail through. It was Mike Mulligan and Mary Anne and some others who cut through the high mountains so that trains could go through. (unpaged, pp. 3–5)

This word pattern is repeated five times in all. Other phrases are also repeated, such as "dig[ging] the cellar for [or of] the new town hall" and "dug [or dig] a little faster and a little better." The variations are as important as the repetition because they alert the reader to phonological distinctions. Memory alone will not enable the child to make the correct word choice, but the pattern is a guide to the reader in divining meaning.

Rhyme and Rhythm

Rhyme and rhythm also act and interact to make stories easier for children to read and remember. The youngest children enjoy nursery rhymes, especially when they are accompanied by actions, as in "Pat a cake, pat a cake, baker's man" or "This little piggy went to market." As early as 1908, Huey (1908/1968) recommended for beginning readers the use of "good old jingles and rhymes and folk stories and fairy tales" (p. 332), together with finger-pointing as the words were read. Stories written in rhyme have a particular appeal. *Noisy Nora* (Wells, 1973) is a clever and amusing story in verse. Another more recent example is *Off Goes the Hose!*, from New Zealand's Ready to Read series:

> Water on the garden.
> Water on the tree.
> Water on the window.
> Water on me!
> (Cowley & Ross, 1997, pp. 2–5)

Here illustrations combine with the rhyme to make the text very predictable and easy to read. The simplicity of the rhyme, the strong rhythm, and the sounds interact to achieve an appealing early reading experience.

Part of the tremendous success of Lynley Dodd's books for young children has been the combination of rhyme with a cumulative effect, building up in *Hairy Maclary from Donaldson's Dairy* (Dodd, 1983) to:

> Off with a yowl / a wail and a howl,
> a scatter of paws / and a clatter of claws,
> went Schnitzel von Krumm / with a very low tum,
> Bitzer Maloney / all skinny and bony,
> Muffin McLay / like a bundle of hay,
> Bottomley Potts / covered in spots,
> Hercules Morse / as big as a horse
> and Hairy Maclary / from Donaldson's Dairy,
> straight back home / to bed. (pp. 31–35)

The ending, safe back home, is another feature that is typical of children's literature (Clausen, 1982).

Books for children in the middle years of childhood may also use rhyme, as do many of the picture books of Bill Peet. These are often read to younger children but are perhaps most popular with readers between ages 7 and 9.

At first all the birds were just too stunned to speak.
But finally a jay blurted out, "It's a freak!
Just look! The thing is half lion, half eagle.
I'm sure that it must be unsafe or illegal."
(Peet, 1963, *The Pinkish, Purplish, Bluish Egg*, p. 13)

The purpose of the rhyme in this book is to make the story both attractive to listen to and easier to read. The rhyme both moves the story along and provides clues as to the sounds of the last word of every second line. The vocabulary, nevertheless, is not particularly simple.

Sound

Some very simple books encourage awareness of sound and of print. Juxtaposition of similarity and contrast arouses interest. For example, Gibbons (1981) reported that when "reading" Suteev's (1972) children's book *The Chick and the Duckling*, one 4-year-old preschool child showed an unexpected awareness of print. She became interested in the word *duckling*, emphasizing in her speech the syllable break /duck-ling/ while pointing to the word in print. The child appeared to recognize the *duck* part of the word and might possibly have been able to read it if it had appeared on its own:

> Researcher: "Why did you point to duckling?"
> Child: "Because that's the word duckling, duck ended."
> Researcher: "Where did duck end? Tell me."
> Child: /kuh/
> (Gibbons, 1981, p. 169)

Later the 4-year-old commented that the printed word *chick* also ended with a "kay" (she used the letter name /kay/), and it was obvious that it was the shared nature of this feature, both words ending in *k*, that interested her. She showed similar interest in *said the duckling* and *said the chick*, which were repeated several times in the book, and compared it with the phrase *cried the chick*, which appears only once. She noticed the difference between the two phrases and recognized that using the word *cried* instead of the word *said* marked out the occasion as special, and she added emphasis to her "reading" of the word (in the story, the chick cries as it sinks into the water).

It was estimated that this 4-year-old had by the time of this incident heard upwards of 5,000 stories. That number was thought by the parent to be conservative, being based on an estimate of around five stories a day for more than 3 years and ignoring stories heard before the age of 18 months. Many of the stories read to her were repetitions of the same books. Rereading stories happens naturally in the home, but it has benefits in the school situation too (Munn, 1995). Morrow (1988) examined the effect of repeated readings of the same story in a one-to-one situation and found that it increased the number, range, and quality of comments that children made compared with those of children hearing different stories each time. Ritchie (1978) incorporated repeated readings into her school-preparation program with New Zealand Maori children with considerable success.

Awareness of Patterns in Language

It was the differences as much as the similarities in the sounds and symbols of the text that the 4-year-old child referred to above was noting; the sameness and differentness of *chick* and *duckling*, the repetition of *said* followed by a change to *cried*. Such surprises are as necessary to texts as are regularities if the story is to capture the child's interest. Awareness of patterns of sound and spelling is increased through the occurrence of discrepant events. Stories or poems that rhyme may demonstrate the variety of spelling patterns that can result in the same sound.

In Margaret Mahy's *Bubble Trouble* poem (1991), which begins "Little Mabel blew a bubble and it caused a lot of trouble," *bubble* and *trouble* rhyme but do not share spelling patterns. Further examples in this poem are *Mabel* and *table, squealing* and *reeling, tense* and *fence, minute* and *in it*. From the last example, children in the 7- to 10-year age range can see that rhyme can be made out of combinations of words as well as single words. Lessons learned from the experience of literature are as valid as those taught by drill or by rule learning and are generally more enjoyable.

Some "discrepancies" in the patterns of language construction are too difficult for children to understand. *The King, the Mice and the Cheese* (Gurney & Gurney, 1965) is popular with preschool children but misunderstood by most children younger than age 7 or 8, who assume that the author has made a mistake when the text refers to " the mice-chasing cats" (p. 20). They make comments such as "But the mice aren't chasing the cats, the cats are chasing the mice!" Most are tolerant of the author's "mistake" but are certain that the text is incorrect, even when similar constructions appear on subsequent pages. Of those who are able to read it by themselves, few children below 8 years of age are able to understand the function of the hyphen in this construction. An understanding of child development can be important to the writing of successful children's books.

UNDERSTANDING DIFFERENT KINDS OF TEXTS

Humor

Humorous stories often have special appeal for children. *The Story of Horace* (Coats, 1937), in which a bear eats all the members of a family one by one, might be thought too violent for children, but few misunderstand the moral of the story—that misplaced leniency can lead to disaster. The continuing pattern of this story results in most children's being able to repeat the words by the end of the book, aided by the decreasing length of the lines as the family diminishes and the pictures that assist in identification of the words. Reading is also assisted by the words being in a similar place on the page each time they appear.

Many favorite stories for young children have humor and a predictable text, which, as in *The Three Billy Goats Gruff* (Blair, 1963), makes them easy to read even when the vocabulary is not particularly "easy." Children's stories also tend to be sympathetic to the underdog. In *The Three Little Pigs* (Galdone, 1970), a pattern is interrupted, and the cautious, sensible little pig conquers the big bad wolf, empowering children who feel that they occupy a similarly powerless position in society.

Humor is also important in longer stories. It contributes to the enormous popularity of writers such as Roald Dahl and Paul Jennings. Humor offers to children (in addition to the vulgarity that is often part of its appeal) the opportunity to encounter irony and multiple meanings. Books such as *The Wolves of Willoughby Chase* (Aiken, 1962), *The BFG* (Dahl, 1982), *McBroom's Wonderful One-Acre Farm* (Fleischman, 1972), and *Agnes the Sheep* (W. Taylor, 1990) represent different kinds of humor, all of which add to children's understanding of what humor is and does.

Complexity in Picture Books

Picture book stories can use simple vocabulary yet have complex meanings. For example, in *Frog and Toad Are Friends* (Lobel, 1970), when Frog calls on Toad a voice replies "I am not here" (p. 7). The child must realize that a literal interpretation of the text is inappropriate. The reader has to work on such stories, and this work is excellent preparation for the later reading of novels. Stories with no gaps for the child to fill in imaginatively tend in the long run to be unrewarding. Iser (1974) argues that readers actively bridge such gaps, constructing sense from the text and from their own knowledge. Lobel's stories have a vocabulary and sentence structure that can be tackled by a child just beginning to read, but at the same time they require thoughtful reading if they are to be appreciated fully.

The best books for young children contain literary devices that you will find in the most sophisticated adult literature but at a level at which they can be enjoyed by the child. In *Where the Wild Things Are*, Sendak (1963) uses repetition of a food motif as a literary device to link the feelings of Max (the little boy who pretends to be a wild thing, and is sent to bed) with his imaginary companions (the wild things that live in his bedroom):

> his mother called him "WILD THING!"
> and Max said "I'LL EAT YOU UP!"
> so he was sent to bed without eating anything. (unpaged, p. 6)

Then Max sends the wild things "off to bed without their supper" (unpaged, p. 30), and when he leaves them they cry,

> "Oh please don't go—
> we'll eat you up—we love you so!"
> And Max said, "No!" (unpaged, p. 32)

He returns home to find his supper waiting for him, still hot. The repetition of the food motif is significant not so much because of any underlying psychological significance (although this is of importance to the adult critic) but because it is recognized, appreciated, and understood by the child reader of around 3 to 7 years old.

These are books with short, simple words and sentences. At the other extreme are books with very complex vocabularies where the sheer pleasure of words is indulged in. These books are enjoyed most by children from 5 to 9 years old who have had positive reading experiences. *Sylvester and the Magic Pebble* (Steig, 1969) contains many examples. Sylvester meets a lion while holding his magic pebble, wishes without thinking, and becomes a rock. The lion goes away "confused, perplexed, puzzled, and bewildered" (unpaged, p. 7). Bill Peet also characteristically uses words that may stretch a child's vocabulary. In *Huge Harold* (Peet, 1961), Father makes a "prediction" about his son's size (p. 1), his mother "wailed in despair" (p. 2), and a wood is "gloomy and dense" (p. 6). Books like this are necessary too, so that a love of language can be kindled and developed.

Reader Response

Reader response is a development in literary criticism (Iser, 1974; Rosenblatt, 1978, 1991) that has struck a special chord among the researchers of children's literature, and this will be examined in detail in Chapter 11.

Educators have long been interested in both children's emotional response to story and their attempts to construct meaning. Martinez and Roser (1991) refer to "the ways that young readers and listeners come to consider, reflect, manipulate, and verbalize their feeling and opinions about text" (p. 643). This aspect of reading is developed to a greater degree through the reading of a variety of literature, especially literature that allows for perceptive appreciation and interpretation. The transaction between the reader and the text involves the reader being both guided by the text and bringing prior knowledge to the text (Rosenblatt, 1978). What children already know contributes to their understanding of the text. It may limit or enhance their understanding, or contribute to misunderstanding.

Applebee (1978) conducted research into children's responses to story and found differences across age levels. Six-year-olds typically described stories by retelling them, 9-year-olds by giving a synopsis or summarizing, and adolescents by analyzing story structures and generalizing about their meanings. While there was some overlap between these descriptive stages, they seldom went above or below more than one age level. That 6-year-olds regarded stories as "primarily a patterning of events" (Applebee, 1978, p. 115) might serve as a guide to what sort of story is appropriate to this age group.

Teachers can help to organize particular types of response. Typically, teachers in New Zealand classrooms ask children to predict what happens next in a story; persuade children to retell, act out, draw, paint, write about, or devise a game from the story; encourage group participation in a shared reading; or discuss the story in large or small groups. Hickman (1981) observed much the same activities in some U. S. classrooms.

EXTENDING CHILDREN'S READING CAPABILITIES

Traditional Stories

Knowledge of traditional stories is necessary to an understanding of other literature. Many stories assume such a knowledge. An 11-year-old will understand *Howl's Moving Castle* (Jones, 1986) better if he or she has previously read stories about being the youngest daughter in the family, magic clothing, and witches. Alternatives to well-known fairy tales provide children's first experiences of intertextuality in literature. Intertextuality refers to aspects of a text that can only be properly understood by reference to another text. In this context, intertextuality refers to what occurs when characters from one story turn up in another, and the author uses the reader's knowledge of how those characters behave in the original story to create expectations of how they will behave or what will happen to them in the second story. The author can then satisfy these expectations or confound them. Janet and Allan Ahlberg's *Each Peach Pear Plum* (1978), *The Jolly Postman* (1986), and *Jeremiah in the Dark Woods* (1977), written for children ranging from 2 to 10 years old, all rely on knowledge of traditional nursery rhyme and fairy tale characters as part of their impact. Children are less likely to enjoy these stories fully if they are unable to bring to the stories their knowledge of traditional nursery rhymes and fairy tales. *The Stinky Cheeseman and Other Fairly Stupid Tales* (Scieszka & Smith, 1992) relies on the child's having a thorough knowledge of how a "traditional" book works. It pulls the traditional book apart and reconstructs it. The general point to be made here is that intertextuality is introduced to children in their earliest reading.

Realism and Fantasy

Another picture book that brings in postmodernist literary devices is *Black and White* (Macaulay, 1990), where one must "read" four stories simultaneously and put them together for a full appreciation of "what happens." Before coming to a complex book such as this, 6- and 7-year-old children can learn about reading both text and pictures in books such as *Aldo* (Burningham, 1991), where the pictures indicate that something is happening other than what is directly communicated through the words of the text. The reader must read both words and pictures to understand the story. Likewise, books such as *Changes* (Browne, 1990) and *Gorilla* (Browne, 1983) provide a rich visual and imaginative experience. Graham Oakley's *The Church Mouse* series (1972–), and his *Once Upon a Time* (1990), abound in visual and verbal humor and irony perhaps most appreciated by children between 6 and 9 years old. *The Wolf* (Barbalet & Tanner, 1991) tests the 8- to 10-year-old readers' interpretation of literal and metaphorical meaning. *The Mousehole Cat* (Barber, 1990), for 6- to 10-year-olds, uses an extended metaphor reinforced by illustrations. "Comprehension" of such stories is helped by an extensive reading background and by discussion with other children or adults who have a similarly enriched background. It involves more than an understanding of the words and phrases used to tell the story.

The early understanding of the complexities of literature, which is achieved by the reading of picture books, assists children when tackling longer and more difficult stories. When children start to read junior novels, they often revert to simpler texts than those in the complex picture books they have been reading recently. This is largely because the additional length of a novel is at first daunting. Short and easy novels have been especially created with this transition period in mind. Books such as *Fuss Finds Out* (Gordon, 1993) and the popular *Pesters of the West* (L. Taylor & Blundell, 1989) border on the vulgarity in which many 6- to 8-year-olds revel. They can be balanced by the exquisitely spine-tingling *Storm* (Crossley-Holland, 1985), humorous books such as *The Brown Felt Hat* (Tulloch, 1990) or *The Sugar-Gum Tree* (Wrightson, 1991), or the serious conservation plea of *Chen Li and the River Spirit* (Holcroft, 1990). Books such as these will provide a rich variety of reading that serves as an introduction to the longer stories children later read independently.

Series fiction, that is, a series of stories about the same characters, has a place in the development of children's capacity to read in "bulk," but quality need not be neglected. Beverly Cleary has for some decades provided young readers with a series of full-length junior novels in a realistic vein. The recommended approach to her fiction is for children to start with a character who is the same age as themselves and then move forward or backward from there. The 6-year-old who is reading junior novels will enjoy *Ramona the Pest* (Cleary, 1974) or *Ramona the Brave* (Cleary, 1978), where the chief character experiences problems common to all 6-year-olds. Children who come to this level of reading ability at 9 or 10 years will probably prefer to start with the *Henry Huggins* (Cleary, 1950–) books and move back to Ramona, viewing her in a younger sibling capacity, once they have read about the characters who are their own age. The Ramona books, written in the late 1970s, were short-listed for the Newbery medal, and Cleary won this award with *Dear Mr. Henshaw* (1983), a book for more established readers.

Another series that develops with the reader, and that may be enjoyed by children with a taste for history, is the *Little House* books by Laura Ingalls Wilder (1956–). Readers who have been captivated by characters and events in the first books can extend their reading skills as Laura grows up and demands on the reader become more challenging. The series by Lloyd Alexander, which begins with *The Book of Three* (1973), provides a developing reading experience for children from 10 years upward. Other series writers with potential to extend children's reading include Joan Aiken, Susan Cooper, Lois Lowry, Margaret Mahy, Edith Nesbit, and Arthur Ransome.

Reading fantasy requires techniques different from those needed for other fiction, and these techniques can be acquired at different levels. *Charlotte's Web* (White, 1952), which is enjoyed by most relatively new readers of novels, provides a fine introduction to fantasy. Books such as *Rowan of Rin* (Rodda, 1993) can be seen as precursors to books such as *The Hobbit* (Tolkien, 1937).

More Mature or More Complex

Many children who are exceptionally good readers are urged by parents and teachers to read books designed for teenagers and adults. A 9-year-old with a reading age of 16 can certainly read works of almost any textual difficulty, but the content of adult or "young adult" books is not always suitable for them. Neither are the texts of young adult books necessarily more complex than those in books for 9-year-olds; it may be *only* their subject matter that is more advanced. Teaching the good reader to read the more complex material designed for his or her age group can be a harder task than providing easy adult material, but it is also more rewarding and paves the way for the enjoyment of complex adult novels. Modern authors who cater to advanced young readers of 9 to 12 years old include Nina Bawden, Sid Fleischman, Virginia Hamilton, Diana Wynne Jones, Ursula Le Guin, Lois Lowry, Patricia MacLachlan, Margaret Mahy, Jan Mark, William Mayne, Katherine Paterson, and Philippa Pearce. Such authors may provide a more intellectually challenging and a more deeply satisfying reading experience for children than do many authors of literature for adults.

Nonfiction

Nonfiction books require different approaches. Some are organized to be read straight through, others designed so that use of the table of contents and index lead directly to the specific information required. Children can be taught how to select the right kind of book for their particular purpose. Accuracy can be checked by investigating an aspect covered by the book about which they know already, or by comparing information in several books. It should be possible to check the credentials of authors. Tables of contents and selected pages can be investigated to see whether the information is presented in a coherent manner and in what ways the information might be biased. Children can soon learn to recognize conventional nonfiction styles.

Some nonfiction books are presented in ways that make the information more accessible to the young without losing any accuracy or focus. Books such as *What Is a Wall, After All?* (Allen, 1993) and *Think of an Eel* (Wallace & Bostock, 1993) are fun to read but also impart accurate information. The Sunshine science series, such as *How Spiders Live* (Biddulph & Biddulph, 1991), conveys accurate science information to 6- to 8-year-old readers. *The Way Things Work* (Macaulay, 1988) provides a mine of assorted information for the browser as well as the seeker of specific information.

Information is easier to extract from a book with a readable style. Exceptionally good books always seem to find keen readers, even where the topic seems at first unlikely.

Nonfiction also provides a suitable entrance to adult literature for the advanced young reader. Nonfiction usually avoids the involvement with adult emotional states so common in adult light fiction. It is quite common for gifted readers to be reading advanced adult nonfiction books side by side with children's novels.

Access to Books

School and public libraries provide access to children's literature for low-income families who cannot afford books, as well as to children whose families do not buy books (see Chapter 1). Schemes have been set up from time to time to provide books to children who might otherwise lack access to them. Some examples are schemes managed through hospitals to provide books to new babies and the "book-floods" which have provided books to many low socio-economic groupings internationally. School book clubs can also provide books at cheaper than usual rates.

While advances in computer technology have led to the wider use of CD-ROMs as reading materials, it appears that, for the moment, these may be of more use in developing word-level reading skills than in developing sustained reading habits or comprehension of texts. Web pages are available to stimulate children's interest in books, including sites available from The Children's Literature Web Guide—http://www.acs.ucalgary.ca/~dkbrown/—and the Association for Library Service to Children—http://www.ala.org/alsc/

GUIDES TO THE BEST

There are a number of guides to children's books available. Most are good, but possibly the best is Landsberg's *The World of Children's Books* (1988). The Thimble Press publishes regular guides (Chambers, 1987), including special guides to areas such as classics (Fisher, 1986) and picture books (Bennett, 1982; Moss, 1992). Butler's *Babies Need Books* (1995) is the best guide available to books for preschool children. *At the Cutting Edge* (Nicholson, 1994) includes some useful booklists for early reading development.

A growing number of awards for children's books are available. Some of these awards are for literary merit, others, often termed "children's choice" awards, are for popularity. The Newbery medal, Boston Globe award,

Carnegie medal, Guardian award, and Whitbread award are prestigious literary awards. The Caldecott and Kate Greenaway medals are awarded to picture books of quality in America and Britain, respectively. (A list of recent winners is available on http://www.acs.ucalgary.ca/~dkbrown). The Smarties prize is a British award that takes into account both literary merit and popularity, and is awarded in several categories. There is a tendency for literary awards to go to books for teenagers rather than to books for younger children, because of the greater scope for complexity in the area of young adult novels. The appearance of awards for books for younger readers is therefore a welcome trend. Australia, New Zealand, Canada, and other countries also have their own awards for children's books. The Phoenix award is granted to a book published 20 years earlier that has stood the test of time.

CONCLUSIONS

Reading to children and talking with them about what they have read increases the likelihood that they will appreciate the pleasures of imaginative literature. Skills that are useful when reading factual books are also developed by reading to children and by letting children read for themselves, followed by discussion. The greater the variety of literature read, the greater the base individuals may draw on to learn. Reading children's literature is both one of the aims and one of the rewards of learning to read.

REVIEW

Literature plays a necessary part in the teaching of reading. Understanding literature generally starts with listening to stories and talking about them. Through hearing, reading, and discussing stories, children begin to understand the nature of texts. Understanding different ways in which books are read and exploring the various ways in which meaning is expressed is a reading task that does not end with childhood; it continues for as long as the reader continues to tackle new kinds of reading experiences.

Literature takes learning to read a text beyond the level of reading words and knowing what they mean to thinking about what the words do, working out how they come to have the effects they have, and seeing how parts of the text interact to make up the whole. This aspect of reading can be learned only by reading literature (whether fiction or nonfiction). The use of quality literature is recommended because it contains more of those literary devices and practices that need to be explored if an understanding of literature is to be developed.

Children's literature has distinctive features that separate it from adult literature, but these are a collection of features, some of which are always present, rather than definite prerequisites. Many books for young children are simple, repetitious, and rhythmic—features that can make a book a great deal easier to read.

Readers must decide on appropriate ways of reading and interpreting each text. A child does not always read at the same level of difficulty, so a variety of material is recommended. Readers respond to text in different ways. Teachers aim to extend the responses that they perceive. As children's reading ability develops, the literature that they have read or have had read to them in the past contributes to the enjoyment and appreciation of the literature they are currently reading.

Reading nonfiction requires the development of techniques appropriate to factual material. Children learn to test accuracy and reliability, and to read for information as well as for enjoyment.

Children with exceptional ability in reading can be encouraged to attempt more complex books that require greater intellectual effort but are designed for their age group. There are suitable books available at every level from early childhood onward. Many guides to appropriate fiction are available. Literary awards also serve as guidelines to good fiction.

STUDY AND DISCUSSION QUESTIONS

1. What is meant by "knowing how to read a novel"? Discuss how you would teach this aspect of reading to children of different ages.
2. Why are books with rhyme and rhythm popular with children? How do rhyme and rhythm help reading progress?
3. What purposes does repetition serve in learning to read?
4. What advantages are there in using popular books as reading materials?
5. How would you encourage children to read more difficult books? Why should you encourage able children to read more complex texts?
6. Discuss the general characteristics of children's literature. What characteristics do you think are essential to children's books?

FURTHER READING

Bradford, C. (1990). *Genre in perspective: A whole language approach.* Gosford, New South Wales, Australia: Bookshelf.

Galda, L., & Cullinan, B. E. (1991). Literature for literacy: What research says about the benefits of using trade books in the classroom. In J. Flood, J. M. Jensen, D. Lapp, & J. R. Squire (Eds.), *Handbook of research on teaching the English language arts* (pp. 529–535). New York: Macmillan.

Hoogstad, V., & Saxby, M. (1988). *Teaching literature to adolescents.* Melbourne: Nelson.

Mallett, M. (1992). *Making facts matter: Reading non-fiction 5–11.* London: Chapman.

Nodelman, P. (1992). *The pleasures of children's literature.* New York: Longman.

Russell, D. L. (1991). *Literature for children: A short introduction.* New York: Longman.

CHILDREN'S BOOKS REFERRED TO IN THIS CHAPTER

Ahlberg, J., & Ahlberg, A. (1977). *Jeremiah in the dark woods.* London: Kestrel.

Ahlberg, J., & Ahlberg, A. (1978). *Each peach pear plum.* Harmondsworth, UK: Kestrel.

Ahlberg, J., & Ahlberg, A. (1986). *The jolly postman, or, other people's letters.* London: Heinemann.

Aiken, J. (1962). *The wolves of Willoughby Chase.* London: Cape.

Alexander, L. (1973). *The book of three.* London: Collins.

Allen, J. (1993). *What is a wall, after all?* London: Walker.

Barbalet, M., & Tanner, J. (1991). *The wolf.* Ringwood, Victoria, Australia: Viking.

Barber, A. (1990). *The mousehole cat.* London: Walker.

Barrie, J. M. (1988). *Peter Pan.* London: Viking Kestrel. (Original work published 1911)

Berenstain, S., & Berenstain, J. (1971). *Bears in the night.* New York: Random House.

Biddulph, F., & Biddulph, J. (1991). *How spiders live.* Hong Kong: Applecross.

Blair, S. (1963). *The three billy goats gruff: A Norwegian folk tale.* New York: Ashton.

Breslin, T. (1994). *Whispers in the graveyard.* London: Methuen.

Browne, A. (1983). *Gorilla.* London: Julia MacRae.

Browne, A. (1990). *Changes.* London: Julia MacRae.

Burningham, J. (1991). *Aldo.* London: Cape.

Burton, V. L. (1942). *Mike Mulligan and his steam shovel.* London: Faber.

Cleary, B. (1950). *Henry Huggins.* New York: Morrow.

Cleary, B. (1974). *Ramona the pest.* New York: Morrow.

Cleary, B. (1978). *Ramona the brave.* New York: Morrow.

Cleary, B. (1983). *Dear Mr. Henshaw.* New York: Morrow.

Coats, A. M. (1937). *The story of Horace.* London: Faber.

Cowley, J. (1983). *Greedy cat.* Wellington, New Zealand: School Publications, Department of Education.

Cowley, J., & Ross, C. (1997). *Off goes the hose!* Wellington, New Zealand: Learning Media.

Crossley-Holland, K. (1985). *Storm.* London: Heinemann.

Dahl, R. (1982). *The BFG.* London: Cape.

Dodd, L. (1983). *Hairy Maclary from Donaldson's dairy.* Wellington, New Zealand: Mallinson Rendel.

Fleischman, S. (1972). *McBroom's wonderful one-acre farm.* London: Chatto & Windus.

Gag, W. (1929). *Millions of cats.* London: Faber.

Galdone, P. (1970). *The three little pigs.* Tadworth: World's Work.

Gordon, G. (1993). *Fuss finds out.* Auckland, New Zealand: Harper Collins.

Gurney, N., & Gurney, E. (1965). *The king, the mice and the cheese.* New York: Random House.

Hoban, R. (1969). *The mouse and his child.* London: Faber.

Hoban, R. (1974). *How Tom beat Captain Najork and his hired sportsmen.* London: Cape.

Holcroft, A. (1990). *Chen Li and the river spirit.* Auckland, New Zealand: Hodder & Stoughton.

Hutchins, P. (1972). *Titch.* London: Bodley Head.

Jones, D. W. (1986). *Howl's moving castle.* London: Methuen.

Le Guin, U. (1971). *A wizard of Earthsea.* London: Gollancz.

Lobel, A. (1970). *Frog and toad are friends.* New York: Harper & Row.

Macaulay, D. (1988). *The way things work.* London: Dorling Kindersley.

Macaulay, D. (1990). *Black and white.* Boston: Houghton Mifflin.

Mahy, M. (1991). *Bubble trouble and other poems and stories.* London: Hamish Hamilton.

Mayne, W. (1985). *Drift.* London: Cape.

Oakley, G. (1972). *The church mouse.* London: Macmillan.

Oakley, G. (1990). *Once upon a time.* London: Macmillan.

Peet, B. (1961). *Huge Harold.* Boston: Houghton Mifflin.

Peet, B. (1963). *The pinkish, purplish, bluish egg.* Boston: Houghton Mifflin.

Rodda, E. (1993). *Rowan of Rin.* Norwood, South Australia: Omnibus.

Rubinstein, G., & James, A. (1991). *Dog in, cat out.* Norwood, South Australia: Omnibus Books.

Scieszka, J., & Smith, L. (1992). *The stinky cheeseman and other fairly stupid tales.* New York: Viking.

Sendak, M. (1963). *Where the wild things are.* New York: Harper & Row.

Seuss, Dr. (1958). *The cat in the hat.* Glasgow: Collins.

Steig, W. (1969). *Sylvester and the magic pebble.* New York: Windmill Books/Simon & Schuster.

Suteev, V. (1972). *The chick and the duckling* (M. Ginsberg, Trans.). New York: Macmillan.

Taylor, L., & Blundell, T. (1989). *Pesters of the West.* London: Young Lions.

Taylor, W. (1990). *Agnes the sheep.* Auckland: Ashton Scholastic.

Tolkien, J. R. R. (1937). *The Hobbit.* London: Allen & Unwin.

Tulloch, R. (1990). *The brown felt hat.* Norwood, Australia: Omnibus.

Wallace, K., & Bostock, M. (1993). *Think of an eel.* London: Walker.

Wells, R. (1973). *Noisy Nora.* New York: Scholastic.

White, E. B. (1952). *Charlotte's web.* London: Hamish Hamilton.

Wilder, L. I. (1956). *Little house in the big woods*. London: Methuen.
Wrightson, P. (1991). *The sugar-gum tree*. Ringwood, Victoria, Australia: Viking.

REFERENCES

Applebee, A. (1978). *The child's concept of story*. Chicago: University of Chicago Press.
Bennett, J. (1982). *Learning to read with picture books* (2nd ed.). Stroud, UK: Thimble Press.
Butler, D. (1995). *Babies need books* (3rd ed.). London: Penguin.
Chambers, N. (Ed.). (1987). *Fiction 6 to 9: A Signal bookguide*. Stroud, UK: Thimble Press.
Clark, M. M. (1976). *Young fluent readers*. London: Heinemann Educational.
Clausen, C. (1982). Home and away in children's fiction. *Children's Literature, 10*, 141–152.
Cullinan, B. (1981). *Literature and the child*. New York: Harcourt Brace Jovanovich.
Durkin, D. (1966). *Children who read early: Two longitudinal studies*. New York: Teachers College Press.
Fisher, M. (1986). *Margery Fisher recommends classics for children and young people*. Stroud, UK: Thimble Press.
Francis, D. (1993). *Decider*. London: Michael Joseph.
Gibbons, J. (1981). *The effects of book experience on the responses of four-year-olds to texts*. Unpublished master's thesis, University of Waikato, Hamilton, New Zealand.
Hickman, J. (1981). A new perspective on response to literature: Research in an elementary school setting. *Research in the Teaching of English, 15*, 353–354.
Huck, C. S., Hepler, S., & Hickman, J. (1987). *Children's literature in the elementary school* (4th ed.). New York: Holt, Rinehart & Winston.
Huey, E. B. (1968). *The psychology and pedagogy of reading*. Cambridge, MA: MIT Press. (Original work published 1908)
Iser, W. (1974). *The implied reader: Patterns of communication in prose fiction from Bunyan to Beckett*. Baltimore: Johns Hopkins University Press.
Landsberg, M. (1988). *The world of children's books: A guide to choosing the best*. London: Simon & Schuster.
Martinez, M. G., & Roser, N. L. (1991). Children's responses to literature. In J. Flood, J. M. Jensen, D. Lapp, & J. R. Squire (Eds.), *Handbook of research on teaching the English language arts* (pp. 643–654). New York: Macmillan.
Morrow, L. M. (1988). Young children's responses to one-to-one story readings in school settings. *Reading Research Quarterly, 23*, 89–107.
Moss, E. (1992). *Picture Books 9 to 13* (2nd ed.). Stroud, UK: Thimble Press.
Munn, P. (1995). What do children know about reading before they go to school? In P. Owen & P. Pumfrey (Eds.), *Emergent and developing reading: Messages for teachers* (pp. 105–114). London: Falmer.
Nicholson, T. (1994). *At the cutting edge: Recent research on learning to read and spell*. Wellington: New Zealand Council for Educational Research.

Nicoll, V., & Roberts, V. (1993). *Taking a closer look at literature-based programs.* Newtown, New South Wales, Australia: Primary English Teaching Association.

Nodelman, P. (1992). *The pleasures of children's literature.* New York: Longman.

Norton, D. E. (1987). *Through the eyes of a child: An introduction to children's literature* (2nd ed.). Columbus, OH: Merrill.

Ritchie, J. (1978). *Chance to be equal.* Whatamongo Bay, New Zealand: Cape Catley.

Rosenblatt, L. (1978). *The reader, the text, the poem: The transactional theory of the literary work.* Carbondale: Southern Illinois University Press.

Rosenblatt, L. (1991). Literary theory. In J. Flood, J. M. Jensen, D. Lapp, & J. R. Squire (Eds.), *Handbook of research on teaching the English language arts* (pp. 57–62). New York: Macmillan.

Rudd, D. (1992). *A communications studies approach to children's literature.* Sheffield, UK: Pavic.

Teale, W. H. (1978). Positive environments for learning to read: What studies of early readers tell us. *Language Arts, 55,* 922–932.

Teale, W. H. (1981). Parents reading to their children: What we know and need to know. *Language Arts, 58,* 902–911.

Townsend, J. R. (1971). *A sense of story: Essays on contemporary writers for children.* London: Longman.

Wall, B. (1991). *The narrator's voice: The dilemma of children's fiction.* Basingstoke, UK: Macmillan.

Watson, V. (1992). Irresponsible writers and responsible readers. In M. Styles, E. Bearne, & V. Watson (Eds.), *After Alice: Exploring children's literature,* London: Cassell.

ACKNOWLEDGMENTS

The extracts on pp. 198–200 and p. 203, from the following publications, are reprinted with permission:

Burton, V. L. *Mike Mulligan and his steam shovel.* Copyright © 1939 by Virginia Lee Burton, copyright renewed 1967 by Virginia Lee Demetrios. Reprinted by permission of Houghton Mifflin Company. All rights reserved.

Cowley, J. *Greedy cat.* Wellington, New Zealand: School Publications, Department of Education. Copyright 1983 by Joy Cowley.

Cowley, J., & Ross, C. *Off goes the hose!* Wellington, New Zealand: Learning Media. Copyright 1997 by Joy Cowley.

Dodd, L. *Hairy Maclary from Donaldson's dairy.* Wellington, New Zealand: Mallinson Rendel. Copyright 1983 by Mallinson Rendel.

Peet, B. *The pinkish, purplish, bluish egg.* Copyright © 1963 by Bill Peet. Reprinted by permission of Houghton Mifflin Company. All rights reserved.

Sendak, M. *Where the wild things are.* Copyright © 1963 by Maurice Sendak. Reprinted by permission of HarperCollins Publishers.

Chapter 10

Engaging in Recreational Reading

DEBORAH A. M. WIDDOWSON, DENNIS W. MOORE,
AND ROBYN S. DIXON

a) What is the need for recreational reading in school?
b) What are children's attitudes toward recreational reading?
c) What are the effects on reading achievement?
d) How may we encourage children to read for recreation?

One of the aims of education is to engender in students a natural liking for reading and to cultivate a voluntary recreational reading habit (Greaney, 1980; Wheldall & Entwistle, 1988). However, the purposes and practices associated with much of the reading done in schools may not always directly reflect this aim. Children are required to read in school and normally something is expected of that reading, usually some measure of proficient oral performance and/or evidence of text comprehension. As a result, reading may come to be viewed by children primarily as an academic activity and the mastery of reading skills an end in itself. It is therefore possible that in our pursuit of competence the purely pleasurable aspects of reading are lost.

Research tends to support this suggestion. It has shown that children spend little time reading either for pleasure or for information (Morrow, 1985). Greaney (1980) found that fifth-grade students in Ireland devoted on average only 5% of their leisure time to recreational reading (of that time, 62% was spent reading books, compared with 31% spent reading comics and 7% spent reading newspapers), while 22% of students reported that they never read during their leisure time. It also seems that even students who are skilled readers may not read voluntarily (Morrow, 1985).

RECREATIONAL READING IN SCHOOL

One practice designed to foster a recreational-reading habit that has become a component of many school reading programs in several countries—including New Zealand, the United States, and Canada—is referred to as uninterrupted sustained silent reading (USSR) or, as it is more commonly known, sustained silent reading (SSR). Essentially, SSR involves the allotment of a special time, preferably each day, for independent, uninterrupted, silent, recreational reading. During this time students and the teacher are expected to quietly read a book of their own choosing. Students do not normally read printed materials other than books (e.g., newspapers, comics). The aim is for children to read extended text, and a book fits this requirement nicely, since reading a book requires a considerable amount of sustained reading time. Another feature of sustained silent reading is that it is meant to be enjoyable, with no follow-up study tasks required of pupils. For example, children are not required to answer comprehension questions or write a book report. Hunt (1970) described USSR as a key reading skill, "the essence of reading power; the ability to keep going with ideas in print" (p. 150). It has been recommended as a way of developing students who are not only capable of reading but who do read.

It is important to note that SSR is not a reading-instruction program. It is intended as a supplementary activity to enhance reading instruction and promote reading growth. However, SSR should not be thought of as a frill. Sadoski (1984) believes that sufficient opportunity to read, such as that provided by regular SSR periods, is essential for the integration and application of the principles and practices learned from reading instruction. This helps children to assimilate and transfer their learning and to internalize their reading skills in cognitively meaningful ways. Sadoski (1984) notes that

> Developmental learning theory holds that students need to build independence and mastery at a given level before going on to the next one, and educators agree that supplementary reading is an important aspect of learning to be a reader. Typically, however, time constraints and the pressures of testing give short shrift to this aspect. All too frequently both the "real-book" practice and interest components of reading instruction receive reduced or even insignificant attention. (p. 121)

THE RATIONALE FOR SUSTAINED SILENT READING

The incorporation of SSR into school reading programs is based on four premises: (1) that the ability to read silently is not automatically acquired, (2) that reading should be viewed as a holistic activity, (3) that silent reading is at least as important as oral reading, and (4) that readers need to develop independence and expertise in self-selecting reading material and in determining their own purposes for reading.

Allington (1975) suggests that classroom experience in reading silently for prolonged periods of time should be encouraged by the teacher. While substantial periods of time are allotted to teaching the various subskills of reading, it appears that relatively little time is provided for sustained practice of the total act of reading for enjoyment alone (Mork, 1972; Morrow, 1985). In the development of any skill, regular practice is required if we are to gain expertise (see Chapter 7). It has been suggested that in order for readers to develop independence, the ratio of practice to direct instruction in reading should be as high as 80% to 20% (Mork, 1972). The rationale for this claim is that reading power is built through the application and consolidation of skills during prolonged encounters with recreational reading material.

While many teachers urge students to read for pleasure at home, students may lack a quiet place free from distractions to do so or may have no adult role model to stimulate the desire to read (see Chapter 1). If the home environment does not actively endorse the value of reading and provide regular opportunities to engage in silent reading, it is unlikely that the child will choose to read at home, despite teacher exhortation, unless the child has already developed a love of reading elsewhere. SSR speaks to these concerns by providing regular quiet times at school when children can engage in silent reading in the presence of a positive adult role model.

The second premise is that reading should be viewed as a holistic activity. In order to avoid the development of a narrow perception of the act of reading, which may result from a focus on the teaching of isolated skills, proponents of SSR emphasize the need to provide time for children to engage in the total process of reading in its most natural form (Wiesendanger & Birlem, 1984). A separate-skills approach to reading may lead children to view the accomplishment of these skills as the goal of reading, leaving the discovery of reading as a holistic and recreational activity to occur incidentally, if at all. It is possible that failure to view reading in this way may provide an explanation for the finding that children can be skilled readers and yet not choose to read.

It is part of our cultural use of reading skills that silent reading is the norm and that oral reading is for news readers and beginning readers. Sadoski (1984) argues that the premise that silent reading is at least as important as oral reading is based on the belief that oral reading may contribute to feelings of incompetence and stigmatization, particularly for low-progress readers. It has been suggested that poor readers would experience more success if teachers treated them as if they were proficient readers by providing them with more silent and less oral reading time. This reduces the likelihood of the student experiencing the feelings of incompetence often associated with public failure by those who are required to read aloud in front of peers. In addition, the opportunity to practice their reading skills privately may result in the development of more positive attitudes toward reading.

The fourth premise is that readers need to develop independence and expertise in self-selecting reading material and in determining their own purposes for reading (Berglund & Johns, 1983). Moreover, students need to be given the opportunity to respond individually to ideas in print without constant teacher direction (Mork, 1972). According to Berglund and Johns (1983), such factors may contribute to the development of independent, mature readers who read for their own enjoyment and information. They claim that SSR gives readers the chance to self-regulate their reading, freeing them from the constraints of reading at a certain pace or reading every word perfectly. During SSR students are able to speed up or slow down their reading when they want to or even skim over sections. Thus SSR affords students the opportunity to read in the manner that more closely matches adult performance.

Benefits

Although many benefits have been attributed to SSR by its advocates, unfortunately little empirical research has been conducted that might substantiate the various claims. Despite this, there has been speculation that SSR leads to greater levels of concentration in students, an increasing ability to screen out distractions, and the ability to sustain silent reading for longer periods of time (Berglund & Johns, 1983). Manning-Dowd (1985) notes that SSR should also lead to more responsibility and greater sophistication in the self-selection of reading material. She also identifies other possible benefits of SSR, such as increased acceptance and enjoyment of reading, along with enhanced reading skills. It is also suggested that the positive effects of greater concentration and increased resistance to distraction that could accrue through involvement in SSR might spill over into other subject areas, resulting in increased effort and performance in other curriculum areas (Berglund & Johns, 1983).

The paucity of empirical research relating to SSR has often been lamented (Collins, 1980; Dwyer & Reed, 1989; Evans & Towner, 1975; Langford & Allen, 1983; Moore, Jones, & Miller, 1980; Summers & McClelland, 1982), and because of this the claims concerning benefits attributed to SSR must be regarded as tentative. The research that has been undertaken has focused mainly on the effects of SSR on reading achievement and attitudes toward reading. However, as Summers and McClelland (1982) point out, the available research is inclined to be

> ex cathedra, provide minimal data on restricted populations, and ignore valid research methodology and program evaluation paradigms. . . . Most of the reported research thus far involves vague definitions, strong promises, limited application of evaluation methodology, and weak estimates of effect. (p. 101)

In addition, comparisons of the findings of studies are made difficult by the fact that there is little consistency between studies as to the length of time over which the programs were implemented and the frequency and duration of SSR periods. It is important to keep such criticism in mind when evaluating research in this area.

Effects on Attitudes toward Reading

One of the objectives of school reading programs should be to engender in students a favorable attitude toward reading (Langford & Allen, 1983; Weisendanger & Birlem, 1984). Some authorities believe that students' attitudes toward reading may not only affect their willingness to read but may also impact on reading achievement. It is assumed that if students have a positive attitude toward reading, then they will read more, and that increases in the amount read will result in greater reading proficiency. Teacher practices that have been suggested as contributing to more positive attitudes toward reading include allowing time for recreational reading without requiring the students to report on what they have read and indicating by example the value of reading (Langford & Allen, 1983; Weisendanger & Birlem, 1984). These practices are components of SSR.

Overall, it appears that SSR has a positive effect on attitudes toward reading. Of the eleven studies reviewed by Weisendanger and Birlem (1984), nine indicated that SSR had a positive effect on students' attitudes toward reading. Manning-Dowd (1985) reached similar conclusions, based on five different studies indicating that SSR had a positive effect on reading attitudes, though in three other studies cited there appeared to have been no effect on students' attitudes toward reading.

It is possible that the effects of SSR on attitudes toward reading may differ according to the age of the children studied. Weisendanger and Birlem (1984) noted that the two studies that found that SSR had a negative effect on reading attitudes both involved high school students, whereas the studies that reported positive attitudes toward reading following in-volvement in SSR included elementary grade students. However, an em-pirical study by Summers and McClelland (1982)—which involved 1,400 fifth-, sixth-, and seventh-grade children from nine schools and was con-ducted over a 5-month period—found that attitudes toward reading did not appear to be enhanced through participation in SSR. Posttesting, using both standardized and informal instruments, indicated that the at-titudes of children who participated in SSR were not significantly differ-ent from those of the children in the control group who had not partici-pated in SSR.

In conclusion, while the majority of the studies undertaken suggest that SSR has a positive effect on attitudes toward reading, more empirical research is needed to clarify the nature of these effects for both elemen-tary and secondary school students.

Effects on Achievement

SSR has also been purported to have a positive effect on reading achievement when it is combined with a program of reading instruction (Moore et al., 1980; Weisendanger & Birlem, 1984). However, on closer examination of the research it becomes evident that, as with the research on reading attitudes, results are inconclusive. Manning-Dowd (1985) re-viewed eleven studies that had examined the effects of SSR on reading achievement and found that six of the studies reported that SSR was as-sociated with significant increases in reading scores, while the remaining five studies showed no significant gains. Meanwhile, Weisendanger and Birlem (1984) note that studies reporting no significant differences in read-ing achievement scores between groups of students exposed to SSR and control groups have all been conducted over relatively short periods of time (1 to 5 months), whereas studies conducted over more extended time periods have found significant differences in favor of SSR. They suggest that changes in reading achievement may not be realized until exposure to SSR has exceeded 6 months or more.

Another explanation for the inconsistent findings of studies examin-ing the effects of SSR on achievement may lie in the observation that such studies do not appear to have obtained objective measures of the degree to which students engage in reading during SSR periods. Factors that have been shown to moderate the effectiveness of SSR include the extent to which the guidelines or rules for SSR are followed. One of the basic guide-lines for SSR is that both teachers and students must read during SSR ses-sions. Therefore sufficient reading material for students must be available in the classroom if this is to occur. McCracken and McCracken (1978) state, based on thousands of anecdotal reports from teachers, that SSR appears to fail when students do not have a wide selection of books to choose from.

ENCOURAGING SUSTAINED SILENT READING

There are several generally accepted guidelines for the implementation of SSR. These include: (1) Regularly scheduled sessions are provided. It is suggested that short daily periods of 5 to 10 minutes should be employed at first and that these should be lengthened gradually according to student readiness to sustain longer periods of silent reading. (2) Students must read silently. (3) Teachers must also read recreationally during SSR, thereby providing a model for recreational reading. (4) Readers should choose their own reading material. (5) A wide variety of reading material must be available to readers in the classroom. To this end students may be encouraged to bring books from home or a library. (6) There should not be any requirements arising from the reading. Reports and records must not be made contingent on material read during SSR periods. These rules should be established prior to the implementation of SSR.

As noted earlier, one of the problems that becomes evident in reading the SSR literature is that researchers have not measured the extent to which students actually engage in reading during SSR sessions. Allocating time for reading does not of itself ensure that children actively engage in reading during that time. When Herbert (1987) asked 636 students what they did during SSR, half of them reported that they did not actually participate in silent reading. Not surprisingly, these children did not hold positive attitudes toward SSR. By contrast, in a study by Combs and Van Dusseldorp (1984) in which they found that 84% of students surveyed said that they read most or all of the time during SSR sessions, there was overwhelming support from participants for the continuation of SSR.

It is obvious that any changes in attitudes toward reading or effects on reading achievement are dependent on participation in SSR. Research suggests that what the teacher does during SSR sessions is a crucial factor with respect to students' participation. McCracken and McCracken (1978) suggest that in the majority of cases where problems arise in SSR programs, teachers are not reading with the children.

Social learning theory, as outlined by Bandura (1977), helps us understand why what the teacher does during these times is so important. Bandura and others claim that observational learning, learning through observation of others' behavior, is the way much of children's learning occurs. Those people whom young children hold in high regard, particularly parents and teachers, can be powerful models for learning. Thus a teacher modeling reading for pleasure during SSR is likely to serve as a strong model for this activity.

In a study carried out in New Zealand, Pluck, Ghafari, Glynn, and McNaughton (1984) investigated the effects of concurrent modeling of recreational reading on five low-achieving and five high-achieving readers in a standard 2 (third-grade) class. Pluck and colleagues defined concurrent modeling as involving a competent model providing a continual display of the target behavior. Observations of subjects' "on-task" behavior during recreational reading sessions were conducted twice weekly over a period of 16 weeks. Results showed increases in on-task behavior for both groups when the teacher modeled recreational reading, with increases being greatest for the low-achieving readers. This study and another by Wheldall and Entwhistle (1988) have drawn our attention to the important role teachers play in encouraging recreational reading.

More recently, Widdowson, Dixon, and Moore (1996) reported a replication and extension of the study by Pluck and colleagues (1984). In addition to low- and high-achieving readers, a third group of average-achieving readers was included. This was because Weisendanger and Bader (1989) had reported that SSR had the greatest long-term effects on students of average reading ability. They reported that when they interviewed subjects about their reading habits during the summer holidays, the average-ability readers who had been exposed to SSR reported they had read on average 40 minutes more each week than had those not exposed to the SSR. By contrast, prior exposure to SSR had no effect on the time spent reading over the summer by above-average readers and below-average readers. Further, because it seems that what the teacher does during SSR is central to the success of the program, Widdowson and colleagues (1996) closely monitored the teacher's behavior throughout their study.

Four students at each of the high, average, and low achievement levels participated in this study, in which on-task behavior was observed during SSR sessions with and without concurrent modeling of recreational reading by the teacher. The researchers report that concurrent modeling of recreational reading increased participation in SSR for both low- and average-achieving readers but not high-achieving readers. In attempting to explain why SSR appears to have differential effects according to the student's reading ability, Widdowson and colleagues (1996) suggest that average-achieving readers already possessed the necessary reading skills but had not spent sufficient time reading, prior to the introduction of concurrent modeling of recreational reading by the teacher, to discover the enjoyment associated with reading. When average readers observed a competent, valued adult reading for enjoyment, they were encouraged to imitate this behavior and were thereby given the opportunity to discover that sustained engagement in reading can be enjoyable. This possibility is strengthened by the fact that when the teacher ceased to model reading, the average readers continued to remain on-task during SSR sessions.

While low-achieving readers spent more time on-task when the teacher modeled recreational reading, when the teacher stopped modeling reading on-task rates for this group fell. It therefore seems important that the teacher continue to provide a model for this group until such time as their reading skills improve to a level that enables them to gain enjoyment from sustained independent reading.

High-achieving readers, on the other hand, did not appear to need an adult model in order to be on-task most of the time during SSR. This could have been because these students already found reading enjoyable. It is interesting to note that on-task rates of two students in this group actually fell when the teacher modeled reading. This suggests that for some students concurrent modeling might be counterproductive.

A possible explanation for this finding is that these high achievers may have been praised by the teacher for engaging in reading before she herself started to model reading. By modeling reading, the teacher was unable to give personal attention to these pupils. Knowing that the teacher was not attending to them any longer, and was instead reading a book for herself, these high achievers may have reacted to the change in her behavior by spending less time reading. These findings add credence to the suggestion that what the teacher does during SSR is crucial to the success or otherwise of SSR. It would also seem important, based on the findings of Widdowson and colleagues (1996), that we do not assume that outcomes of SSR will necessarily be the same for all students and that researchers continue to investigate possible differential effects according to the student's reading ability.

CONCLUSIONS

SSR properly implemented is a useful way to introduce children to recreational reading as part of the classroom reading program. Though the empirical evidence is limited, it is clear that the teacher's modeling of recreational reading is central to the success of SSR. It seems that generally SSR has a positive impact on children's attitudes toward reading and reading achievement, with some evidence that poor and average readers benefit the most. However, there is need for further research in order to further clarify which of our students have the most to gain from participating in SSR.

REVIEW

Recreational reading is seen to be a key part of the overall reading program in schools, since it is in such activity that the learner practices particular reading skills and builds autonomy in reading. Up to 4 hours of practice with recreational reading material for every hour of instruction has been recommended for the consolidation of reading skills. Sustained silent reading (SSR) or the daily scheduling of time specifically for independent, uninterrupted, silent, recreational reading during school time is one procedure designed to provide students with such regular and ongoing practice. It is not to be viewed as a substitute for instruction, but as opportunity for skill rehearsal.

Four premises underlie the allocation of class time to recreational reading in SSR:

1. The ability to read silently is learned, not acquired automatically.
2. Reading should be viewed as a holistic activity, not as a series of isolated skills.
3. Silent reading is at least as important as oral reading.
4. Readers need to develop independence and expertise in self-selecting reading materials and in determining their own purposes for reading.

Much has been written on the benefits of SSR, though unfortunately little empirical research has been done to substantiate these claims. The weight of the evidence available supports the claim that SSR enhances students' attitudes toward reading and, in combination with effective instruction, may have a positive effect on reading achievement, particularly if the SSR has been properly implemented and has been in place for more than 6 months. Student participation in the SSR process is a necessary precondition to attitudinal or performance gains and should be planned and structured by the teacher, not simply expected to occur automatically. Six components have been identified as critical in the proper implementation of SSR:

1. Regularly scheduled sessions are provided.
2. The students read silently.
3. Teachers provide a model for reading by also reading recreationally during the session.
4. Readers choose their own reading material.
5. A wide variety of reading material is available to readers in the classroom.

6. There are no performance requirements, comprehension exercises, or reports arising from the reading.

STUDY AND DISCUSSION QUESTIONS

1. In what ways is SSR considered to contribute to a classroom reading program?
2. Identify the premises underlying SSR.
3. What effects does SSR have on students' attitudes toward reading and their reading performance?
4. What does Bandura's work tell us about the importance of teacher modeling of SSR?
5. Consider why the study by Widdowson and colleagues (1996) found differential outcomes for SSR according to the ability of the students.

FURTHER READING

Pluck, M., Ghafari, E., Glynn, T., & McNaughton, S. (1984). Teacher and parent modelling of recreational reading. *New Zealand Journal of Educational Studies, 19*, 114–123.

Sadoski, M. C. (1984). SSR, accountability and effective reading instruction. *Reading Horizons, 24*, 119–123.

Wheldall, K., & Entwistle, J. (1988). Back in the USSR: The effect of teacher modelling of silent reading on pupils' reading behaviour in the primary school classroom. *Educational Psychology, 8*, 51–66.

Widdowson, D. A. M., Dixon, R. S., & Moore, D. W. (1996). The effects of teacher modelling on students' engagement during sustained silent reading. *Educational Psychology, 16*, 171–180.

REFERENCES

Allington, R. (1975). Sustained approaches to reading and writing. *Language Arts, 52*, 813–815.

Bandura, A. R. (1977). *Social learning theory.* Engelwood Cliffs, NJ: Prentice-Hall.

Berglund, R. L., & Johns, J. L. (1983). A primer on uninterrupted sustained silent reading. *Reading Teacher, 36*, 534–539.

Collins, C. (1980). Sustained silent reading periods: Effects on teachers' behavior and students' attainment. *Elementary School Journal, 81*, 108–114.

Combs, C., & Van Dusseldorp, R. (1984). *Student and teacher attitudes to uninterrupted sustained silent reading.* (ERIC Document Reproduction Service No. ED248488).

Dwyer, E. J., & Reed, V. (1989). Effects of sustained silent reading on attitudes toward reading. *Reading Horizons, 29*, 283–293.

Evans, H. M., & Towner, J. C. (1975). Sustained silent reading: Does it increase skills? *Reading Teacher, 29*, 155–156.

Greaney, V. (1980). Factors related to amount and type of leisure reading. *Reading Research Quarterly, 15*, 337–357.

Herbert, S. S. (1987). Open to suggestion. *Journal of Reading, 30*, 648–651.

Hunt, L. C. (1970). The effect of self-selection, interest, and motivation upon independent, instructional, and functional levels. *Reading Teacher, 24*, 146–158.

Langford, J. C., & Allen, E. C. (1983). The effects of USSR on students' attitudes and achievement. *Reading Horizons, 23*, 194–200.

Manning-Dowd, A. (1985). *The effectiveness of SSR: A review of the research.* (ERIC Document Reproduction Service No. ED276970)

McCracken, R. A., & McCracken, M. J. (1978). Modeling is the key to sustained silent reading. *Reading Teacher, 31*, 406–408.

Moore, J. C., Jones, C. J., & Miller, D. C. (1980). What we know after a decade of sustained silent reading. *Reading Teacher, 33*, 445–450.

Mork, T. A. (1972). Sustained silent reading in the classroom. *Reading Teacher, 25*, 438–442.

Morrow, L. M. (1985). Developing young voluntary readers: The home—the child—the school. *Reading Research and Instruction, 25*, 1–8.

Pluck, M., Ghafari, E., Glynn, T., & McNaughton, S. (1984). Teacher and parent modelling of recreational reading. *New Zealand Journal of Educational Studies, 19*, 114–123.

Sadoski, M. C. (1984). SSR, accountability and effective reading instruction. *Reading Horizons, 24*, 119–123.

Summers, E. G., & McClelland, J. V. (1982). A field-based evaluation of sustained silent reading (SSR) in intermediate grades. *Alberta Journal of Educational Research, 28*, 100–112.

Wheldall, K., & Entwistle, J. (1988). Back in the USSR: The effect of teacher modelling of silent reading on pupils' reading behaviour in the primary school classroom. *Educational Psychology, 8*, 51–66.

Widdowson, D. A. M., Dixon, R. S., & Moore, D. W. (1996). The effects of teacher modelling on students' engagement during sustained silent reading. *Educational Psychology, 16*, 171–180.

Wiesendanger, K. D., & Bader, L. (1989). SSR: Its effects on students' reading habits after they complete the program. *Reading Horizons, 29*, 162–166.

Wiesendanger, K. D., & Birlem, E. D. (1984). The effectiveness of SSR: An overview of the research. *Reading Horizons, 24*, 197–201.

Chapter 11

Learning to Evaluate Literature

CHANDA K. PINSENT

a) What is literary evaluation?
b) What does the process of literary evaluation require of the reader?
c) What evidence is there that young readers are capable of literary evaluation?
d) How can literary criticism be practiced in the classroom?

When educators are considering the acquisition of a skill, such as reading, they should take into account not only how that acquisition is to be achieved but also why the acquisition is a priority. In other words, why teach children to read? This may seem an unnecessary question to ask with reference to reading. After all, educated people are literate people, and an educator's task is to assist in development of a literate population. However, reading is often defined in terms of the ability to decode print, not in terms of the ability to deal with the ideas in print and with the process of reading itself.

> The literate person, however, is not one who knows *how* to read, but *one who reads*: fluently, responsively, critically, and because he wants to. Reading involves an engagement with print and an active personal involvement with the ideas expressed in it. (Sloan, 1975, p. 1)

If we use Sloan's description of literacy, then the fluent reader is one who would be expected to read with competent decoding and comprehension skill; the responsive reader would be able to interact intellectually with the text and express his or her feelings about reading experience; and the critical reader would be able to evaluate the reading, that is, apply criteria and express a supported opinion about what is read. Finally, the literate person reads because he or she wants to, or finds something inherently rewarding about the experience.

These issues have been considered by theorists, researchers, and educators within the context of learning to read and the role of children's literature in that learning process (Gardner & Gardner, 1971; Hancock, 1993; Sutherland & Arbuthnot, 1991). In this book, the acquisition of decoding and comprehension skills has been dealt with in earlier chapters. The chapters on children's literature and recreational reading deal with the issues of providing reasons to read literature. It is the purpose of this chapter to address what it is to be a critical reader of literature and, more specifically, a critical child reader of children's literature.

WHAT IS LITERARY EVALUATION?

Reader Experience and Reader Response

There are two components to the process of reading literary works: experience and response. The *reader's experience* of literature, and this includes the young child's experience of hearing literature read aloud, is the internal private creation of meaning. The reading experience is known fully only to the reader. Rosenblatt (1970) describes the reading experience as a "transaction," or an exchange, between the reader and the text.

On the one hand, the reader brings to the process of creating meaning all his or her prior knowledge about the world, reading, and texts. On the other hand, the text sets constraints on the possible meanings the reader can create. In educational terms, educating the reading experience can be seen as developing a reader's meaning-making ability. This development will be assisted by the reader's expanding knowledge about the world, about reading, and about texts. For example, increasing one's vocabulary and exposure to many and varied types of books is believed to enrich one's reading experience. This is referred to sometimes as "educating the imagination." How a reading experience can be changed as a result of an "educated imagination" could be seen in the example of you, as an adult reader, rereading a book that was a childhood favorite. Often the rereading produces a different experience from the one you remember having with this book as a child. Part of what contributes to the different experience is your adult knowledge and experience associated with reading, books, and the world.

The second component to the process of reading is that of *reader response*. A reader response is the reflective expression about the reading experience. The reader reflects on the experience and forms a response that can be communicated either verbally or nonverbally to the world external to the reader. For example, a verbal response could be a reader's written summary of a storybook's plot. A nonverbal response could be a drawing done by the reader of his or her favorite character or simply the action of a reader setting aside a disappointing book before it is finished. A reader's response is the component accessible to the educator. It is through the reader's response that one may measure comprehension, achieve insight into the reader's experience, or engage the reader in discussion. Response to literature is a large area of research and theory (Beach & Hynds, 1991). However, the rest of this chapter will focus on one particular type of response: the evaluation by the reader of what is read.

Evaluative Response

Reader response can be distinguished from reading experience in that the response process distances the meaning created as something separate from the self, something that can be reflected upon. This differs from the experience of creating meaning when the self is engaged in the world of the text or "immersed in the text's reality." Langer (1990) refers to the reader response process as one of "stepping out" of the world of the text. While there appears to be a limitless number of forms of reader response—from the classic book report, to a letter to the author, to an interpretation of the story through dance—Vandergrift (1990) identifies six broad categories of types of response based on the purpose the reader has for communicating his or her reading experience. These categories can also be seen as the step-by-step procedure for criticizing a literary work. These categories are:

1. *Personal*: the reader's affective reaction to the reading. This may be seen, for example, in the impulsive "starting again" by a reader of a book that he or she has really enjoyed and just finished, or a reader's answer to the question "Did you like this book?" The purpose of the personal response is to identify one's subjective feeling about the reading.
2. *Descriptive*: an early step in objectifying the text. This is characterized by the description and identification of surface elements by a recalling or retelling of the reading, as when a reader responds to a question such as "What is that book about?" or to comprehension questions such as "Who are the main characters?" The purpose of the descriptive response is to relate some basic information about the content.
3. *Classificatory*: placing the reading within a context so that it can be compared or contrasted to other books or experiences. This is a step outside of the single reader–text consideration and an extension of the experience to considering the reading within a wider context of reading experiences. This type of response is seen in discussion about genre or when a reader compares the works of an author.

4. *Analytic*: the writing process of the author and the text as a literary entity are central to the analysis as the reader considers the use of literary elements and the structure of the work itself. This is a dive beneath the surface structures, which were the object of the descriptive responses, to analyze the deep structures and workings of the text. For example, a reader may analyze the use of figurative language, or the pacing, or the order of events in a work. The purpose of the analytic response is to communicate one's understanding of the structure of the work.
5. *Interpretive*: the making of inferences about a reading. It involves the reader's expressing interpretations about theme, recognizing influences of other works on the author, or exploring symbolic, mythological, or psychological elements. It is an "I think this means this because . . . " type of response. Interpretive responses thrust the reader into a debate where alternatives can be proposed and considered. Whereas analysis is about textual structure, interpretation is about textual ideas.
6. *Evaluative*: the opportunity to judge the reading experience on its merit or quality, based on the consideration of criteria. These criteria may be personal, literary, social, or moral. This is the point at which the initial personal response comes together with the support built up by a thorough exploration of the reading experience. The purpose of the reader's evaluative response is to make a supported decision about the value of this reading.

   In summary then, Vandergrift's (1990) model of reader response can be viewed as a

> form of reader-response criticism, one begins with a subjective response (personal), moves to a more objective position (descriptive, classificatory, analytic) in an attempt to identify the characteristics of a work that triggered personal responses and then to a combination of subjective and objective responses (interpretive, evaluative) to use both personal and external criteria in interpreting and judging a text. (p. 40)

   Within a theoretical framework such as this, the reader who evaluates a literary work does so by applying criteria to the reading experience in order to judge its success or quality. In order to formulate an evaluative response, a reader must be able to reflect on the parties that were part of the meaning-making process and consider the interrelations between them. As F. Smith (1982) states: "There are three parties to every transaction that written language makes possible: a writer, a reader, and a text" (p. 87). Therefore, in order for the young reader to evaluate the reading experience, he or she must be able to consider the reading from a number of different perspectives: the perspective of the author, the one who writes the text; the perspective of the text, the literary world and the structures and conventions that define it; and the perspective of the reader, the one who has created the meaning.

In this model, the job of the literary critic is to approach reader response by extending the comprehension of a literary work to an evaluation of a literary work. This requires an objectification of the work and the reader's experience of it (Langer, 1990). By objectification it is meant that the experience, the meaning created while reading the work, must be viewed as an "object," as if one could hold the meaning created still or static (Vandergrift, 1990) while one examines it. The reading experience can be considered as an entity distanced to some extent from each of three parties involved in its creation: the author, the text, and the reader. It is almost as if the reading experience must have some static shape, like a sculpture, so that the critic can "walk around" it, viewing it from a number of different but overlapping perspectives.

For an example of this process, consider the following statement by a 10-year-old reader evaluating a picture book:

> It was a really great book. The story line was short and simple.
> The words in the book were really describing, it would not
> have mattered if the pictures were there or not because you
> could have imagined what the characters looked like. It was
> like you knew what was going to happen but it ended up very
> different from what you expected it to. The author had a sense
> of humor.

The reader's response seems to reflect that "circling" or "walking around" process outlined above, as she holds the experience "still" and considers the meaning created, after first making a personal assertion about the quality. Then she proceeds to build a case for her evaluation of it as "a really great book." She goes to the text, describing the story line, the words and characters, and then to the reader, the experience of the surprise ending, and then to the author, making an inference about his personality or style of writing.

The critic, whether child or adult, evaluates the reading experience by considering its relations to:

1. Personal experience and knowledge, or how believable the work is
2. Other texts and other readings, or how successful this work is in comparison to other works

3. The motivation of the author, or why this work was written
4. The actual structure and conventions of the text itself, or how it
   was written

The evaluation is a *reader* response and is therefore based on the *reader's* knowledge of both the external world and the literary world.

At this point, the issues of why and how one would apply such a model to reading instruction arise. This is worthy of consideration given the development and widespread implementation of literature-based curricula. In the next section, the issue of "Why literary criticism?" will be addressed. The question of "How?" is considered in the final section on educational practice.

Literature-Based Curricula

The rationale for developing methods to teach literary evaluation, or facilitate its development, is founded on the notion that learning to evaluate what one reads is part of learning to appreciate the art of literature. Learning to evaluate thereby assists in the development of the cognitive processes involved in understanding representation, expression, and aesthetics (Hochberg, 1978). Evaluation as a response goal is central to models of reader response development such as Langer's (1990), where she cites "the role of literature in the development of the sharp and critical mind" (p. 812), or Hade's (1991) "literary approach" to reading that pushes for "rigor" in response, that is, responses that have clarity of expression and justification of personal opinion.

Students are taught to evaluate literature but usually not until adolescence, when adult literature is introduced to the curriculum (Beach & Hynds, 1991). However, with the advent of literature-based curricula in the first 6 years of formal schooling, attention has been directed toward the relationship between processes and operations involved in reader response and the development and teaching of critical thinking skills. It is now quite common for instructional objectives related to the evaluation or criticism of literature to be included in the elementary ("primary") syllabus (New Zealand Draft English Curriculum, 1993; Protherough, 1990).

Literature-based curricula rest on the theoretical principle that children will learn to read best when the central materials used to teach reading are books of literary merit. In practice, this means that the fictional texts used in the elementary or primary classroom are books labeled children's literature: the illustrated picture book and the junior novel. These so-called real books are written by authors whose intention it is to relate a story to a young audience; how the books are used in reading instruction is the task of the educator. This approach differs from the use of a basal reader or excerpt anthology program in which the materials read by the students are created to match the scope and sequence of a specific reading program (see Chapter 4). Literature-based curricula reflect the theoretical assumption that introducing children to the best of writing and illustration as soon as formal reading instruction begins creates an early interest in real books that will be fostered over the child's language arts instruction (Sutherland & Arbuthnot, 1991). The goal of this approach is to provide a wide and authentic experience with literature so as to prepare children to become lifelong and independent readers.

In the first few years of school, children's literature is used to *teach* reading. The storybook is the focus of the reading lesson as children participate in shared and guided reading, and the acquisition of skill is meant to piggyback on the process of reading for meaning. However, once the child has acquired the skills necessary to read independently, by third grade on average, much of the rest of the elementary or primary reading curriculum is focused on increasing the level of text difficulty in conjunction with the development of comprehension skills. Reader response activities related to prediction, summarization, and discussion of the story's features allow the educator to assess the student's comprehension achievement. "Describe what happened in this story" can be asked in a thousand different and often very creative ways.

In the first 6 or 7 years of school, literature acts as the handmaiden to the goals of reading acquisition and comprehension. It is used as a tool to teach reading; its value is located in its application to these goals. It is with the introduction of adult literature, in secondary school, that the study of literature begins to resemble the scholarly practice of literary criticism (Young, 1991); that is, the careful and reflective study of literature as an art form with inherent value. Traditionally, this has meant a text-based analysis of classical literature. However, contemporary theories and methods have provided the opportunity for analysis and evaluation of the reader's response in addition to the study of the text itself. Attention in these theories is given to the *interaction* between reader and text, such as how particular textual or structural elements can evoke a particular reaction in a reader, or how the reader's prior experience influences the meaning created. Examples of reader–text interaction can be seen in the following statements made by 10-year-old readers:

Just by reading the title it made me want to get straight into it.
[Words of the title cause reaction in reader and reader
responds with getting "straight into it."]

A boy would not like this book because the main character
was a girl and boys that are younger don't really like girls. [The
reader's experience of gender relations at particular ages
influence his evaluation of the book.]

This book is not a mystery. It is sort of a whispering book. I can
tell by the way the grandmother spoke her story. [Words of
the text attributed to a character cause the reader to create a
new classification, "whispering book," when known genre
label, mystery, does not seem to apply.]

The adolescent reader is also expected to evaluate what he or she reads,
that is, to express and support an opinion about the value or success of the
reading experience. Children's literature is rarely treated in such a scholarly manner in the teaching of young children. The reason for this may lie
in the assumption on the part of educators that literary criticism is too difficult a task for the young reader, or in the belief that an analytical or evaluative approach may rob the young reader of some of the pleasure of reading.

In answer to the first assumption, the balance of this chapter will
address children's abilities as they relate to the two key cognitive operations identified as integral to the evaluation process, those being objectification and the taking of multiple perspectives. In other words, are young
readers cognitively able to tackle the task of literary criticism? In answer
to the second assumption, evaluation of the reading experience need not
be a cruel vivisection of a work but rather part of one's development as a
independent reader (Sloan, 1975). In the classroom, the children's literature used by students is usually selected by teachers or librarians and therefore is of a quality that satisfies some generally accepted criteria related to
value. However, in order to meet the objective of educating readers to be
independent and critical, one must consider how this is to be achieved
without providing opportunity to acquire the knowledge and skill to evaluate what one reads for oneself. After all, the teacher-selector will not always be available.

It is the intention of this chapter to put forward the notion of children's
literature as art, the reading of it as an artistic experience, and the response
to it as motivated by the need not only to understand but also to compare,
analyze, and evaluate. Because reading acquisition and comprehension skills
are central to the definition of what literacy education is in our society, the
children's literature used for reading instruction sometimes loses its relation to the rest of the arts. From the artistic perspective proposed here, one's
literary education is part of one's arts education and, therefore, learning to
appreciate and criticize literature must be part of the literature-based cur-

riculum. The issue of literary criticism in the elementary or primary class-room is really an issue of bridging *language* and *arts* education.

THE COGNITIVE NATURE OF LITERARY EVALUATION

On one hand, reader response theory liberates the process of evalua-tion from that of the traditional handing down of a judgment from the academic critic to become a process within the grasp of any reflective reader. As B. H. Smith (1990) states in her analysis of the role of evalua-tion in contemporary literary theory,

> Literary evaluation is no longer thought of as confined to the discrete verbal statements of journalistic or academic critics. The evaluation of a work is seen, rather, as a continuous process, operating through a wide variety of individual practices. The work's value is seen not as some-thing already fixed. (p. 177)

On the other hand, reader response theory imposes considerable cogni-tive demands on the child reader that it assumes he or she has the ability to meet successfully.

The two key cognitive operations required in the production of the evaluative response are the ability to "distance," or objectify, a reading experience and the ability to consider multiple perspectives and the rela-tionships among them. Both of these operations are involved in the evalu-ative response, which demands thinking about and understanding both the reader's process of reading (how the meaning was created) and the author's process of writing (how the text was created). Therefore the reader's ability to produce an evaluative response is dependent on his or her ability to consider the interactions among the parties of the reader–text–author triangle as they relate to the processes of reading and of writ-ing. This requires both an ability to "distance" oneself from the reading experience in order to reflect on it and an ability to consider the reading experience from alternative perspectives. Consider the earlier example of the reader "circling" the meaning she had created, considering the influ-ence and perspectives of the author, the text, and the reader in that expe-rience as she built a case for making the assertion that it was a "a really great book."

These operations will be considered as they relate to children's cog-nitive abilities in the areas of thinking about texts, thinking about authors, and thinking about readers. The purpose of this section is to develop a profile of children's competence as literary critics, that is, the evidence relating to their possession of required skills, knowledge, or capacities (Dent, 1986) for evaluating the literature they read. Particular attention will be paid to the roles of the operations of objectification and perspective taking in that evaluative process.

Thinking About Texts

When considering the text itself, the critic may consider such things as the use of figurative language, the various devices that enhance the expression of the work; the literary structure of the work, how the work functions as a whole; and intertextuality, the relationship among texts. The reader's consideration of the structural elements of the text draws on his or her competence with literary conventions and devices. For some of these elements, competence is seen to develop as part of normal cognitive development, such as the use and understanding of metaphors (Pollio, Smith, & Pollio, 1990); or is assisted with literary experience, such as the development of story schemata (Black & Siefert, 1985); or may be achieved as the result of direct instruction, such as an analysis of the use of parody in children's stories (Stott, 1990).

"Thinking about texts" relates to the operation of objectification in that the reader, in order to evaluate the reading experience, must consider the role of the text in the reading experience. The text is the concrete referent for subsequent description, analysis, and evaluation. The experience of reading a particular text is the object evaluated. When the text's form and structure are considered, it is their impact on the reader's experience and the meaning created that are being evaluated. To appreciate this experience as the object, the reader must be able to consider the relationship between text and reader and alternate between at least two perspectives: reader considering text, and text influencing reader. It may also include the consideration of the author's role in the production of a text that influenced a reader's experience.

Dealing with texts requires the ability to objectify the experience of reading a particular text and the ability to identify the actual forms, such as a genre, or structures, such as figurative language, so that those elements may be evaluated. The evaluative process involves the consideration of the alternative perspectives of the reader and of the text as players in the reading experience. The young reader's competence with intertextuality, literary structure, and figurative language as examples of dealing with texts will be considered.

Intertextuality. Critical readers make use of the relations among texts to construct an evaluation through the act of comparing the text being read to other texts in their literary experience. The act of comparing textual form is the recognition on the part of the reader that no text is created in a vacuum and that both reading and writing occur within a social and cultural community, historical and contemporary, of texts, authors, and readers who are influenced by one another. The readers in their response to a text may recognize the role of other texts in their experience in forming an interpretation or may recognize the role other texts have played in the author's creation of the text being evaluated. This web of influences is referred to as intertextuality (Stephens, 1990).

Intertextuality requires that the reader "step back from the individual poem or story to see it in the context of literature as a whole" (Sloan, 1975, p. 84). It requires the reader to create enough distance between the self and the text so that the text can be considered in a relational context to other texts. This aspect of textual evaluation is found in the type of classificatory responses outlined previously. For example, a text may be considered as a poor instance of the mystery genre. In order to arrive at such an evaluative response, one text has to be weighed against all other relevant ones in that reader's prior experience, by employing appropriate criteria.

There is very little research in the area of children's intertextual competence, especially as it relates to their ability to form an evaluative response. Intertextuality is a comparative skill and is dependent on both a breadth of literary experience to provide the background knowledge from which to draw, and on the practice of identifying common and contrasting elements of form. Both experience and practice are influenced by the teaching approach: how many and what type of books are presented and the degree to which books are presented as isolated or related entities (Rogers, 1991). There is some evidence (Lowe, 1991; Young, 1991) to suggest that young children are capable of identifying author- and character-based relations among texts, for example, common elements of Beatrix Potter books. Also, by the fifth and sixth year of schooling in a literature-based language arts program, children will have encountered hundreds of stories and had practice identifying patterns and commonalities in other curriculum areas, such as spelling and mathematics. It may be expected, then, that the consideration of literary intertextuality would not be an insurmountable challenge for the student in the fourth to sixth year of schooling.

Textual Structure. The structure of a literary text may be distinguished from its form in the following way:

> A text has *form*: it is a novel, or a poem, or a play; it's probably a particular kind of novel or poem (genre). . . . In addition, a text has its own individual *structure*: it is those words, those sentences, those lines of verse in that order; it's that particular novel, that particular poem. *Form* is

what a text has in common with other texts put together according to
the same rules or conventions. . . . *Structure* is the detailed working out,
within the conventions of the adopted form, of an original idea: structure is what makes a text unique. (Quinn, 1992, p. 29)

As intertextuality relies on breadth of literary experience in order to analyze form, structural competency relies on depth to analyze structure. The
critic of structure, therefore, must be knowledgeable about literary devices
and such structural elements of a literary text as plot, character, style, and
theme.

A structural analysis considers how structures have influenced one's
reading experience. Such an in-depth study is integral to the construction
of a good evaluative response because it is part of the process of putting
forward the evidence or justification for the evaluation. Some theorists
refer to the structural analysis as a "close study," requiring one

to dwell on a book, to read pictures and text closely and with care . . .
[to be] able to discover and discuss such literary patterns as the relation between picture and text, the shape of the story, the development
of character, and the use of language. (Landes, 1981, p. 193)

However, the in-depth study need not be a fragmented or unimaginative
dissection of the "parts" of the story, such as many people remember from
high school or undergraduate literature classes. Instead, it can be seen as
part of the overall process of coming to understand one's reading experience, not simply the last exercise before the book is put aside.

Examples of creative instruction in structuralist consideration of literature by children can be found in the work of Jon Stott (1987, 1990),
who says that "until we have mastered the conventions of a culture's literature—its symbolic vocabulary and its narrative grammar—we cannot
read that literature with true perception" (1990, p. 219). This means that
in order to achieve a rich understanding of literature, one must be knowledgeable about how a literary work "works." Stott cites numerous anecdotal examples at the fourth to fifth year of schooling that use his approach
to teach literary structure to children. The approach involves more than a
simple lesson about a particular structure, for example, the use of parody.
It involves extending children's responses to making comparisons among
works and to learning to cite evidence and justify their responses and criticisms. Stott's (1990) theory centers on the principle that once the literary
patterns are discovered, compared, and criticized, then a better understanding of the "unity" of the work is achieved. Therefore comprehension is
improved with critical consideration of the pattern, or "literary framework,"

because it "provides a coherence for the details" (p. 227). This is a theoretical stance shared by Sloan (1975) in her discussion of a pattern-based critical method for children's responses to literature adapted from Frye's (1957) archetypal criticism, that is, that there are common structures or patterns to the narrative form that define all stories of a culture. Once those structures are understood, then narratives can be compared to one another. The world of literature, in effect, becomes an open book.

In terms of the operations of objectification and perspective taking, the structural analysis of a literary work requires the reader to alternate between a consideration of his or her experience and the actual structures of the text as he or she attempts to locate where one influenced the other. The text as object is something with the potential to have meaning. The act of reading operates within the framework, or structure, of the text to infuse those structures with meaning. The reader must then be able to reflect on the meaning made from the perspective of both text and reader. There can be even further consideration when the role and perspective of the author and his or her motivation for choosing to construct this work in this particular way is addressed.

There is some evidence to suggest that children of very young ages can conceptualize and express consideration of literary structure. In a study of young children's evaluation of storybooks, Young (1991) found that children aged 5 to 8 were able in interviews to "elaborate on theme, conceptualize and sequence key events in a plot, be critical of those stories which do not have a strong story line . . . compare and contrast qualities of character . . . evaluate illustrations . . . [and] comment on style" (p. 58). Consistent with this finding are studies by Lehr (1988, 1991) in which it was found that half of 10-year-old children were able to identify books with shared themes and generate thematic statements linking two books. The theme of a work is the central organizing idea around which a literary work revolves. Such a task is usually expected only of an adolescent reader able to make abstract statements because it involves the reader not only considering one *whole* work but, in this case, two, in order to "step back" from the works and objectify them so that the "main idea" that runs through them as wholes can be identified and then expressed. Lehr's tasks required the children to abstract a theme from each book that could apply to either, and it was found that half of her 10-year-old sample could do so.

In the area of "thinking about texts," one could expect a rather sophisticated evaluative response from a fourth- to seventh-grade student who had a relatively extensive literary knowledge on which to draw. It appears from the evidence that children in the first 6 or 7 years of school are capable of objectifying texts and their structures (Young, 1991), and of considering the relationship between texts (Lehr, 1991; Stott, 1990).

Perspective-taking ability on the part of the reader will be considered further in the section on thinking about readers.

Figurative Language. With regard to figurative language, considerable research has been done in the past 10 years on children's development of what is known as metaphoric competence, the ability to generate and understand metaphors (Pollio et al., 1990; Vosnaidou & Ortony, 1986). Metaphors are a common use of figurative language in literary works and are related to simile and allegory, where the meaning of one word, idea, or story is transferred to another so that the expression is enhanced by the comparison (McLaughlin, 1990). In other words, one word or idea is used to stand for another in order to stress the comparison, for example, "her temper was a storm."

Much of the most recent research has contradicted the Piaget-influenced view that understanding metaphor is only within the grasp, cognitively speaking, of the adolescent in the stage of formal operational thinking. This view holds that the abstract nature of metaphor requires the type of operations available only to the mature thinker in order to generate and appreciate its full meaning. In a review of the literature in this area, Pollio and colleagues (1990) cite several studies that report figurative language, such as metaphor, occurring spontaneously in young children's speech and compositions, indicating that it is not the "special event" of literature but rather a practical linguistic tool of expression.

Comprehension of figurative language appears to precede the ability to explain its meaning by several years, so that the metaphor that is understood by the 8-year-old child may not be able to be explained to others until the age of 12 (Windmeuller, Massey, Blank, Gardner, & Winner, 1986). Competence in the explication of metaphors is necessary for the reader to communicate an evaluation of metaphoric use in a literary work. Therefore, according to this research, one could expect children around 10 years old to be able to begin evaluating the author's use of figurative language because at this age they begin to be able to paraphrase and explain "in their own words" the meaning of metaphors written by other people (Pollio & Pickens, 1980). This aspect of evaluation would be found in the type of analytical and interpretative responses in which a reader considers the influences of the text's structure and ideas on the reading experience.

Thinking About Authors

The reader's conceptualization of the author will have an impact on how the processes of reading and writing are perceived. The text with no author (i.e., if there is no concept of author on the part of the reader) is a work without a past. Understanding that a text is a creation of an author means a reader may turn some of his or her attention to evaluating the writing process that produced the text.

In current language arts theory, much is made of the reading–writing connection, or the interdependent nature of learning to read and learning to write (Tierney & Shanahan, 1991). The critical reader who has a concept of author and an appreciation of the writing process is in a better position to take an authorial perspective in the analysis and interpretation of a work; this, in turn, assists in the formation of an evaluative response. Fitzgerald (1989) has compared the process of critical reading to that of revision in writing, based on the theory that there are reciprocal relationships among readers, authors, and texts. "Critical reading refers to the criticism of one's own thinking and the writer's thinking during meaning construction while reading" (p. 44). As a writer might *revise* a text to meet criteria, a reader may *criticize* a text according to his or her own criteria. According to Fitzgerald, one's understanding of the writing process (derived in part from one's own experience of writing) will feed the development of criticizing the writing process of others, which is accessed through reading their work, just as one revises after reading one's own work.

According to Tierney and Shanahan (1991) in their review of the reading–writing connection research, "Readers, as they read text, respond to what they perceive writers are trying to get them to think of, as well as what readers themselves perceive they need to do" (p. 259). This involves a "mutual awareness" of each other as readers and authors. That is, writers are communicating with potential readers and readers are reading with the writer's communicative purpose in mind. Just consider what a reader needs to be able to do in order to have an "awareness" of author. "It is a matter of linking actions (what the author has done) with goals and intentions (the author's purpose)" (Tierney, LaZansky, Raphael, & Cohen, 1987, p. 208). Or, in other words, the "aware" reader must consider the relationship between the words that the author has written and the author's purpose in choosing to express that idea in that way.

It is difficult to find empirical research on children's abilities in perspective taking and conceptualization of author. However, Tierney and Shanahan (1991) found evidence in their review that a sense of authorship develops with age and literary experience, starting off as somewhat vague in early primary school and becoming more sophisticated and used more often to assist in comprehension processes by the end of elementary school. Tierney and Shanahan note several times the development of an "awareness of author's intention" as central to a maturing conceptualization of author. Another way of approaching this is to say that the child with a concept of author recognizes that

> a literary work illustrates not only the final outcome of the creative process, but the creative process itself. A work of literature is the expression of a conceptual model of reality held in the mind of the writer. It exhibits the schemata of its creator. (Harker, 1981, p. 11)

There is evidence to suggest that many 7-year-old children do not recognize the author as anything other than an identity tag for a book. This derives from the finding that young children do not realize the author has choice with regard to the creation of a story (Applebee, 1978). In Applebee's study he found that young children considered a story as "set"— in existence as a whole before the author writes it—and the author as someone who merely takes down the story as it exists. Recognizing that the story is a creation—that the author was able to *choose* the setting, the characters, the theme, and so forth—is to have some awareness of the writing process; Naming a book "a Beatrix Potter" does not necessarily indicate an awareness of author or of the writing process; it may simply be another way of identifying the book, similar to saying "a scary story" or a "a blue book."

Lowe (1991) cites examples, such as those I have called "identity tags," as purported evidence for the development of a concept of author in preschool children. However, in her study of two children's reading response devclopment over several years, she also cites examples of her subjects' distinguishing between author and narrator as evidence. This may be a more fruitful avenue to explore in this area of development. Being able to distinguish between the person who writes the story (author) and the person who tells the story (narrator) is more representative of the ability to take alternative perspectives. It also indicates an ability to move back and forth between the internal world of the story and the external world of the text. At present, this area of conceptualization of author and its relationship to the evaluation of literature is in need of much more study.

Thinking About Readers

The reader formulating an evaluative response to literature needs to be able to distance the self from the reading experience in order to reflect both on the reader's processes that produced the reading experience and on the text itself. This involves both a subjective reflection on the role of the self in the creation of meaning and a more objective reflection on the role of the text. For example, consider this statement made by an 11-year-old reader:

> I think this book was very imaginative, but it wasn't my type
> of story. I like horror books. It would be great for 6- to 8-year-
> olds because it is an adventure and they like that. I found it
> very interesting that many adults enjoyed this story; they
> would have had a very different reading mind to mine.

In this response the reader reflects on the effect the text would have on different kinds of readers, from himself to younger children to adults. In doing so, he weighs the characteristics of each against the text itself and attempts to make a judgment about the quality of the text. Furthermore, he identifies reading experience as being part of one's "reading mind" and acknowledges that while the text stays constant, an adventure, the experience can vary by reader. Most contemporary literary theorists would agree that there is likely to be an involvement of the reader's personal characteristics in the formulation of any evaluation of a reading experience. Where once the task of literary criticism required the student to objectively evaluate the text as if it were a task of decoding the correct meaning and then applying criteria generated by an academic authority (such as a teacher), now response theory expects variance related to personal differences to be present between critiques.

In a review of the research on response to literature, Beach and Hynds (1991) considered the evidence for reader-based factors influencing response and made the following conclusion:

> Readers' personality characteristics, stances, and attitudes toward read-
> ing, knowledge of social and literary conventions, and experiences in
> social and institutional contexts influence their responses to literature.
> Such reader attributes exist in relationship to a variety of text factors in
> the transaction between reader and text. (p. 468)

This conclusion is in keeping with the theoretical view presented earlier that considers interpretation to be a subjective cognitive process guided by textual cues and constraints. This may be contrasted with a view that holds that all the meaning for a literary work resides in the work itself and readers simply achieve correct or incorrect interpretations. The first component, the personal characteristics of an individual and how they account for similarity and variance in readers' responses, will be addressed in this section. The second component, the reader's knowledge of literary conventions, has been dealt with in the section on thinking about texts. The third component, the reader's experiences, will be dealt with briefly in the section on educational practice.

The content of the evaluative response can be expected to vary as a function of individual differences (Beach & Hynds, 1991). However, it has been found that there is also similarity in responses among readers (Applebee, 1978; Beach & Wendler, 1987; Golden & Guthrie, 1986), which suggests that some common experiences or processes are shared among groups and these can influence the type of response produced. So while the response can be a reflection of a specific reader's experience, it can also be similar enough to those of others to be seen as characteristic of a particular age group or type of reader. The theoretical work of Fish (1980) attributes these similarities to the "interpretative community" to which groups of readers sharing common characteristics belong. On the other hand, Iser (1978) views similarity as accounted for by the textual constraints, which impose a limit on the number of possible interpretations, and variance as created by the individual nature of the cognitive processes involved in constructing the meaning.

How "thinking about readers" relates to the operation of perspective taking is fairly straightforward. A critical reader formulating an evaluation not only must reflect on his or her own experience, thereby taking the perspective of self, but also must take the perspectives of other readers. This is necessary in order to generate such statements as: "The reader who is familiar with the stock characters of the historical romance will immediately recognize this as a parody." Furthermore, a reader considering the alternative interpretations or evaluations of other readers will be able to compare and contrast the points of departure. "Distancing," or objectifying, the reading experience is like an evaluator moving around a sculptured object, taking advantage of many and overlapping perspectives in order to reach an evaluation that considers the whole. In keeping with this analogy, it is impossible to take into account every possible perspective in one's consideration, as they are limitless, but an evaluation will be enhanced by considering several, just as an evaluation would be considered weak if it only took account of one perspective.

One of the factors in similarity of reader response most often studied is that of age or stage of cognitive development. Several researchers have compared age groups in search of similarities in reader response, and many have used a Piaget-influenced model of cognitive development to explain the results of age-group differences (Applebee, 1978; Appleyard, 1990; Gardner & Gardner, 1971; Young, 1991). The conclusions of many of these studies suggest that sophisticated responses that could be considered "literary criticism" only begin to be found in the responses of the adolescent reader using "formal operational thought." Applebee (1978) examined how young adolescent subjects reflected on the interaction between reader and text to analyze the reading experience. Applebee found that it was only the older subjects who were able to untangle the relationships between structural characteristics of a work and the interest or tedium that they felt reading it. Forty percent of the thirteen-year-olds studied attempted some untangling, though it did not appear at all in the responses of the younger [9-year-old] children. (p. 112)

In other words, according to Applebee (1978), the work of literary criticism is an adult endeavor.

Recently, however, some reader response research has begun to focus in depth on the individual's process of responding to literature and the nature of the operations involved, rather than just age comparisons. This research approach has produced examples of young children using operations such as awareness and comparison of theme (Lehr, 1988) and distancing, or objectifying, the literary reading experience (Hancock, 1993), which are operations previously attributed only to adolescents. These results may be due to the amount of time taken to work with each participant and explore the process, time perhaps not afforded in large-group comparison studies or in regular classroom situations, or in some cases it may be due to the high ability of some of the participants drawn from exceptional samples (Galda, 1982; Hancock, 1993).

With regard to the operations of objectification and of perspective taking in "thinking about readers," it is relevant to consider metacognitive awareness, the awareness of one's own thinking. After all, the reader as evaluator has to objectify the reading "experience," or hold it static, and then reflect on how the experience was achieved in order to produce an evaluative response. "I like it" is a response. "I like it because . . . " is an evaluative response. The latter indicates the application of criteria and an awareness of the experience being held for reflection while it is being responded to. The subject of the "because" clause can be seen to represent the perspective being considered. For example, "I like it because the author tried to teach us that war is wrong" takes the perspective of the author by considering the writer's motivation, while "I like it because of the way the animals took over the power of the farm from the people" takes the perspective of the text by considering the action of the characters.

Wellman (1991) has been an active researcher in the area of children's development of the concept of mind. He cites evidence from studies supporting the claim that, by school age, children move from understanding their minds (and the minds of others) as "containers of one's thoughts" to understanding their minds as active processors. This appreciation for the mind as active, combined with the evidence supporting children's ability to take multiple perspectives by the age of 10 to 12 (Fox, 1991; Selman,

1980), would seem to support a case for engaging the reader of this age in the task of literary evaluation.

EDUCATIONAL PRACTICE

> In the teaching act, one makes deliberate choices, both personal and professional, from among many possible teaching behaviors; but it is always the act of knowledgeable choice within teaching boundaries rather than the behavior itself which is the work of teaching. Almost anyone can stand in front of a group of children and read a picture storybook, but when the teacher of children's literature does this, what is important is the intent involved in the selection, presentation, and follow up activities. (Vandergrift, 1990, p. 71)

What constitutes the teaching of evaluative response to literary text will depend on the theoretical approach of the teacher to both the process of reading and the process of literary criticism. It will depend on how the teacher views the roles of the text, the reader, and the educator as participants in those processes and will influence what in the end is considered to be an appropriate response. As Rogers (1991) notes, the authority of the teacher can be seen in the students' processes of interpretation. In a study of the effect of teaching method on reader response, it was found that the way students responded was representative of what they believed was expected by the teacher. Their beliefs about the purpose of reading literature and what comprised a satisfactory response reflected the teacher's approach in instruction. The methods and intentions involved in the teaching of children's literature to children are considered in this section.

The theoretical framework supporting a reader-based approach to literary criticism views the process of evaluation as one of integrating the knowledge of the text and the author with the experience of the self into a comprehensive understanding and statement of how the "reading" has worked. The evaluation can draw on all aspects of the reader's knowledge and experience related to that reading experience. From such a reader–text interactive stance, Langer (1990) describes this process as one of extensive building and uses the metaphor of "scaffolding," in which the reader builds onto the initial understanding with interpretation, comparison, and, finally, evaluation. The reader therefore has to be afforded *time* and *opportunity* to build an interpretation so that he or she may approach the task of evaluation from a position of strength, that is, in possession of a comprehensive understanding. Several authors have emphasized the factors of time and of the type of discussion following a reading in the development of a good critical response (Chambers, 1985; Close, 1990; Hansen, 1992; Langer, 1990).

Based on the anecdotal reporting of literature teachers and the work of theorists, it is proposed by many that comprehensive understanding of a text is possible only after extensive and close study that combines the reader's knowledge of text and the experience of reading, thereby producing a critical response. While the strict reader response methods would limit literary study to the personal-aesthetic response, it is suggested that the more integrative methods, which include both the reader-based and text-based methods, enable the formulation of a complex response that in turn assists in the process of evaluation. Based on this integrative model, various researchers in the teaching of children's literature have developed methods that seek to produce the type of critical process that sees the teacher as the literary guide in the interaction between the reader and text. Examples of these methods include Chambers's (1985) "framework," Langer's (1990) "scaffolding," Stott's (1987) "spiralled sequence," and Sloan's (1975) "archetypal criticism for children."

Many of the above methods have evolved out of a desire on the part of academic researchers interested in children's literature to apply the reader-based theories of literature to children's reading and to chart the cognitive processes and development in responding aesthetically and critically to text. Langer (1990) notes that much of the recent reform in language arts methods has been primarily focused on the process approach to writing instruction. This has led to the practice in many classrooms of a process approach to writing but retention of text-based approaches to reading, which focus on achieving the right answers in literary study. There is an attempt to "catch up" the understanding and application of a process approach to reading instruction to the current status of writing instruction.

The rationale for giving instructional time to teaching the formulation of the evaluative response centers on the personal benefits for the reader. These benefits include learning to form and support criticism (Gambell, 1986); establishing oneself as a self-sufficient and mature reader (Dixon, 1987); acquiring sufficient command of critical skills so as to apply them to other contexts (Sloan, 1975), such as television, advertising, or even computer software; and developing a metacognitive awareness of one's own reading processes (Durrant, Goodwin, & Watson, 1990).

The development of a critical reader, in turn, has benefits beyond those to the individual reader. Studying literature and engaging in critical discussion and exchange as part of a class encourages the social aspects of interpretation to emerge and extends one's personal response. Chambers (1985) notes that not only does talking about books allow for the exchange of ideas but also, at times, the very act of discussion generates new thoughts about the piece that had not been considered before by any of the participants.

> Saying thoughts together creates new thoughts that lie beyond us all. . . .
> By close attention *together*, the text begins to reward us with riches we
> did not know it possessed. . . . [We] come to know by lively understand-
> ing the social importance of literary reading. (Chambers, 1985, p. 143)

The social aspects of the interpretative discussion are noted in the study by Durrant and colleagues (1990) that contrasted the written and oral responses to literature by adolescent readers. Following group discussion, students' original written reactions to the piece had been challenged and refined and the postdiscussion written responses showed not only a better understanding through discovering a range of interpretations but also more confidence in expressing opinions about the piece. Perhaps the 8-year-old girl quoted by Chambers (1985) best describes the social learning nature of interpretation: "We don't know what we think about a book until we've talked about it" (p. 138).

The benefit beyond the classroom is to be found in the support that literature as an accessible art form receives when given a prominent role in education.

> Literature nourishes the imagination and develops the desire to read.
> . . . Literature appeals directly to the emotions and the imagination,
> carrying with it a powerful motivation to participate in its wonders and
> delights. . . . This is not to say that basic skills need not be taught and
> developed. But that they will be more readily learned and used only if
> the child . . . is continuously made aware that reading is worth his time
> and attention. (Sloan, 1975, p. 2)

CONCLUSIONS

The use of children's literature in the elementary language arts curriculum is often accompanied by a text-based approach that does not include the critical process of evaluating what is read (Langer, 1990). Literature in these cases is used as a means to teach reading and writing skills as opposed to the literary teaching of texts as art. But if literature is studied in depth, appreciated, and evaluated for its aesthetic value (Hade, 1991), then a study of language and of the arts is integrated. A literary education feeds the development of reader response, including the process of literary criticism, and in an integrative approach students are taught to combine their knowledge of text (such as the use of structural elements or figurative language) and their personal experience (relating the literary and external "worlds") in order to produce an evaluative response. In this way, literary education is directly linked to development of the literate person as an educational goal for reading instruction.

REVIEW

The two key components of the process of reading literature are experience and response. While the reading experience is the internal and private construction of meaning, the reader's response is the expression about that experience. The response is the part of the reading process that is available to the educator and may be used to gain insight into the individual reading experience. It is through the reader's response that the educator may measure comprehension or engage readers in discussion. However, reader response is not a one-step or a one-dimensional process. Responses may be categorized into several types based on the purpose the reader has for responding. One of these categories is the evaluative response, or expression of criticism.

The purpose of literary criticism is to apply criteria to a reading experience in order to formulate an evaluation that justifies the personal reaction to the work. In an educational context the task of literary criticism is usually first assigned to the adolescent or young adult student when adult literature is introduced into the curriculum. However, with the advent of literature-based curricula in the first 6 years of schooling, research attention has turned to the reader response abilities of young children. This chapter addressed the ability of children to evaluate the literature they read and, in particular, the ability to objectify the reading experience and the ability to take multiple perspectives on the experience. Research in the areas of the reader's thinking about texts, authors, and other readers was presented, and the evidence indicated that, with age-appropriate methods, one would expect children in the fourth to sixth years of schooling to be able to begin responding evaluatively to children's literature.

Literary criticism as an instructional objective may be viewed as dovetailing with other art education objectives. If the children's literature used in the language arts curriculum is treated in an artistic manner, then part of learning to read well is learning about the art of representation, expression, and aesthetics in the written form. Part of that process is the development of a critical approach to text, and in this way "language" and "arts" are truly both part of the reading curriculum.

STUDY AND DISCUSSION QUESTIONS

1. Distinguish between *reader experience* and *reader response* and discuss the implications of each for the educator.
2. Using the analogy of a viewer circling a sculpture, outline the process of literary evaluation, taking into consideration the role of author, text, and reader in the creation of an experience. Make reference to both objectification and perspective taking.
3. Using a children's book, give examples of each of the six types of responses outlined in Vandergrift's model.
4. How might similarity and variance in responses be accounted for among a class of children?
5. Why might a literature-based reading program be considered part of one's arts education?
6. What is the rationale for including literary criticism in the elementary (primary) syllabus?

FURTHER READING

Chambers, A. (1985). *Booktalk*. London: Bodley Head.
Lukens, R. (1990). *A critical handbook of children's literature* (4th ed.). Oxford, OH: HarperCollins.
Pinsent, P. (Ed.). (1993). *The power of the page: Children's books and their readers*. London: Fulton.
Rosenblatt, L. (1970). *Literature as exploration*. London: Heinemann.
Tucker, N. (1981). *The child and the book*. Cambridge, UK: Cambridge University Press.
Vandergrift, K. (1990). *Children's literature: Theory, research, and teaching*. Englewood, CO: Libraries Unlimited.

REFERENCES

Applebee, A. N. (1978). *The child's concept of story*. Chicago: University of Chicago Press.
Appleyard, M. (1990). *Becoming a reader: The experience of fiction from childhood to adulthood*. Cambridge, UK: Cambridge University Press.
Beach, R., & Hynds, S. (1991). Research on response to literature. In R. Barr, M. L. Kamil, P. B. Mosenthal, & P. D. Pearson (Eds.), *Handbook of reading research* (Vol. 2; pp. 453–489). White Plains, NY: Longman.
Beach, R., & Wendler, L. (1987). Developmental differences in response to a short story. *Research in the Teaching of English, 21,* 286–298.

Black, J. B., & Siefert, C. M. (1985). The psychological study of story understanding. In C. R. Cooper (Ed.), *Researching response to literature and the teaching of literature: Points of departure* (pp. 190–211). Norwood, NJ: Ablex.

Chambers, A. (1985). *Booktalk*. London: Bodley Head.

Close, E. (1990). Seventh graders sharing literature: How did we get here? *Language Arts, 67,* 817–823.

Dent, C. (1986). The development of metaphoric competence: A symposium. *Human Development, 29,* 223–225.

Dixon, J. (1987). Becoming a maturer reader. *Reading Teacher, 40,* 761–765.

Durrant, C., Goodwin, L., & Watson, K. (1990). Encouraging young readers to reflect on their processes of response: Can it be done, Is it worth doing? *English Quarterly, 22,* 211–219.

Fish, S. E. (1980). *Is there a text in this class? The authority of interpretive communities.* Cambridge, MA: Harvard University Press.

Fitzgerald, J. (1989). Enhancing two related thought processes: Revision in writing and critical reading. *Reading Teacher, 42,* 42–48.

Fox, R. (1991). Developing awareness of mind reflected in children's narrative writing. *British Journal of Developmental Psychology, 9,* 281–298.

Fyre, N. (1957). *Anatomy of criticism: Four essays.* Princeton, NJ: Princeton University Press.

Galda, L. (1982). Assuming the spectator stance: An examination of the responses of three young readers. *Research in the Teaching of English, 16,* 1–20.

Gambell, T. J. (1986). Growth in response to literature. *English Quarterly, 19,* 130–141.

Gardner, H., & Gardner, J. (1971). Children's literary skills. *The Journal of Experimental Education, 39,* 42–46.

Golden, J. M., & Guthrie, J. T. (1986). Convergence and divergence in reader response to literature. *Reading Research Quarterly, 21,* 408–421.

Hade, D. (1991). Being literary in a literature-based classroom. *Children's Literature in Education, 22,* 1–17.

Hancock, M. R. (1993). Exploring the meaning-making process through the content of literature response journals: A case study investigation. *Research in the Teaching of English, 27,* 335–368.

Hansen, J. (1992). The language of challenge: Readers and writers speak their minds. *Language Arts, 69,* 100–105.

Harker, W. J. (1981, May). *Teaching the language of literature.* Paper presented at the 14th annual conference of the Canadian Council of Teachers of English, Vancouver, British Columbia. (ERIC Document Reproduction Service No. ED209672)

Hochberg, J. (1978). Visual art and the structures of the mind. In S. S. Madeja (Ed.), *The arts, cognition and basic skills* (pp. 151–172). St. Louis, MO: Cermel Inc.

Iser, W. (1978). *The act of reading: A theory of aesthetic response.* Baltimore: Johns Hopkins University Press.

Landes, S. (1981). Teaching literary criticism in the elementary grades: A symposium. *Children's Literature in Education, 12,* 192–206.

Langer, J. (1990). Understanding literature. *Language Arts, 67,* 812–816.

Lehr, S. S. (1988). The child's developing sense of theme as a response to literature. *Reading Research Quarterly, 23,* 337–357.

Lehr, S. S. (1991). *The child's developing sense of theme: Responses to literature.* New York: Teachers College Press.

Lowe, V. (1991). 'Stop. You didn't read who wrote it': The concept of author. *Children's Literature in Education, 22,* 79–88.

McLaughlin, T. (1990). Figurative language. In F. Lentricchia & T. McLaughlin, (Eds.), *Critical terms for literary study* (pp. 80–90). Chicago: University of Chicago Press.

New Zealand Draft English Curriculum. (1993). *Draft: English in the New Zealand Curriculum.* Wellington, NZ: Ministry of Education.

Pollio, M., & Pickens, J. D. (1980). The developmental structure of figurative competence. In R. Honeck & R. Hoffman (Eds.), *Cognition and figurative language* (pp. 311–340). Hillsdale, NJ: Erlbaum.

Pollio, H., Smith, M. K., & Pollio, M. (1990). Figurative language and cognitive psychology. *Language and Cognitive Processes, 5,* 141–167.

Protherough, R. (1990). Ten levels of response? *English in Education, 24,* 44–49.

Quinn, K. (1992). *How literature works.* London: Macmillan.

Rogers, T. (1991). Students as literary critics: The interpretive experiences, beliefs, and processes of 9th grade students. *Journal of Reading Behavior, 23,* 391–423.

Rosenblatt, L. (1970). *Literature as exploration.* London: Heinemann.

Selman, R. (1980). *The growth of interpersonal understanding.* London: Academic Press.

Sloan, G. D. (1975). *The child as critic: Teaching literature in the elementary school.* New York: Teachers College Press.

Smith, B. H. (1990). Value/Evaluation. In F. Lentricchia & T. McLaughlin (Eds.), *Critical terms for literary study* (pp. 177–185). Chicago: University of Chicago Press.

Smith, F. (1982). *Writing and the writer.* London: Heinemann.

Stephens, J. (1990). Intertextuality and 'The Wedding Ghost'. *Children's Literature in Education, 21,* 23–36.

Stott, J. (1987). The spiralled sequence story curriculum: A structuralist approach to teaching fiction in the elementary grades. *Children's Literature in Education, 18,* 148–161.

Stott, J. (1990). 'Will the real dragon please stand up?' Convention and parody in children's literature. *Children's Literature in Education, 21,* 219–228.

Sutherland, Z., & Arbuthnot, M. H. (1991). *Children and books.* New York: HarperCollins.

Tierney, R. J., LaZansky, J., Raphael, T., & Cohen, P. (1987). Author's intentions and reader's interpretations. In R. J. Tierney, P. L. Anders, & J. N. Mitchell (Eds.), *Understanding readers understanding: Theory and practice* (pp. 205–226). Hillsdale, NJ: Erlbaum.

Tierney, R. J., & Shanahan, T. (1991). Research on the reading–writing relationship: Interactions, transactions, and outcomes. In R. Barr, M. L. Kamil, P. B.

Mosenthal, & P. D. Pearson (Eds.), *Handbook of reading research* (Vol. 2; pp. 246–280). White Plains, NY: Longman.

Vandergrift, K. (1990). *Children's literature: Theory, research, and teaching.* Englewood, CO: Libraries Unlimited.

Vosnaidou, S., & Ortony, A. (1986). Testing metaphoric competence of the young child: Paraphrase versus enactment. *Human Development, 29,* 226–230.

Wellman, H. (1991). *The child's theory of mind.* Cambridge, MA: MIT Press.

Windmeuller, G., Massey, C., Blank, P., Gardner, H., & Winner, E. (1986). Unpacking metaphors and allegories. *Human Development, 29,* 236–240.

Young, E. R. (1991). *Can children be critics? A participant observational study of children's responses to literature.* Unpublished doctoral dissertation, Claremont Graduate School, Claremont, CA.

Author Index

255

Subject Index

Subject Index

About the Contributors

Jillian M. Castle, Takapuna Grammar School, Takapuna, Auckland, New Zealand. Jill Castle is a reading and special needs teacher currently teaching special education students and English at a state secondary school. She spent 10 years working as a primary teacher and is a trained Reading Recovery teacher. She completed her M.A. in Education at the University of Auckland in 1993.

James W. Chapman, Department of Learning and Teaching, College of Education, Massey University, Palmerston North, New Zealand. James Chapman received his Ph.D. in educational psychology from the University of Alberta in 1979. The following year he took up a lectureship in the Faculty of Education at Massey University, and in 1996 he was appointed professor and head of the Department of Educational Psychology. He is now head of the Department of Learning and Teaching.

Vincent Connelly, Department of Psychology, University of Southampton, Southampton, England. Vince Connelly completed his Ph.D. at the University of St. Andrews, Scotland, in 1994. This work was an examination of how children learn to read under different instructional approaches and involved the study of children in Scotland and New Zealand. He took up his present post as lecturer in 1995.

Robyn S. Dixon, School of Education, University of Auckland, Auckland, New Zealand. Robyn Dixon received her Ph.D. in Education from the University of Auckland in 1996. She is currently a lecturer in developmental psychology and applied behavioral analysis. She is associate director of the Centre for Child and Family Policy Research in the School of Education.

Susan J. Dymock, Hamilton, New Zealand. Sue Dymock received her master's degree in education from the University of Waikato, Hamilton, New Zealand. For 7 years she taught in primary and intermediate schools. In 1997 she received a Ph.D. in education from the University of Auckland. She was a winner of the 1997 National Reading Conference (U.S.A.) Student Outstanding Research Award.

Joan Gibbons, School of Education, University of Waikato, Hamilton, New Zealand. Joan Gibbons worked as a teacher before becoming deputy librarian at Hamilton Teachers' College. She is currently senior librarian at the Education Library, University of Waikato, and is working on a doctoral thesis in children's literature.

Rhona S. Johnston, School of Psychology, University of St. Andrews, St. Andrews, Fife, Scotland. Rhona Johnston received her Ph.D. from the University of Hull, England. For 2 years she worked as a remedial teacher in secondary schools in Fife, Scotland. Since 1979 she has been a lecturer at the School of Psychology, University of St. Andrews, Scotland.

Dennis W. Moore, School of Education, University of Auckland, Auckland, New Zealand. Dennis Moore worked for several years as an educational psychologist in the New Zealand school system. He then moved to Papua New Guinea, where he completed a Ph.D. while lecturing in the Psychology and Education Departments at the University of Papua New Guinea. Since 1985 he has been a senior lecturer at the University of Auckland.

Tom Nicholson, School of Education, University of Auckland, Auckland, New Zealand. Tom Nicholson was a teacher in New South Wales, Australia, and subsequently a research officer in the Education Department of South Australia. From there he went to the United States, where he completed a Ph.D. in education at the University of Minnesota. Since moving to New Zealand, he has lectured at the University of Waikato and is now an associate professor in the School of Education at the University of Auckland.

Chanda K. Pinsent, St. Andrew's Independent School, George Town, Exuma, Bahamas. Chanda Pinsent received her M.A. in education at Victoria University of Wellington, New Zealand, in 1995. Her thesis was on children's evaluative responses to literature. She is currently the sole teacher at a multigrade school on the Bahamian island of Exuma.

Annette Tan, American International, Auckland Central, New Zealand. Annette Tan began her career in Singapore, where she completed a teaching diploma. She received her M.A. in education from the University of Auckland. She is currently a marketing manager for American International, which specializes in insurance.

G. Brian Thompson, School of Education, Victoria University of Wellington, Wellington, New Zealand. Brian Thompson worked as a psychologist in the

New Zealand school system for 7 years before taking up a position as senior teaching fellow in the Faculty of Education at Monash University, Melbourne, Australia. He received his Ph.D. from Monash University; since 1978 he has been a senior lecturer in the Department of Education at Victoria University of Wellington, New Zealand.

William E. Tunmer, Department of Learning and Teaching, College of Education, Massey University, Palmerston North, New Zealand. William Tunmer received his Ph.D. in experimental psychology from the University of Texas at Austin in 1979. From 1980 to 1988 he held the posts of research fellow, lecturer, and senior lecturer in the Faculty of Education of the University of Western Australia. In 1988 he took up the position of professor of education at Massey University, New Zealand.

Deborah A. M. Widdowson, University of California, School of Education, Berkeley, California. Deborah Widdowson completed her M.A. in education at the University of Auckland in 1994 and is currently a graduate student at the University of California, Berkeley, where she is conducting research on conceptual development and literacy.